THE RHETORIC OF
FAITH

Irenaeus and the Structure of
the *Adversus Haereses*

Scott D. Moringiello

The Catholic University of America Press
Washington, D.C.

Cataloging-in-Publication Data available from the Library of Congress

ISBN 978-0-8132-3260-7

FOR JOHANNA

✠

Io era tra color che son sospesi
e donna mi chiamò beata e bella,
tal che di comandare io la richiesi

CONTENTS

PREFACE

What are the limits of metaphor? At what point does exegesis become eisegesis? How does the community of interpreters establish norms for interpretation? When does a new set of norms form a new community of interpretation? These are questions that intrigue literary scholars, sociologists, theologians, and scholars of religion.

Although Irenaeus of Lyon, the second-century Christian scriptural exegete, does not ask these questions directly, I will argue that his answers to these questions are precisely what is at issue between him and his opponents. Irenaeus offers a way of interpreting scripture that draws on the Greco-Roman rhetorical tradition. He uses the faith of the church to distinguish what in the scriptures ought to be read literally and what ought to be read metaphorically. This faith, as a hermeneutical tool, helps Irenaeus to navigate interpretations that we call allegorical and typological.

Irenaeus is unique among Christian writers in the first centuries A.D. because he casts the Christian *kerygma* in rhetorical terms.[1] Irenaeus deliberately uses an idiom found in rhetoric, so the question before us is simple to state but has not fully been addressed in previous literature on Irenaeus; namely, why did Irenaeus choose this format to interpret scripture? He did not write letters like Ignatius of Antioch, or *apologiae* like Justin Martyr, or relate a personal visionary experience like the author of the *Shepherd of Hermas*. Many early Christian

---

1. For excellent introductory studies on Irenaeus, see John Behr, *Irenaeus of Lyons: Identifying Christianity* (New York: Oxford University Press, 2013); D. Jeffrey Bingham, "Irenaeus of Lyons," in *Routledge Companion to Early Christian Thought*, ed. D. Jeffrey Bingham (London: Routledge, 2010); Robert M. Grant, *Irenaeus of Lyons* (New York: Routledge, 1997); Denis Minns, *Irenaeus: An Introduction* (New York: T and T Clark, 2010); Eric F. Osborn, *Irenaeus of Lyons* (Cambridge: Cambridge University Press, 2001).

theologians, like Justin, found Greek philosophical categories to be particularly beneficial for proclaiming the Christian message; Irenaeus does not. He views Greek philosophical thought as the progenitor of the heresies he opposes.

Irenaeus, so I will argue, borrows tools from "literary studies" to interpret the scriptural text: whatever else it is, Christian theology is a work of literary criticism. Unfortunately, it is all too easy to forget this and cast Christianity as ersatz philosophy or primarily as a subject to be studied in sociological terms. Of course, there is good reason to mine sociology for insights into early Christian thought and practice. After all, we live in an age obsessed with identity. We divide ourselves along questions of race, gender, class, nationality, "religion," and the like. What we buy and what we eat classify us in myriad ways. As a result, these questions also interest the academic world. The field of early Christian studies is full of discussions of various Christianities and Christian teachers. The trend in academic scholarship is to focus on notions of hybridity and to eschew most value judgments. Sociology ends up being a helpful tool to discuss these matters. Scholars explore how Christian groups of the first two or three centuries A.D. identified themselves through their actions and rituals and how these identifications worked to differentiate one group from another.

No intellectual endeavor is value-neutral, however, and so it is worth examining the limits of focusing scholarly attention on sociological questions of identity. The most obvious problem is that, unlike contemporary sociologists who can do field work and interact with the groups they study, the scholar of early Christianity only has texts (and a few inscriptions) that through the centuries have been transmitted, copied, redacted, translated, lost, and found. Those texts themselves clearly employ certain rhetorical strategies. These rhetorical strategies push up against another problem in early Christian studies. The quest for a value-neutral, sociologically-based scholarly agenda ends up castigating those early Christians who make normative—and often highly rhetorically charged—claims. This should be no surprise.

What we have, then, are texts written in the first three centuries A.D., and these texts—whether "canonical" or not and whether "orthodox" or not—usually offer interpretations of other texts. Those other texts are chiefly, or at least most consequentially, the texts that make up the Hebrew scriptures and what came to be known as the New Testament or the New Covenant. How this testament or covenant was new, how it related to the "old" testament or covenant, and what continuities, if any, existed between them are exactly the sorts of questions these texts of the first centuries A.D. explored. Irenaeus is interested in these issues, as are the people whose interpretations he opposes. Both Irenaeus and his opponents are interested in these questions—so I will argue—as, at least in part, literary. That is, both Irenaeus and his opponents discuss how certain texts relate to other texts and what rhetorical strategies these texts employ.

There is no doubt that a whole range of sociological factors influenced the authors of these texts, and that these texts point to a range of social and ritual practices outside themselves. We can intelligently discuss the theologies of texts like Paul's letter to the Romans, the *Didache*, or the *Gospel of Truth*. Thus, we can rightly talk about, for example, Justin, Valentinus, Marcion, or Irenaeus being theologians, and even talk about each of those authors having his own theology. When we say that each of those authors has his own theology, what we ultimately mean is that each of them interprets the scriptural text in a certain way. These ways need not be contradictory, but each author understandably varies in the elements of the text that he highlights.

Amid important discussions of social practice, community, rituals, or ethics, we often lose sight of the literary aspect of early Christian literature. The flip side of this approach is to view these early Christian texts *only* in literary terms. That is, one can examine the rhetorical techniques the texts employ without being attentive to the theological vision that those techniques serve. Both approaches occur because scholars discuss one understanding of rhetoric at the expense of another. We should remember that "rhetoric" denotes a method of persuasive argumentation, even though "rhetoric" is often opposed to a disinterested pursuit of truth that supposedly comes through the name "philosophy." But we forget that in the ancient world the rhetor had two tasks, and that besides offering persuasive arguments, it was his job to interpret texts. What today we might call literary criticism was, in the ancient world, the domain of rhetoric. Irenaeus understands the message of scripture, which has been handed down by the Apostles, in rhetorical terms. Thus, in an important sense, theology—which is first and foremost the exegesis of scripture in the community in faith—is rhetorical.[2]

Before I go any further, let me step back and define what I mean by "rhetoric." Today there is no shortage of inspiring speakers: they are actors, lawyers, and politicians, among others. And when we discuss them we normally discuss the power of their words. We might think of Cicero denouncing Catiline, Lincoln debating Douglas, or King announcing his dream. In this context, it makes little sense to describe theology as rhetorical, unless we mean a particularly good preacher. But for Irenaeus, his educational context, and the tradition that formed him, giving speeches came part and parcel with interpreting texts. This education focused on how a student could learn what literary techniques an author used so that the student himself could use them when he gave his own speech. The student would learn when and how to make contrasts, when and how to appeal to his audience's hopes and fears, when and how to announce the plan for his speech, and when and how to conclude it. Irenaeus employs just these techniques in his text. He has learned from his Greco-Roman educational context and he has employed this education in the service of interpreting and proclaiming scripture.

In this book I argue that Irenaeus structured the *Adversus Haereses* in accordance with Greco-Roman rhetorical techniques and in accordance with the faith of the church. This argument stands in contrast to those who have argued that the *Adversus Haereses* evinces no clear structure.[3] For a start, though, I want to make it clear that I believe Ire-

---

2. Irenaeus's use of rhetoric has not been established by all scholars. Indeed, many of Irenaeus's defenders do not consider him to be a great stylist. See John Lawson, *The Biblical Theology of St. Irenaeus* (London: Epworth Press, 1948), 4; André Benoit, *Saint Irénée: introduction à l'étude de sa théologie* (Paris: Presses universitaires de France, 1960), 57; André Gouilloud, *Saint Irénée et son temps: deuxième siècle de l'église* (Lyon: Briday, Libraire-Éditeur, 1876), 42. Bengsch discusses the structure of the *Adversus Haereses* but does not look to forensic discourse. See Alfred Bengsch, *Heilsgeschichte und Heilswissen: eine Untersuchung zur Struktur und Entfaltung des theologischen Denkens im Werk "Adversus Haereses" des hl. Irenäus von Lyon* (Leipzig: St. Benno Verl, 1957).

3. Those who have argued that the *Adversus Haereses* evinces no clear structure, and indeed that at major points Irenaeus's thought is incoherent, include Hans Hinrich

naeus understands "rhetoric" in both senses I have just described. He offers what he believes is a persuasive account of Christian truth, and he does so in a way that focuses on the interpretation of the texts of the Hebrew scriptures and what came to be known as the New Testament. He employs techniques that were common in rhetorical handbooks and discussed by the great theorists of rhetoric in the Greek and Latin traditions. He sees the same techniques at work in the scriptures he discusses.

The corollary of my thesis is a negative one. Most of what scholars discuss about Irenaeus turns out to be, at best, a secondary concern to him. Such secondary concerns include the identity of "gnostic" teachers, Valentinus's perfidy, the authority of bishops or presbyters, the Eucharist, the *homo vivens*, and eschatology. Now to be clear, Irenaeus is interested in all of these issues, and most scholars who have written on Irenaeus's treatment of these issues know they are not his primary concern. The problem is that when we take Ireneaus's thoughts on these issues out of the context in which he wrote them, out of the structure of his well-structured argument, we quickly take Irenaeus on our own terms rather than his. I do not want my argument to focus on what Irenaeus says about any given theological topic. Instead, I want to offer a reading of Irenaeus that tries to understand him on his own terms and in his own context. Only then can we understand what he says about any particular topic.

Wendt, *Die christliche Lehre von der menschlichen Vollkommenheit* (Göttingen: Vanden-hoeck and Ruprecht, 1882), 21–26 and 29; Adolf von Harnack, *History of Dogma* (New York: Russell and Russell, 1958), 2:269–74; Friedrich Loofs, *Theophilus von Antiochen Adversus Marcionem und die anderen theologischen Quellen bei Irenaeus* (Leipzig: J. C. Hinrichs, 1930), 1–4; Anthony Briggman, *Irenaeus of Lyons and the Theology of the Holy Spirit* (Oxford: Oxford University Press, 2012), 3–4; B. Reynders, "Paradosis: le progrès et l'idée de tradition jusqu'à saint Irénée," *Recherches de théologie ancienne et medieval* 5, no. 2 (1935): 5–27, esp. 26–27. The scholarly consensus changed thanks to Philippe Bacq's *De l'ancienne à la nouvelle alliance selon s. Irénée: unité du livre IV de l'Adversus Haereses* (Paris: Lethielleux, 1978). Winfried Overbeck, in his *Menschwerdung: eine Untersuchung zur literarischen und theologischen Einheit des fünften Buches 'Adversus Haereses' des Irenäus von Lyon* (New York: P. Lang, 1995), followed Bacq in showing the coherence of Book Five. Although some scholars, most notably Robert Grant, have noted the importance of rhetoric to Irenaeus's thought, no scholar has argued that the rhetorical framework makes the most sense of the structure of the *Adversus Haereses*. See Grant, *Irenaeus of Lyons*.

Part of the problem that we face when we approach Irenaeus is to understand who his opponents were. A lot turns on how we answer that question. We can safely say that Irenaeus believes there are Christian teachers who say that Christ only saves human souls and not human bodies. Irenaeus believes that those teachers do this, furthermore, through secret knowledge rather than through God's love. Irenaeus refers to these teachers as disciples of Valentinus, who lived in Rome, and traces Valentinus's doctrine back to Simon Magus in Acts.[4] Irenaeus also refers to these teachers as "so-called gnostics," a term meant to be wider than those Valentinus has influenced. The term "gnostic" has generally fallen out of favor with scholars thanks to the work of Michael Williams and others who question if the name was historically applied to any specific group. Indeed, Christoph Markschies has even gone so far as to argue that Valentinus himself was neither a Valentinian nor a gnostic.[5]

I understand the scholarly interest in Irenaeus's description of his opponents, but I fear that it has moved us away from Irenaeus's text and his goal in that text. The goal is to present Christian teaching, which is to say, the goal is to show how the Apostles interpreted scripture. So yes, Irenaeus is concerned with Christian identity. But his concern with Christian identity reveals itself through the ways the Christian community is united in interpreting the scriptural text. Now anyone interested in how Christians identify themselves through the texts they read will also want to know how one can misread these texts. This is the context in which to understand Irenaeus's discussion of "heresy."

I do not mean for my interpretation of Irenaeus to replace other

---

4. See Acts 9:8–24.

5. For examples of books that question the use of the term "gnostic" see Michael A. Williams, *Rethinking "Gnosticism": An Argument for Dismantling a Dubious Category* (Princeton, N.J.: Princeton University Press, 1996); Christoph Markschies, *Valentinus Gnosticus?: Untersuchungen zur Valentinianischen Gnosis mit einem Kommentar zu den Fragmenten Valentins* (Tübingen: J. C. B. Mohr, 1992); Karen L. King, *What Is Gnosticism?* (Cambridge, Mass.: Belknap Press of Harvard University Press, 2003); Elaine H. Pagels, *The Gnostic Paul: Gnostic Exegesis of the Pauline Letters* (Philadelphia: Fortress Press, 1975); David Brakke, *The Gnostics: Myth, Ritual, and Diversity in Early Christianity* (Cambridge, Mass.: Harvard University Press, 2010).

interpretations. I do not think that if my interpretation is true, any others are necessarily false. With that said, I think it does mean that some interpretations are less plausible. Instead, I hope my argument will reframe our discussion of Irenaeus in terms that would have been familiar to him and can be intelligible to his readers today. Of course, this is the challenge: part of my burden will be to show how my argument can be intelligible to readers of this book and to Irenaeus himself. Thus, although there are many contemporary literary theorists whose methods might come into fruitful conversation with Irenaeus, their work will not be my focus here. I will also refrain, to the extent that I can, from importing ideas that have become normative for Christian thought but which only appear *in nuce*, if at all, in Irenaeus's writing. We should not expect Irenaeus to be a proto-Nazianzen when it comes to the Christian understanding of the Trinity or a proto-Balthasar when it comes to Christian critiques of philosophical gnosticism. But only when we understand Irenaeus's context and aims properly will we be in a position to make such comparisons.

Throughout the book, I will argue that part of the difference between Irenaeus and his opponents comes from the backgrounds they bring to their interpretations. This will be a particular focus in chapter 2. Now, though, I want to highlight Irenaeus's own educational background. Irenaeus was born in Smyrna, which is present-day Izmir, Turkey. Both Smyrna and Lyon were places where Greco-Roman culture flourished. Irenaeus not only was a man of his community of Christians, he was an educated member of the community of Lyon.[6] In their schooling, young boys learned grammar and then they

6. Robert M. Grant, "Irenaeus and Hellenistic Culture," *Harvard Theological Review* 42, no. 1 (1949): 41. Irenaeus described his fellow Gauls as barbarians. See *Adversus Haereses* (hereafter, *AH*) 1.P.1. *Paideia*, as the work of Peter Brown, among others, has pointed out, both joined its students to the culture around them and allowed them to stand out as individuals. See Peter Brown, *The World of Late Antiquity: From Marcus Aurelius to Muhammed* (London: Thames and Hudson, 1971); Maud Gleason, *Making Men: Sophists and Self-Presentation in Ancient Rome* (Princeton, N.J.: Princeton University Press, 1995); George Kennedy, *A New History of Classical Rhetoric* (Princeton, N.J.: Princeton University Press, 1994), 49. On ancient education more generally, see Henri Irénée Marrou, *Histoire de l'éducation dan l'antiquité* (Paris: Seul, 1956); Raffaella Cribiore, *Gymnastics of the Mind: Greek Education in Hellenistic and Roman Egypt* (Princeton, N.J.: Princeton University Press, 2001); Heinrich Lausberg, *Handbook of Literary*

learned rhetoric. That is, they learned how to interpret texts and give speeches.[7] Irenaeus absorbed his rhetorical education so thoroughly that it shows not only in the form of his work (i.e., how he makes arguments), but also in the content of his work (i.e., he understands biblical theology to be primarily educative).[8] In these pages, I will argue that this dual aspect of rhetoric is key to understanding Irenaeus's texts.

Irenaeus is not an interesting figure because he was rhetorically trained. He is an interesting figure because he combines this rhetorical training with the Christian proclamation. We should be aware, however, that there is an important distinction between classical rhetoric and what George Kennedy has called "radical Christian rhetoric." For Greek and Roman writers the ability of the audience to understand what the rhetor presented through his words depended on intelligence. For Irenaeus and Christian rhetors like him, the ability of the audience to understand what they heard depended on God's grace.[9]

Rhetoric: A Foundation for Literary Study, trans. Matthew T. Bliss (Leiden: Brill, 1988). And for education in the context of Judaism and Christianity, see Wilhelm Bousset, *Jüdisch-Christlicher Schulbetrieb in Alexandria und Rom: Literarische Untersuchungen zu Philo und Clemens von Alexandria, Justin und Irenäus* (Göttingen: Vandenhoeck and Ruprecht, 1915).

7. As Woolf has pointed out, education "followed the pattern outlined in the works of Quintilian and the Elder Seneca, beginning with the study of language and proceeding to that of rhetoric." Greg Woolf, *Becoming Roman: The Origins of Provincial Civilization in Gaul* (Cambridge: Cambridge University Press, 1998), 73. Woolf goes on to say that "rhetorical training dominated education in the West" (ibid.).

8. Grant, "Irenaeus and Hellenistic Culture," 47–48. For the context of Irenaeus's education, see ibid., 48–49. Through this education, Gauls became Roman. Woolf writes, "Becoming Roman was not a matter of acquiring a ready-made cultural package ... so much as joining the 'insiders' debate about what the package did or did not consist of at that particular time." See Woolf, *Becoming Roman*, 54–60. One could view Irenaeus's purpose in the *Adversus Haereses* in much the same way. In the *Adversus Haereses*, Irenaeus joined a debate about what it meant to be a Christian and how scriptural interpretation both shaped and was shaped by that definition.

9. As Kennedy writes, "The Christian orator, like his Jewish predecessor, is the vehicle of God's will to whom God will supply the necessary words, and his audience will be persuaded, or not persuaded, not because of the capacity of their minds to understand the message, but because of God's love for them which allows their hearts to be moved or withholds that grace." George Kennedy, *New Testament Interpretation through Rhetorical Criticism* (Chapel Hill: University of North Carolina Press, 1984), 8. I have found Kennedy's work extremely helpful. See also his *The Art of Persuasion in Greece* (Princeton, N.J.:

In fact, as we shall see, Irenaeus both uses elements of the rhetorical tradition in his presentation of Christian truth and shows how this tradition cannot fully convey that truth. Ultimately, it is God who, through the economy of creation and salvation in his Son, persuades Christians to interpret scripture correctly. Irenaeus's task is to show the rules by which proper interpretation can take place.

As I end this preface, it is appropriate to discuss the general plan of the book. Because, as I have said, my basic argument is that Irenaeus's structure *is* his argument, the structure of the *Adversus Haereses* is the basis for all that I write here. In the appendix, I offer an outline of the *Adversus Haereses*, and I will refer to that outline throughout my argument.[10] As noted above, scholars have argued that the *Adversus Haereses* lacks a coherent argument, and those scholars who claim that the text does have a coherent organization have proposed a different scheme from the one presented here. I give this outline in an appendix so that I can make substantive thematic points in the text. Each chapter of this book will examine one of the books of the *Adversus Haereses* under a particular theme appropriate to that book: silence, fiction, manifestation, prophecy, and judgment. The themes also line up with the structure of a forensic speech, as the Roman orator Quintilian describes that order.

I should underline that Irenaeus does not, at any point in his argument, refer to Aristotle, Quintilian, or any other Greco-Roman rhetorician. And I should also emphasize that Irenaeus tells his readers what he is doing at different moments in his text, usually in the preface of each book. Thus my interpretation of Irenaeus's structure is just that—an interpretation. Of course, I will track what Irenaeus says he is doing, and his remarks usually come in the preface of each book. But I will suggest that when Irenaeus tells his readers what he

Princeton University Press, 1963); *The Art of Rhetoric in the Roman World* (Princeton, N.J.: Princeton University Press, 1972); *Classical Rhetoric and Its Christian and Secular Tradition from Ancient to Modern Times* (Princeton, N.J.: Princeton University Press, 1989); *A New History of Classical Rhetoric*; *Progymnasmata: Greek Textbooks of Prose Composition and Rhetoric* (Atlanta: Society of Biblical Literature, 2003). For the distinction between "rhetor" and "sophist" and "orator" see G. W. Bowersock, *Greek Sophists in the Roman Empire* (Oxford: Clarendon Press, 1969), 12–14.

10. Compare my outline with Behr, *Irenaeus of Lyons*, 85–103.

is doing he can still be understood in the context of the framework I offer here. My argument is the faith of the church structures Irenaeus's argument, and that the format Quintilian offers and the issues with which Aristotle and Quintilian (among others) were concerned give us a helpful context to understand the faith and the structure of the *Adversus Haereses*.[11] In each chapter I also argue that in each book of the *Adversus Haereses*, Irenaeus writes a brief section on what we might call theological methodology, and each of these sections is appropriate to its own book. I devote a section of each chapter to those parts of Irenaeus's argument. These parts also fit into the structure for which I argue.

In my conclusion, I examine some Irenaean approaches to scripture and the theological tradition. In some ways, Irenaeus's method lost out to other more philosophically-based or historically-based methods of interpretation. In other ways, though, Irenaeus's method has remained a vital force in the history of interpretation and scholarship, perhaps most especially in those scholars most dubious of the content of Irenaeus's argument. All scholars of early Christianity and historians of Christian theology owe Irenaeus a great deal, but in order to recognize this debt we must first attend to how he shapes his argument.

11. I have used the Sources Chrétiennes (hereafter, SC) texts of Irenaeus. Irenaeus of Lyon, *Contre Les Hérésies: Livre I* (Paris: Cerf, 1979); *Contre Les Hérésies: Livre II* (Paris: Cerf, 1982); *Contre Les Hérésies: Livre III* (Paris: Cerf, 2002); *Contre Les Hérésies: Livre IV* (Paris: Cerf, 1965); *Contre Les Hérésies: Livre V* (Paris: Cerf, 1969). Translations are my own, but I have benefited from *Against the Heresies: Book 1*, trans. Dominic Unger and James Dillon, Ancient Christian Writers (hereafter, ACW) 55 (New York: Paulist Press, 1992); *Against the Heresies: Book 2*, trans. Dominic Unger and John Dillon, ACW 65 (Mahwah, N.J.: Paulist Press, 2012); *Against the Heresies: Book 3*, trans. Dominic Unger, John Dillon, and Ireaneus Steenberg, ACW 64 (Mahwah, N.J.: Paulist Press, 2012). I have included the original Greek and Latin in the footnotes so that readers can check my translations.

ACKNOWLEDGMENTS

As with all book projects, this one could not have been completed without the support of many. I would like to thank my teachers John Cavadini, Brian Daley, Kevin Hart, Cyril O'Regan, and especially Robin Darling Young.

Friends Corey Barnes, Kristin and Shawn Colberg, Brian FitzGerald, Rita George-Trikovic, Kate Gibbons, Kevin Kalish, Greg Hoskins, Lance Jenot, David Jorgensen, Jeanne-Nicole Mellon Saint Laurent, Sheryl Overmyer, John-Paul Spiro, Jack Tannous, and Leah Whittington helped this project in many and various ways. Teachers and mentors such as Bill Darrow, Meredith Hoppin, David Meconi, Frank Oakley, John O'Keefe, Mark Roche, Bob Sullivan, and Mark Taylor provided endless encouragement, often when I needed it most.

Jack Doody of the Villanova Center for Liberal Education, Thomas Levergood of the Lumen Christi Institute, and my colleagues at DePaul University provided institutional support without which I would not have been able to complete this project.

Lewis Ayers, John Behr, Jeff Bingham, and Elaine Pagels are among the many scholars of Irenaeus and the second century who offered helpful advice. I do not expect that they will agree with everything written here, and I know I have a lot more to learn from them.

John Connelly of Regis High School and Matthew Rose of the Berkeley Institute each read an earlier draft of this book. Their comments helped me reshape and refine my argument.

John Martino of the Catholic University of America Press guided this from an idea to a proposal to drafts to the final product. I am grateful to the anonymous reviewers for their comments.

I am sorry that Wm. Theodore de Bary, Fr. Joseph Dorgan, SJ, and

Louis Macchiarulo passed away before this book came to completion.

I would like to thank my family, including my parents, siblings, and in-laws. Our sons, Theodore and Marco, have helped keep things in perspective. My wife, Johanna Heinrichs, read through the final draft of the manuscript. Her comments have been invaluable. Without her friendship, encouragement, and love, this project would never have been completed. I dedicate this book to her.

ABBREVIATIONS

ACW   Ancient Christian Writers

AH   *Adversus Haereses* (Irenaeus)

EH   *Ecclesiastical History* (Eusebius)

JTS   *Journal of Theological Studies*

SC   Sources Chrétiennes

VC   *Vigiliae Christianae*

THE RHETORIC OF
FAITH

INTRODUCTION

This book is entitled *The Rhetoric of Faith: Irenaeus and the Structure of the* Adversus Haereses. I began my discussion of rhetoric in the preface, and before I go any further, I want to discuss how Irenaeus understands the faith, which he defines in Book One of the *Adversus Haereses*. The faith has three points. First, the church has received faith in one God, the Father, in one Jesus Christ, and in the Holy Spirit. Second, the Holy Spirit has proclaimed through the prophets the economies of God's salvation. Third, these economies conclude with the just judgment of Christ, who will raise the dead, cast the wicked into eternal fire, and bestow life on those who kept his commandments and persevered in his love.[1] Even in this paraphrase, we can see how the faith is not simply a list of propositions. It certainly is not a "feeling" that lacks evidence. Instead, the faith has a structure that tracks the narrative of the scriptures. The three parts of this structure are God, God's creation and plan for salvation, and God's judgment. To understand the scriptures, one must understand the structure (we could even say the narrative) that the faith provides.

In this book, I focus on the structure of Irenaeus's argument in the *Adversus Haereses* because I believe that the structure is the argument. That is, Irenaeus has structured his argument in the way that he has because he believes this structure does justice to the message of the scriptures. Irenaeus's argument throughout the text spirals. He always begins with a discussion of God, and then he moves to a discussion of of the economy of salvation, and then he concludes with a discussion of Christ's judgment. This structure is, according to Irenaeus, the *true* hypothesis, the true key to understanding the scriptures. His princi-

---

1. See *AH* 1.9.1 and the discussion of this passage in chapter 1.

ples of interpretation come to the fore through this structure, so in order to do justice to Irenaeus's interpretation we must take the structure of his text seriously.

I do not want my argument to be an exercise in purely formal criticism. And I do not want it to be an overreaction against the scholarship that I think too often focuses on what ancient Christian texts might say about the society around them rather than what those texts say. I began my preface by arguing that much of the study of early Christianity has been reduced to discussions of identity in a sociological sense. In saying that, though, I would not want to argue that identity is not important. I hope to make the case that Irenaeus interprets the scriptures in the way that he does because he wants to establish Christian identity in a certain way. After all, he bases the structure of his argument on the faith of the church, and so the identity of the church is paramount.

Of course, there remains an essential place for discussing extratextual issues when discussing identity. To that end, I will make a few points about Irenaeus's life as well as his world: the Roman city of Lugdunum (present-day Lyon) and the lives of Christians in Lugdunum. Irenaeus did not write in a cultural vacuum, and some background about his social situation will enrich our understanding of his work. An important part of Irenaeus's social situation is the writings of those scriptural exegetes he opposes. These exegetes used to be called "Gnostics," and I will introduce them here.[2] Finally, I will conclude my introduction with a discussion of the type of education one would receive in Irenaeus's time and place. In the preface I offered a preview of Irenaeus's education, and I want to fill out the picture in this introduction. His educational background, as I will show, illuminates both the form and the content of Irenaeus's argument.

We know very little about Irenaeus's life and even less from him directly. Today we know him as Irenaeus of Lyon, but his "Western" location should not obscure that he was a Greek speaker with a Greek name. Unfortunately, although Irenaeus wrote in Greek, only fragments of his writings in Greek survive. We have an almost full Latin

---

2. Throughout my argument, I avoid the word "Gnostic/gnostic." Instead, I refer to "Irenaeus's opponents."

translation of the *Adversus Haereses*. His *Demonstration of the Apostolic Preaching* comes down to us in an Armenian translation.[3]

Most of what we know about Irenaeus actually comes from Eusebius of Caesarea, who discusses the former at length in his *Ecclesiastical History*.[4] Eusebius goes so far as to note that Irenaeus earned his name as a peacemaker when he intervened in a dispute between Victor, who was the bishop of Rome, and Christians in Asia, who wanted to celebrate Easter on a different date.[5] Thanks to Eusebius, we know that there were eight works attributed to Irenaeus: a letter *Against Blastus: On Schism*;[6] a letter *Against Florinus: On the Monarchy* or *On the Fact that God is not the Maker of Evil*;[7] *On the Ogdoad*;[8] a letter to Victor of Rome;[9] *On Knowledge against the Pagans*;[10] *Book of Various Discourses*;[11] *Demonstration of the Apostolic Preaching*; and the *Adversus Haereses*.

Both in the *Adversus Haereses* and in his letter to Florinus (which Eusebius records), Irenaeus writes that, as a young boy (παῖς), he knew Polycarp.[12] Polycarp was the bishop of Smyrna in Asia Minor, and so we can be reasonably sure that Irenaeus came from that region. As his letter to Victor and his catalogue of bishops of Rome in *Adversus Haereses* 3.3.1 shows, Irenaeus was familiar with the church in Rome. Although it is unlikely that Irenaeus and Valentinus would have been in Rome at the same time, it is likely that Irenaeus would have learned of Valentinus's teachings and his followers—especially Ptolemy—

---

3. The *Adversus Haereses* was likely translated into Latin in North Africa in the early fourth century and into Armenian in the sixth century. See John Behr, *Asceticism and Anthropology in Irenaeus and Clement* (Oxford: Oxford University Press, 2000), 26–27; Jacques Fantino, *L'Homme, Image de Dieu, chez Saint Irénée De Lyon* (Paris: Cerf, 1986), 47–48.

4. Eusebius, *The Ecclesiastical History* (hereafter, *EH*), trans. Kirsopp Lake (New York: G. P. Putnam's Sons, 1926). Eusebius probably finished this work around 323 or 324.

5. *EH* 5.24.8–13.

6. *EH* 5.20.1.

7. *EH* 5.20.1 and 5.20.4–8.

8. *EH* 5.20.1 and 5.20.2.

9. *EH* 5.24.11, 5.24.12–13, 5.24.14–17.

10. *EH* 5.16.

11. *EH* 5.26.

12. *AH* 3.3.4.

while he was in Rome or in contact with the Christian community in Rome.[13]

As I will show throughout this book, Irenaeus places great emphasis on the relationship between teachers and students. Although Valentinus is his main opponent, Irenaeus traces Valentinus's teaching back to Simon Magus in Acts 8 and ultimately sees Satan as the progenitor of Simon's teaching. Whereas Satan, so Irenaeus argues, began "their" tradition of teaching, Jesus began Irenaeus's, and then passed that teaching on to the Apostles. Because he has set up the importance of a tradition of teachers, Irenaeus must show his personal connection to the interpretation of the Apostles. This connection comes through Polycarp, Irenaeus's teacher, who taught him to see the vision of God's love offered in the scriptures. Irenaeus's description of Polycarp makes his admiration for the bishop of Smyrna clear. Polycarp lived to an old age and "he left life in the most glorious martyrdom."[14] Irenaeus says that Polycarp "always taught the things that were taught by the Apostles, which the Church handed down, which alone is true."[15] Polycarp was a witness to the truth through his martyrdom, which "all the Churches in Asia and those who succeeded Polycarp witnessed." These successors "were more faithful and trustworthy witnesses to the truth than Valentinus and Marcion and all the rest who have bad opinions."[16] Not only does Irenaeus favorably compare Polycarp to Valentinus and Marcion, he also mentions Polycarp's Roman sojourn, which obviously underscores the importance of the Roman church. In fact, Polycarp once met Marcion, as Irenaeus relates it, and when he did, he called Marcion "the first born of Satan."[17] Polycarp links Irenaeus

13. Peter Lampe, *From Paul to Valentinus: Christians at Rome in the First Two Centuries* (Minneapolis, Minn.: Fortress Press, 2003).
14. ἐπὶ πολὺ γὰρ παρέμεινεν καὶ πάνυ γηραλέος ἐνδόξως καὶ ἐπιφανέστατα μαρτυρήσας ἐξῆλθεν τοῦ βίου. *AH* 3.3.4.
15. ταῦτα διδάξας ἀεὶ ἃ καὶ παρὰ τῶν ἀποστόλων ἔμαθεν, ἃ καὶ ἡ ἐκκλησία παραδίδωσιν, ἃ καὶ μόνα ἐστὶν ἀληθῆ. *AH* 3.3.4.
16. Μαρτυροῦσι τούτοις αἱ κατὰ τὴν Ἀσίαν ἐκκλησίαι πᾶσαι καὶ οἱ μέχρι νῦν διαδεδεγμένοι τὸν Πολύκαρπον, πολλῷ ἀξιοπιστότερον καὶ βεβαιότερον ἀληθείας μάρτυρα ὄντα Οὐαλεντίνου καὶ Μαρκίωνος καὶ τῶν λοιπῶν κακογνωμόνων. *AH* 3.3.4.
17. Καὶ αὐτὸς δὲ ὁ Πολύκαρπος Μαρκίωνί ποτε εἰς ὄψιν αὐτῷ ἐλθόντι καὶ φήσαντι· «Ἐπιγίνωσκε ἡμᾶς», ἀπεκρίθη· Ἐπιγινώσκω, ἐπιγινώσκω τὸν πρωτότοκον τοῦ Σατανᾶ.» *AH* 3.3.4.

to the Apostles, but more specifically, thanks to his location in Ephesus, he links Irenaeus to John and Paul. Polycarp is "a true witness to the tradition of the Apostles."[18] The authority for Polycarp's teaching comes from the way Polycarp lived his life. He lived as he taught. He understood what ought to be read literally and what ought to be read metaphorically in the scriptures, and this understanding shaped his life and gave his teaching authority. For Irenaeus, as we will see, the interpretation of scripture ought to be lived out. His teachers and the martyrs to the faith are proof of that.

Eusebius tells us that during the controversy between Rome and the churches in Asia about the dating of Easter, Irenaeus was the bishop of the diocese of Gaul.[19] Irenaeus came to oversee the community in Gaul because Ponthius, the previous leader, was killed in a violent persecution that occurred in the city around 177. We do not know how Irenaeus escaped the persecution but he seems to have been sent as an envoy from Gaul to Rome. Eusebius notes that Irenaeus was a presbyter in Lyon during the persecution and came to Eleutherius, the bishop of Rome.[20] Eusebius further tells us that Irenaeus was "zealous for the covenant of Christ."[21]

We learn of the martyrdoms because of Eusebius, who compiled an *Acts of the Martyrs*.[22] He quotes selections from the *Martyrs of*

18. Ἀλλὰ καὶ ἡ ἐν Ἐφέσῳ ἐκκλησία ὑπὸ Παύλου μὲν τεθεμελιωμένη, Ἰωάννου δὲ παραμείναντος αὐτοῖς μέχρι τῶν Τραϊανοῦ χρόνων, μάρτυς ἀληθής ἐστιν τῆς τῶν ἀποστόλων παραδόσεως. *AH* 3.3.4.

19. ὁ Εἰρηναῖος ἐκ προσώπου ὢν ἡγεῖτο κατὰ τὴν Γαλλίαν ἀδελφῶν. *EH* 5.24.11. About the relationship between the churches of Lyon and Vienne and the churches of Asia, see Pierre Nautin, *Lettres et écrivains chrétiens des iie et iiie siècles* (Paris: Éditions du Cerf, 1961), 102. See also Frank D. Gilliard, "Apostolicity of Gallic Churches," *Harvard Theological Review* 68, no. 1 (1975): 17–33. I should note here that Irenaeus was the leader of the Christian community in Lyon, but the role of bishop was obviously quite different from a bishop's role today. It is also worth noting that Irenaeus would not have had any power to "enforce" "orthodoxy."

20. *EH* 5.4.1.

21. *EH* 5.4.1. Οἱ δ' αὐτοὶ μάρτυρες καὶ τὸν Εἰρηναῖον, πρεσβύτερον ἤδη τότ ὄντα τῆς ἐν Λουγδούνῳ παροικίας, τῷ δηλωθέντι κατὰ Ῥώμην ἐπισκόπῳ συνίστων, πλεῖστα τῷ ἀνδρὶ μαρτυροῦντες, ὡς αἱ τοῦτον ἔχουσαι τὸν τρόπον δηλοῦσι φωναί· 'χαίρειν ἐν θεῷ σε πάλιν εὐχόμεθα καὶ ἀεί, πάτερ Ἐλεύθερε. ζηλωτὴν ὄντα τῆς διαθήκης Χριστοῦ.

22. For the text see Herbert Musurillo, *The Acts of the Christian Martyrs* (Oxford: Clarendon Press, 1972).

Lyon and Vienne in the *Ecclesiastical History*. Paul Foster notes that it is somewhat strange that Irenaeus does not mention the martyrdoms in either the *Adversus Haereses* or the *Demonstration of the Apostolic Preaching*.[23] Although Eusebius does not attribute the *Martyrs of Lyon and Vienne* to Irenaeus, I agree with those scholars who argue that Irenaeus himself wrote the text. I will not offer a full analysis of my agreement here, but I see similarities not only between the language of the *Adversus Haereses* and the *Martyrs* but more importantly in the connection between God's love and the economy of salvation in both texts.[24] Whether or not Irenaeus wrote the martyrdom accounts, there is no question that martyrdom is central to his thinking about the interpretation of scripture and the life of the church.

Rome, of course, was a center of Christian teaching and the site of the oldest Christian community in the West, but for Irenaeus, the most consequential Christian site was Lugdunum. We know very little about Gaul in the second century after Christ, and most of what we can say about Lyon, its provincial capital, remains conjecture, largely based on writings and inscriptions from later periods.[25] We know that Lugdunum was one of the few manufacturing centers in Gaul, and the city was a node for a network of roads that spread throughout Gaul. Irenaeus's community did not loom very large in this city of 35,000. Lugdunum was also the center of an imperial cult. A full consideration of Roman Gaul is beyond the scope of my argument here. I should note, though, that issues of identity were never far from the minds of the Romans living in Gaul. Indeed, Romans living in Asia Minor faced similar questions.

23. *Irenaeus: Life, Scripture, Legacy*, ed. Sara Parvis and Paul Foster (Minneapolis, Minn.: Fortress Press, 2012), 16.
24. These are largely the reasons why Nautin believes Irenaeus wrote the *Martyrs*. Nautin, *Lettres et écrivains chrétiens*, 54–61. Tremblay disagrees, basing his judgment on the dating of the *Martyrs*. Real Tremblay, "Le Martyre selon saint Irénée de Lyon," *Studia Moralia* 16 (1978a): 172n27.
25. See Woolf, *Becoming Roman*. This monograph paints a vivid portrait of Roman Gaul, on which I have relied. Unfortunately for our purposes, Woolf does not discuss the Christian presence in Gaul. See also *Les Martyrs de Lyon (177)*, ed. Jean Rougé and Robert Turcan, Colloques Internationaux Du Centre National De La Recherche Scientifique, no. 575 (Paris: Éditions du C.N.R.S, 1978); Jean Colson, *Saint Irénée: Aux Origines du Christianisme en Gaule* (Paris: Ouvrières, 1993).

One way to negotiate questions of identity was to show that one was as educated as the Romans were. Irenaeus and his community faced a double bind. First, because they did not worship at the imperial cult, their *romanitas* could always be called into question. Second, Irenaeus's opponents interpreted the scriptures in a way that he believed was incompatible with Christian identity. Irenaeus's writing is an attempt to forge (or reassert) Christian identity through reading techniques taken from the Greco-Roman rhetorical tradition.[26] Irenaeus could put his education to use as a way of asserting his place among those scholars—"pagan" or Christian—who were educated the same way he was. Indeed, we can place Irenaeus in one cultural context in particular.

Irenaeus was not alone in his concern about questions of interpretation and identity. One important (if neglected) context in which to understand Irenaeus is the Second Sophistic movement in Greek literature (ca. 50–250 A.D.). Scholars debate the exact contours of the "Second Sophistic," a term that Philostratus originally coined in his *Lives of the Sophists*.[27] Writers in the period often debated the status of philosophy.[28] As we shall see, at different points in the *Adversus Haer-*

26. See Paul Foster, "Who Was Irenaeus? An Introduction to the Man and His Work," in *Irenaeus: Scripture, Life, Legacy* (ed. Foster and Parvis), 13–24.

27. Philostratus, *The Lives of the Sophists*, Loeb Classical Library (Cambridge, Mass.: Harvard University Press, 1961). Laurent Pernot, for example, argues, that the Second Sophistic "was not so much an organized movement as a multitude of individual initiatives, linked by a common spirit, a shared educational and intellectual practice, and numerous personal contacts." Laurent Pernot, *Rhetoric in Antiquity* (Washington, D.C.: The Catholic University of America Press, 2005), 187. See also G. W. Bowersock, *Approaches to the Second Sophistic* (University Park, Penn.: American Philological Association, 1974), and *Hellenism in Late Antiquity* (Ann Arbor: University of Michigan Press, 1990); Graham Anderson, *The Second Sophistic: A Cultural Phenomenon in the Roman Empire* (New York: Routledge, 1993); Tim Whitmarsh, *The Second Sophistic* (Oxford: Oxford University Press, 2005).

28. For studies on this see George R. Boys-Stones, *Post-Hellenistic Philosophy: A Study of Its Development from the Stoics to Origen* (Oxford: Oxford University Press, 2001); J. M. Andre, "Les Ècoles Philosophiques aux Deux Premiers Siecles de l'Empire," *Aufstieg und Niedergang der romischen Welt* 36, no. 1 (1987): 5–77; John Whittaker, "Platonic Philosophy in the Early Centuries of the Empire," *Aufstieg und Niedergang der romischen Welt* 36, no. 1 (1987): 81–123; Johannes Hahn, *Der Philosoph und die Gesellschaft: Selbstverstandnis, Offentliches Auftreten und populare Erwartungen in der hohen Kaiserzeit* (Stuttgart: Steiner, 1989). Two doctoral dissertations have focused on the role that

eses, Irenaeus argues that his opponents borrow from Greek literary and philosophical categories to interpret the scriptures. To enter into a debate about the ability of any of the various philosophical schools to offer persuasive interpretations is to engage in questions very much alive in this period.[29] Of course, that is not to say that the Bible did not need certain principles to understand it correctly. Both Irenaeus and his opponents agree that it did. The question, as we shall see, is the source of those principles.

Concerns about the nomenclature of the Second Sophistic notwithstanding,[30] three aspects of the period resonate with Irenaeus's work. First, rhetors of the Second Sophistic often wrote poems or speeches of praise or blame.[31] Second, these rhetors often focused their attention on the past, on the great glories of Greek history and literature.[32] Their concern for the past links closely with the third aspect of Second Sophistic rhetoric, which is its concern for Greek identity. Greek-speaking sophists, who lived under Roman political authority, saw themselves as the inheritors of the language and culture of classical Greece and, as such, the guardians of the Hellenic legacy.[33] Preserving Greek identity was not simply a matter of copying certain

---

Plato played in the authors of the Second Sophistic, and both note that the line between philosophy and rhetoric in this period was not as finely demarcated as it was in Plato's *Gorgias*. See Ryan Coleman Fowler, "The Platonic Rhetor in the Second Sophistic" (PhD diss., Rutgers University, 2008); Katarzyna Anna Jazdzewska, "Platonic Receptions in the Second Sophistic" (PhD diss., Ohio State University, 2011).

29. As we shall see in chapter 2, Irenaeus was well aware of the various philosophical schools alive in the second century; see especially *AH* 2.14. Of course, thanks to the work of Pierre Hadot among others we know these various schools offered different ways of life to their adherents. See Pierre Hadot, *Philosophy as a Way of Life: Spiritual Exercises from Socrates to Foucault*, ed. Arnold Davidson (Oxford: Wiley-Blackwell, 1995).

30. Simon Goldhill, "Rhetoric and the Second Sophistic," in *The Cambridge Companion to Ancient Rhetoric*, ed. Erik Gunderson (Cambridge: Cambridge University Press, 2009), 229.

31. Later, we will show the categorization of speeches with which Irenaeus would have been familiar.

32. See Whitmarsh, *The Second Sophistic*, 1. On the connection between the Second Sophistic and education, see Barbara Borg, *Paideia: The World of the Second Sophistic* (New York: Walter de Gruyter, 2004).

33. Pernot, *Rhetoric in Antiquity*, 191; Whitmarsh, *The Second Sophistic*, 1.

books and teaching them. Instead, the authors in the Second Sophistic debated who should be studied and why. Like these Second Sophistic authors, Irenaeus would have been trained in methods we now call "rhetorical" and "philosophical," but his training does not entail a full-scale endorsement of any one of the philosophical or rhetorical schools.[34]

Irenaeus might not have been part of a network of pagan sophists, but on these basic points his concerns align him with the Second Sophistic. As a Greek speaker in a land where the Greek-speaking population was a minority, and as someone rhetorically trained with a deep concern for religious identity, he obviously shares the sophists' concerns.[35] In Irenaeus's case, Christian identity is forged through an understanding of the person and work of Christ and the related issue of the interpretation of scripture. In reaction to those teachers who disregard the writings of the Jewish scriptures, Irenaeus argues forcefully that these scriptures are part of the Christian past. This identity and this past are the proper objects for praise. Indeed, the only appropriate response to the economy of salvation that is recapitulated in Christ is praise for God. By guarding both the scriptures and the memory of the martyrs, Irenaeus establishes a specifically Christian identity based on the Law given by God, taught by Jesus, and handed down by the Apostles. I will return to these major issues throughout my argument.

At this point, allow me to step back. To contemporary ears, the word "rhetoric" itself is a problem. Often it denotes style over substance, subterfuge over clarity. For my purposes, we can think of rhetoric in one of two ways: either as a theory of how to speak or as the theory and practice of speech together. Irenaeus would have been fa-

34. I will return to this point in chapter 2.

35. George Kennedy notes "as early as the second century a Christianized version of sophistry had begun to emerge" (*A New History of Classical Rhetoric*, 230). See also Hans Conzelmann, *Gentiles, Jews, Christians: Polemics and Apologetics in the Greco-Roman Era* (Minneapolis, Minn.: Fortress Press, 1992); Willi Braun, *Rhetoric and Reality in Early Christianities* (Waterloo: Wilfrid Laurier University Press, 2005); Erik Gunderson (ed.), *The Cambridge Companion to Ancient Rhetoric* (New York: Cambridge University Press, 2009).

miliar with rhetoric in both senses.[36] We cannot witness Irenaeus's speech, but we do have two of his texts. Irenaeus would have shaped his argument in these texts with techniques he learned in the rhetorical education he received. Two of the most important figures whose writings helped shape that education were Aristotle and Quintilian.

In this book, I draw on Aristotle and Quintilian because their texts—especially Aristotle's *On the Art of Rhetoric* and Quintilian's *The Orator's Education*—help us make sense of how Irenaeus structures his argument in the *Adversus Haereses*. I do not draw on these texts because I think Irenaeus read them; in fact, the opposite is likely the case. I hope to offer an account of Irenaeus's argument that would have made sense of his understanding *both* of the scriptures and the faith that interprets those scriptures *and* of the education Irenaeus would have received. I should note here that according to Quintilian, when an orator composed his speech, he needed to worry about five things.[37] One of these five was the *dispositio*, which is the translation of the Greek *oikonomia*.[38] Each of these five parts is integral to giving a speech, but I can only discuss the *dispositio*, how the orator ordered his speech.[39] In the following chapters I shall examine how the *dispo-*

36. We can follow Pernot in understanding that rhetoric has two uses: "a restrained use, which designates only the theory of discourse ... and a wider use, which covers theory and practice together" (*Rhetoric in Antiquity*, vi). Averil Cameron has a similarly wide understanding of rhetoric. See Averil Cameron, *Christianity and the Rhetoric of Empire: The Development of Christian Discourse* (Berkeley: University of California Press, 1991).

37. These were: invention, ordering (*dispositio*), style (*elocutio*), memory, and pronunciation. "Omnis autem orandi ratio, ut plurimi maximeque auctores tradiderunt, quinque partibus constat: inventione dispositione elocutione memoria pronuntiatione sive actione (utroque enim modo dicitur)." Quintilian, *The Orator's Education,* trans. D. A. Russell (Cambridge, Mass.: Harvard University Press, 2001), 3.3.1.

38. I will fill out this picture in chapter 4, but for now it is enough to flag the connection one might draw between God's *oikonomia* and the way a rhetor would order his speech. Aristotle also includes these five steps.

39. Kennedy distinguishes between what Aristotle and Quintilian mean by rhetoric. For Aristotle, rhetoric is "the faculty of discovering in each case the available means of persuasion," and for Quintilian it is "the knowledge of how to speak well." Kennedy, *New Testament Interpretation through Rhetorical Criticism*, 13. These two definitions denote a difference in emphasis. Aristotle is concerned with proof and Quintilian is interested in "a variety of rhetorical features which does not neglect proof, but gives increased attention to style." Even in translation, though, Irenaeus's "invention," which Kennedy

sitio of the *Adversus Haereses* fits within a rhetorical framework and how Irenaeus uses this framework to argue for a particular understanding of scriptural interpretation.

In order to get a better hold on this rhetorical framework, we should note the three kinds of speeches a rhetor could give. Aristotle lists deliberative speech as the first kind. Today we would associate deliberative speeches with politicians. They urge their audience to take a particular action. We would associate lawyers with the second kind of speech, the forensic. This type of speech accuses or defends. After the deliberative and the forensic, Aristotle lists the epideictic, which we would associate with eulogies. The the rhetor giving an epideictic speech either praises or blames his subject.[40] All three types of speech aim to persuade their audience to make a judgment, but Aristotle refers to the audience in a epideictic speech as spectators.[41] Irenaeus fills his text with discussions of visions to be seen. He does this in large

---

describes as "the treatment of subject matter, the use of evidence, the argumentation, and the control of emotion" shines through. In fact, Kennedy goes on to say that invention "is often of greater importance and is central to rhetorical as understood by Greeks and Romans" (*New Testament Interpretation through Rhetorical Criticism*, 3). For Hellenistic views on rhetoric see James Kinneavy, *Greek Rhetorical Origins of Christian Faith* (New York: Oxford University Press, 1987), 40–44.

40. "The deliberative kind is either hortatory or dissuasive; for both those who give advice in private and those who speak in the assembly invariably either exhort or dissuade. The forensic kind is either accusatory or defensive; for litigants must necessarily either accuse or defend. The epideictic kind has for its subject either praise or blame." (συμβουλῆς δὲ τὸ μὲν προτροπή, τὸ δὲ ἀποτροπή· ἀεὶ γὰρ καὶ οἱ ἰδίᾳ συμβουλεύοντες καὶ οἱ κοινῇ δημηγοροῦντες τούτων θάτερον ποιοῦσιν. δίκης δὲ τὸ μὲν κατηγορία, τὸ δ' ἀπολογία· τούτων γὰρ ὁποτερονοῦν ποιεῖν ἀνάγκη τοὺς ἀμφισβητοῦντας. ἐπιδεικτικοῦ δὲ τὸ μὲν ἔπαινος τὸ δὲ ψόγος.) Aristotle, *The "Art" of Rhetoric*, trans. John Henry Freese (Cambridge, Mass.: Harvard University Press, 1959), 1358b.

41. "Now the employment of persuasive speeches is directed towards a judgment; for when a thing is known and judged, there is no longer any need of judgment ... and similarly in epideictic speeches, for the speech is put together with reference to the spectator as if he were a judge." (Ἐπεὶ δὲ ἡ τῶν πιθανῶν λόγων χρῆσις πρὸς κρίσιν ἐστί περὶ ὧν γὰρ ἴσμεν καὶ κεκρίκαμεν οὐδὲν ἔτι δεῖ λόγου, ἔστι δ' ἐάν τε πρὸς ἕνα τις τῷ λόγῳ χρώμενος προτρέπῃ ἢ ἀποτρέπῃ, οἷον οἱ νουθετοῦντες ποιοῦσιν ἢ πείθοντες οὐδὲν γὰρ ἧττον κριτὴς ὁ εἷς· ὃν γὰρ δεῖ πεῖσαι, οὗτός ἐστιν ὡς εἰπεῖν ἁπλῶς κριτής, ἐάν τε πρὸς ἀμφισβητοῦντας, ἐάν τε πρὸς ὑπόθεσιν λέγῃ τις, ὁμοίως τῷ γὰρ λόγῳ ἀνάγκη χρῆσθαι καὶ ἀναιρεῖν τὰ ἐναντία, πρὸς ἃ ὥσπερ ἀμφισβητοῦντα τὸν λόγον ποιεῖται, ὡσαύτως δὲ καὶ ἐν τοῖς ἐπιδεικτικοῖς ὥσπερ γὰρ πρὸς κριτὴν τὸν θεωρὸν ὁ λόγος συνέστηκε.) Aristotle, *Rhetoric* 1391b.

part because the scriptures do the same thing. And so in this way he follows a major theme in the tradition that precedes him.

Irenaeus uses all three categories of speech throughout the *Adversus Haereses*. We shall further see that Irenaeus begins each book with a forensic discourse, moves to epideictic discourse, and concludes with deliberative discourse. That is, Irenaeus begins each book with either an accusation or a defense, which is the mark of forensic discourse. He either accuses his opponents' tradition of misinterpreting God or defends the Apostolic tradition for understanding God correctly. He then shifts to epideictic discourse in order to praise (or blame) the economy of salvation offered by his tradition or that of his opponents. Then he shifts to deliberative discourse to encourage his audience to make a decision. They can choose either his opponents' interpretation of Christ's salvific work or defend the interpretation that comes from the Apostles.

All of this fits well with Aristotle's general point about the function of rhetoric: "to deal with things about which we deliberate, but for which we have no systematic rules."[42] Although I shall argue throughout this book about the principles of scriptural interpretation that Irenaeus and his opponents use, neither Irenaeus nor his opponents would see those principles as thoroughly systematic. Aristotle argues that the goal of rhetoric is "the power to persuade each one to see what is admitted."[43] Irenaeus's goal is to help his audience understand how scripture recounts God's economy of creation and salvation and how the end of this economy will result in a vision of God. Irenaeus, like Aristotle, sees a deep connection between rhetoric and vision. I will return to this theme throughout the book.

If Aristotle describes the three different categories of speech, Quintilian discusses the effect the speech should have on the audience. For Quintilian, the three aims of the orator are to teach, to move, and to delight.[44] When the orator exposes his opponent's argument

---

42. ἔστιν δὲ τὸ ἔργον αὐτῆς περί τε τοιούτων περὶ ὧν βουλευόμεθα καὶ τέχνας μὴ ἔχομεν. Aristotle, *Rhetoric* 1357a.

43. Ἔστω δὴ ἡ ῥητορικὴ δύναμις περὶ ἕκαστον τοῦ θεωρῆσαι τὸ ἐνδεχόμενον πιθανόν. Aristotle, *Rhetoric* 1355b25.

44. "Tria sunt item quae praestare debeat orator, ut doceat moveat delectet." Quintilian, *The Orator's Education* 3.5.2.

and argues against it, he is teaching. When an orator appeals to his audience's emotions, he is moving them. The orator can delight his audience while he teaches and moves them, but delight is most properly reserved for the orator's delivery.[45] Quintilian also lists three styles of speech: the subtle, the robust, and a combination of the two. That is, the orator should use the subtle style to teach, the robust style to move, and the mixed style to delight.[46] The good orator will use all three of these styles throughout his speech. Irenaeus, as we shall see, does exactly this. In each of the five books of the *Adversus Haereses*, we can find examples of subtle, robust, and mixed discourse.[47] In fact, we can map the three goals onto Aristotle's three kinds of speech. The forensic speech needs to instruct, the epideictic to delight, and the deliberative to move.

George Kennedy, the great scholar of ancient rhetoric, has written that the sophist acted as a virtuoso by structuring his work around a small number of themes. The images that the orator used "are presented to the mind and are woven into changing visual patterns."[48] In his vast *oeuvre*, Kennedy does not discuss Irenaeus, but the description he offers here fits Irenaeus well. Irenaeus structures his *Adversus Haereses* around a small number of themes. Through his interpretation of scrip-

---

45. "Oratoris officium docendi movendi delectandi partitibus contineri, ex quibus ad docendum expositio et argumentatio, ad movendum adfectus pertineret, quos per omnem quidem causam sed maime tamen in ingressu ac fine dominari. Nam delectationem, quamvis in utroque sit eorum, magis tamen proprias in elocutione partes habere." Quintilian, *The Orator's Education* 8.1.7.

46. "Altera est divisio, quae in tribus partis et ipsa discedit, qua discerni posse etiam recta dicendi genera inter se videtur. Namque unum subtile, quod ἰσχνον vocant. alteram grande atque robustum, quod ἁδρον dicunt. constituent tertium alii medium ex duobus, alii floridum (namque id ἀνθρόν appellant) addiderunt." Quintilian, *The Orator's Education* 12.10.58.

47. Of course, each of the three styles has a purpose: "Quorum tamen ea fere ratio est, ut primum docendi, secundum movendi, tertium illud, utrocumque est nomine, delectandi sive, ut alii dicant, conciliandi praestare videatur officium, in docendo autem acumen, in conciliando lenitas, in movendo vis exigi videatur." Quintilian, *The Orator's Education* 12.10.59. A good orator should make use of all three styles: "ita in eadem oratione aliter conciliabit, non ex isdem haustibus iram et misericordiam petet, alias ad docendum, alias ad movendum adhibebit artis. Non unus color prohoemii narrationis argumentorum egressionis perorationis servabitur" (12.10.71).

48. Kennedy, *A New History of Classical Rhetoric*, 232.

ture he shows that the God and Father of Jesus Christ is the creator of the universe. He contends that the scriptures cannot be interpreted properly unless one has a proper understanding of the normative role that the church, as the community of interpreters, plays in that interpretation. He also argues that Christ's salvation extends to the entire human being, flesh and soul.

My point in this introduction is not to offer a catalog of different types of speeches and different views of ancient theorists of rhetoric. After all, we must remember that the *Adversus Haereses* was not meant to be delivered orally and that Greek rhetors were not concerned with Valentinian teaching.[49] It is helpful, I want to argue, to know how Aristotle thought speeches should be organized.[50] It is even more helpful to know how Quintilian understood the parts of a forensic speech because Irenaeus's goal in the *Adversus Haereses* is to expose and refute his opponents' teaching. Quintilian argues that a forensic speech should include the *prohoemium*, which acts as a preface; a *narratio*, which is the statement and refutation of the opponent's case on its own terms; the *probatio* or proof, which is the statement of one's own case; the *refutatio*, which is the refutation of the opponent based on the speaker's own argument; and the *recapitulatio*, where the speaker reca-

---

49. William Schoedel argues that the that the *Adversus Haereses* "follows no pattern since it is much more than a speech and since Hellenistic rhetoricians did not concern themselves with heretics." William R. Schoedel, "Philosophy and Rhetoric in the Adversus Haereses of Irenaeus," *Vigiliae Christianae* (hereafter, *VC*) 13, no. 1 (1959): 27. Schoedel points to Ciceronian antecedents for Irenaeus, but I think Quintilian's division of the forensic speech is more apt. I disagree with Schoedel that the *Adversus Haereses* lacks a peroration or a recapitulation.

50. According to Aristotle, there are only two essential parts of a speech, the statement of the case and the proof. He recognizes, however, that speeches usually come in four parts and so he adds the prologue before the statement of the case and the epilogue after the proof. διήγησις γάρ που τοῦ δικανικοῦ μόνου λόγου ἐστίν, ἐπιδεικτικοῦ δὲ καὶ δημηγορικοῦ πῶς ἐνδέχεται εἶναι διήγησιν οἵαν λέγουσιν, ἢ τὰ πρὸς τὸν ἀντίδικον, ἢ ἐπίλογον τῶν ἀποδεικτικῶν; προοίμιον δὲ καὶ ἀντιπαραβολὴ καὶ ἐπάνοδος ἐν ταῖς δημηγορίαις τότε γίνεται ὅταν ἀντιλογία ᾖ (Rhetoric 1414a). About the parts of speech, Aristotle continues, ἀναγκαῖα ἄρα μόρια πρόθεσις καὶ πίστις. ἴδια μὲν οὖν ταῦτα, τὰ δὲ πλεῖστα προοίμιον πρόθεσις πίστις ἐπίλογος· τὰ γὰρ πρὸς τὸν ἀντίδικον τῶν πίστεών ἐστι, καὶ ἡ ἀντιπαραβολὴ αὔξησις τῶν αὐτοῦ, ὥστε μέρος τι τῶν πίστεων (ἀποδείκνυσι γάρ τι ὁ ποιῶν τοῦτο), ἀλλ᾽ οὐ τὸ προοίμιον, οὐδ᾽ ὁ ἐπίλογος, ἀλλ᾽ ἀναμιμνήσκει (1414b).

pitulates his own argument and urges his audience to side with him.[51] I shall address each of these in relation to each of the five books.[52] We should also note that Irenaeus follows the rhetorical precedent that calls for starting with the weakest arguments and ending with the strongest.[53]

Within Irenaeus's overall forensic goal, however, we can find moments of epideictic and deliberative discourse as well as forensic discourse. For example, the forensic discourse in Books One and Two shifts to an epideictic discourse in Books Three and Four. In these books Irenaeus offers an *epideixis* of praise, praising Christ (in Book Three) and the economy of salvation (in Book Four). Irenaeus gives his positive account of Apostolic teaching and "proves" that teaching through an exegesis of select Old Testament passages. In Book Five,

---

51. "Nunc de iudicale genere, quod est praecipue multiplex sed officiis constat duobus, intentionis ac depulsionis. Cuius artes, ut plurimus auctoribus placuit, quinque sunt: prohoemium narratio probatio refutatio peroratio. His adiecerunt quidam partitionem propositionem excessum quorm priores duae probationi succidunt." Quintilian, *The Orator's Education* 3.9.1. For the more on the order of speeches see Kennedy, *New Testament Interpretation through Rhetorical Criticism*, 24.

52. Quintilian recognizes, though, that the rules he puts forth are not hard and fast. "Nemo autem a me exigat id praeceptorum genus quod est a plerisque scriptoribus artium traditum, ut quasi quasdam leges immutabili necessitate constrictas studiosis dicendi feram" (*The Orator's Education* 2.13.1). Just as Irenaeus's rhetorical skill has been the subject of scholarly debate, so too has the structure of the *Adversus Haereses* as a whole. Minns argues that it does not seem like Irenaeus planned the five books. Denis Minns, *Irenaeus* (Washington, D.C.: Georgetown University Press, 1994), 6–8. Fantino has also argued that the structure of the *Adversus Haereses* is not Irenaeus's strongest point; see Jacques Fantino, *La Théologie d'Irénée: Lecture des ecritures en réponse à l'exégèse gnostique: une approche trinitaire* (Paris: Editions du Cerf, 1994), 390.

53. Vallée writes, "The very order of the arguments in Books II to V betrays such an acquaintance, for it was a common rhetorical technique to hold back the decisive arguments for the later parts of the development and to present the weaker ones first. Irenaeus follows this pattern by presenting first his philosophical arguments against the Gnostics and then by offering the most decisive scriptural arguments." Gérard Vallée, *A Study in Anti-Gnostic Polemics: Irenaeus, Hippolytus, and Epiphanius* (Waterloo: Wilfrid University Press, 1981), 13. Schoedel writes the following about the structure of the *Adversus Haereses*: "According to Theon authorities are to be arranged κατὰ αὔξησιν, i.e. in order of significance from the last to the greatest (Progymn. 12,122 Spegel). This is precisely what Irenaeus does when he devotes book ii to arguments from reason, book ii to arguments from the apostolic tradition and book iv to arguments based on the words of the Lord." Schoedel, "Philosophy and Rhetoric," 28.

although he is still attacking the false teaching of his opponents, Irenaeus presents a deliberative discourse that shifts his audience's attention. Having provided them with an exposition of his opponents' teaching and a praise of Apostolic teaching, Irenaeus recapitulates his argument and offers his audience the choice between the two systems of scriptural interpretation. He also describes the consequences of that choice. Irenaeus's strongest arguments, then, come from his exegeses of the scriptures and his comparisons with what his opponents say. These arguments are more likely to make his audience choose the Apostolic teaching than if he were merely to lay out his opponents' teaching and refute it on its own terms. Each of the five books can be further broken down into sections of *probatio*, *refutatio*, and *recapitulatio*. The *probatio* in each book is a moment of forensic rhetoric. It sets the terms of the debate. These terms, as we shall see, focus on how best to understand God. The *refutatio* in each book is a moment of epideictic rhetoric. It seeks to refute his opponents' claims by focusing on the economy of the scriptural text. If the *probatio* focuses on God, the *refutatio* focuses on the economy of creation and salvation. The *recapitulatio* in each book is a moment of deliberative rhetoric. It looks to the future and urges the audience to consider the competing claims about salvation that his opponents and Irenaeus make in their interpretation of scripture, and specifically focuses on the role Christ plays in salvation.

As we will see, these three moments also line up with the faith as Irenaeus presents it in Book One. The church's faith begins with discussing who God is. It then addresses how God has worked through the economy of salvation. The statement of faith concludes with Christ as the recapitulator of God's work through history, especially Christ's work of salvation. Therefore, each time Irenaeus discusses God or God's power, he is addressing the *probatio*, the case in dispute between him and his opponents. Each time he discusses the economy of salvation and Christ's role in the economy of salvation, he is addressing the *refutatio*. And each time he addresses human salvation, he is addressing the *recapitulatio*. In fact, we shall see that throughout the *Adversus Haereses*, Irenaeus's argument spirals in exactly this way. Within each book, we find these major sections, and each section is further divided into three. Hence we see (as we shall throughout our discussion of the *Adversus Haereses*) the *probatio*, the *refutatio*, and the *recapitulatio*.

At all points in the *Adversus Haereses*, Irenaeus offers an interpretation of scriptural texts. Each *probatio*, *refutatio*, and *recapitulatio* is the site for and fruit of scriptural interpretation. I will not delineate this structure now, but I will say here that Irenaeus's argument spirals as it builds to a climax. I have organized each of the chapters around the three moments of *probatio*, *refutatio*, and *recapitulatio*. In each chapter, I also examine those sections of Books One through Five of the *Adversus Haereses* where Irenaeus offers what I call a "theological methodology" or a scriptural hermeneutics. In these sections, I step back and examine the principles Irenaeus uses when he interprets the scriptures.

If these are the divisions we find in a speech, we still need to discuss what makes such a speech persuasive. According to Aristotle, there are three aspects of a rhetor's speech that make it likely that the audience will be swayed by it: the rhetor's character, his ability to put the audience into a certain frame of mind, and the speech itself insofar as it can persuade.[54] In short, we can follow Aristotle and name these three respectively as *ethos*, *pathos*, and *logos*. As we will see, Irenaeus employs all three aspects throughout the *Adversus Haereses*. In order for the rhetor to have a persuasive character, according to Aristotle, he must have "good sense, virtue, and good will."[55] Quintilian goes even further than Aristotle, saying not only that an orator must be a good man "but that no one can be an orator unless he is a good man." Someone who expects people to take his counsel "must be, and be thought to be, very wise and very good."[56] As we shall see, in his *probationes*

---

54. τῶν δὲ διὰ τοῦ λόγου ποριζομένων πίστεων τρία εἴδη ἔστιν· αἱ μὲν γάρ εἰσιν ἐν τῷ ἤθει τοῦ λέγοντος, αἱ δὲ ἐν τῷ τὸν ἀκροατὴν διαθεῖναί πως, αἱ δὲ ἐν αὐτῷ τῷ λόγῳ διὰ τοῦ δεικνύναι ἢ φαίνεσθαι δεικνύναι (Aristotle, *Rhetoric* 1356a1).

55. τοῦ μὲν οἷ αὐτοὺς εἶναι πιστοὺς τοὺς λέγοντας τρία ἐστὶ τὰ αἴτια τοσῦτα γὰρ δῑ ἃ πιστεύομεν ἔξω τῶν ἀποδείξεων. ἐστὶ δὴ τὰ ταῦτα φρόνησιν καὶ ἀρετὴ καὶ ἔθνοια (Aristotle, *Rhetoric* 1387a).

56. "Oratorem autem instituimus illum perfectum, qui esse nisi vir bonus non potest, ideoque non dicendi modo eximiam in eo facultatem sed monis animi virtutes exigimus" (Quintilian, *The Orator's Education* 1.1.9–10). "Neque enim tantum id dico, eum qui sit orator virum bonum esse oportere, sed ne futurum quidem oratorem nisi virum bonum" (12.1.3).

and his *recapitulationes* and especially in his *refutationes*, Irenaeus goes to great lengths to connect himself to upstanding teachers and to show the moral depravity of those teachers whose interpretations he rejects.

But the rhetor's own character—his own *ethos*—is only one part of the story. The rhetor must consider the character of the audience, and he must know how to put them into a frame of mind so that he can be persuasive.[57] He must know, in other words, their *pathos*. *Pathos* refers both to the audience's frame of mind and to the speaker's ability to engage them. One key way to do this is through the use of witnesses. Both Aristotle and Quintilian recognize that the character of witnesses lends credibility to one's argument and therefore makes it more persuasive. For example, Aristotle notes that even a single witness can be useful and that ancient witnesses are more trustworthy because they cannot be corrupted.[58] Quintilian argues that it is customary to begin one's speech with a discussion of witnesses. That way, while the prosecutor can argue "that there is no firmer proof than that which depends on personal knowledge," the defense, trying to "detract from witnesses' credibility, lists the reasons for which false evidence is commonly given."[59] For both Aristotle and Quintilian, then, witnesses serve both as proof for the orator when he tries to make his case and as a point of contention when orators disagree with each other.

57. "But since the object of rhetoric is judgment—for judgments are pronounced in deliberative rhetoric and judicial proceedings are a judgment—it is not only necessary to consider how to make the speech itself demonstrative and convincing, but also that the speaker should show himself to be of a certain character and should know how to put the judge into a certain frame of mind." (ἐπεὶ δὲ ἕνεκα κρίσεώς ἐστιν ἡ ῥητορική (καὶ γὰρ τὰς συμβουλὰς κρίνουσι καὶ ἡ δίκη κρίσις ἐστίν), ἀνάγκη μὴ μόνον πρὸς τὸν λόγον ὁρᾶν, ὅπως ἀποδεικτικὸς ἔσται καὶ πιστός, ἀλλὰ καὶ αὐτὸν ποιόν τινα καὶ τὸν κριτὴν κατασκευάζειν.) Aristotle, *Rhetoric* 1377b. As Walker writes, "Aristotle describes all audiences as *akroatai*: *akroatai* subdivide into *kritai* and *theôroi* with *kritai* further subdivided into *dikastai*, *bouletai* and *ekklesiastai* for dikanic and symbouleutic/demeogic discourse." Jeffrey Walker, *Rhetoric and Poetics in Antiquity* (Oxford: Oxford University Press, 2000), 322n14.

58. πιστότατοι δ᾽ οἱ παλαιοὶ ἀδιάφθοροι γάρ (Aristotle, *Rhetoric* 1394a).

59. "In actionibus primum generaliter pro testibus atque in testis dici solet. Est hic communis locus, cum par altera nullam firmiorem probationem esse contendit quam quae sit hominum scientia nixa, altera ad debrahendam illis fidem omnia per quae fiere soleant falsa testimonia enumberat." Quintilian, *The Orator's Education* 5.7.4.

Greek and Roman theorists of rhetoric saw witnesses as individuals who could "take the stand" in a judicial proceeding. Irenaeus saw witnesses as the Christian martyrs who died for their faith. I will return to the theme of martyrdom throughout my argument, but here I want to point to the way we can understand martyrs as witnesses in the tradition of Greco-Roman rhetoric. Witnesses serve both as proof for the orator when he tries to make his case and as a point of contention when orators disagree with each other. Rhetors can use them for both *ethos* and *pathos*. Scholars of Irenaeus have understood the importance that the bishop of Lyon places on martyrs, with one scholar going so far as to describe martyrdom as intrinsic to Irenaeus's thought.[60] They, however, have focused their attention on the martyr as the perfected Christian.[61] Although this is an important theme, it neglects a possible connection with the way in which the rhetorical tradition understood witnesses. Irenaeus's invocation of martyrs connects him to the tradition of Apostolic teaching. Through his invocation of Ignatius and Papias and Polycarp as interpreters of scripture and members of the body of Christ, Irenaeus establishes the connection between following Christ in life and death and following Christ's church in interpreting the scriptures.

When Irenaeus offers his witnesses he does so because of the specific way they interpreted the scriptures. To be sure, Irenaeus sees these interpreters as models of Christian living, but he also admires the consistency of their interpretation. Indeed, the consistency of their interpretation is shown through how they live their lives. Unlike his opponents, those Christians who understand the scriptures in light of the faith recognize that the scriptures recount the love of God the Father shown forth in the life, death, and resurrection of Jesus Christ who was offered as salvation for human beings. These human beings

60. Tremblay, "Le martrye selon saint Irénée de Lyon," 177.

61. See, for example, Ysabel de Andia, *Homo Vivens: Incorruptibilite et Divinisation de l'Homme selon Irenée de Lyons* (Paris: Etudes augustiniennes, 1986), 338. Gustaf Wingren, *Man and the Incarnation: A Study in the Biblical Theology of Irenaeus* (Philadelphia: Muhlenberg Press, 1959), 34–35, 55, 138; and Behr, *Asceticism and Anthropology*, 78. For a study of martyrdom in the early church more generally see William Hugh Clifford Frend, *Martyrdom and Persecution in the Early Church: A Study of a Conflict from the Maccabees to Donatus* (Grand Rapids, Mich.: Baker Book House, 1981).

receive the Spirit of God because of Christ's work, and this reception makes them spiritual human beings whose bodies and souls will be saved.[62]

Even the title helps us to understand the goal of Irenaeus's work. One way to read the title, of course, would be to focus on the fact that Irenaeus is interested in detecting and overthrowing knowledge falsely so-called. If we were to take this route, then Irenaeus's interest in "Gnosticism" seem to be the most important part of the text. But a stronger interpretation of the title would begin by recognizing that the "detection and overthrow of knowledge falsely so-called" alludes to Paul's first letter to Timothy.[63] Irenaeus wants to identify himself with Paul. Indeed, Book Five of the *Adversus Haereses* focuses on the proper interpretation of Paul. The heart of Irenaeus's presentation is the proper identification of the witness of the books of the New Covenant. Yes, Irenaeus is interested in "defeating" his opponents, but he is interested in defeating them as Paul would defeat them. That is, Irenaeus is concerned with passing down Paul's teaching, and Irenaeus sees himself in the same position that Paul found himself in, combating false teachings about Jesus.[64]

If Irenaeus connects his writing to Paul, he also connects it to John, and for the same reason. According to Irenaeus, false teaching compelled John to write his Gospel. (I will discuss this at greater length in chapter 3.) My point here, though, is straightforward. Irenaeus wants to assert Christian identity through the proper interpretation of scriptural texts. In order to do this, he aligns his interpretation with two past Christian teachers: Paul and John. Irenaeus is interested in "false teaching" not for its own sake and certainly not as some sociological study, but because teachers such as Paul, John, and Polycarp were. These teachers were witnesses to the Apostolic interpretation of scripture on which Christian identity is based.

---

62. This is especially important in Irenaeus's exegesis of 1 Cor 2:15, where Paul discusses the spiritual man.

63. See 1 Tm 6:20.

64. Jared Secord suggests that like Paul, Irenaeus saw himself going to the ends of the world to proclaim the Gospel. Jared Secord, "The Cultural Geography of a Greek Christian: Ireaneus from Smyrna to Lyons," in *Irenaeus: Life, Scripture, Legacy* (ed. Foster and Parvis), 25–34.

Irenaeus's goal is to help his audience understand how scripture recounts God's economy of creation, and that salvation and the end of this economy will be a vision of God. We have already seen how Aristotle connected rhetoric and vision. I will say much more about vision throughout my argument, but here I want to flag a text that Irenaeus might have known. When Plutarch, in his work *On the Glory of the Athenians*, describes Thucydides's skill, he writes that the historian "desired to make the listener like a spectator."[65] For Plutarch, the rhetorical ideal was to present one's case so clearly that the most apt metaphor was vision. I have no proof that Irenaeus read Plutarch, who was a generation older than the Christian exegete, but I do want to argue that Irenaeus also wanted to make his hearers seers. For Irenaeus, the visions of scripture come from the Word of God, but they can only be seen if the scriptures are properly interpreted, that is, if they are read with the faith. Needless to say, there is much to unpack here, and I will spend a great deal of time in my argument discussing how Irenaeus's interpretations—following those of the Apostles—make the readers of scripture seers of the economy of salvation.

The structure of the *Adversus Haereses* is the argument of the *Adversus Haereses*. Irenaeus bases the structure of his argument on the structure of the faith of the church. Thus my own argument about Irenaeus tracks Irenaeus's structure closely. I begin each chapter with a scriptural verse that Irenaeus either discusses at length or that resonates with Irenaeus's project. The faith of the church, after all, is a guide to reading the scriptures correctly. I will discuss, in turn, five major themes: silence, fabrication, manifestation, prophecy, and

65. The best historian makes his narrative an image like a painting with events and people. Thucydides, for example, aimed for a vivid description with his speech. "He desired to makes the listener like a spectator and desired that the disturbing and astounding things that occurred for the people who saw them be produced for his listeners to know well." (τῶν ἱστορικῶν κράτιστος ὁ τὴν διήγησιν ὥσπερ γραφὴν πάθεσι καὶ προσώποις εἰδωλοποιήσας. ὁ γοῦν Θουκυδίδης ἀεὶ τῷ λόγῳ πρὸς ταύτην ἁμιλλᾶται τὴν ἐνάργειαν, οἷον θεατὴν ποιῆσαι τὸν ἀκροατὴν καὶ τὰ γινόμενα περὶ τοὺς ὁρῶντας ἐκπληκτικὰ καὶ ταρακτικὰ πάθη τοῖς ἀναγινώσκουσιν ἐνεργάσασθαι λιχνευόμενος.) Plutarch, *De Gloria Atheniensium*, trans. Jean-Claude Thiolier (Paris: Presses de l'Université de Paris-Sorbonne, 1985), 347a. For more on this theme, see Jasi Elsner, *Roman Eyes: Visuality and Subjectivity in Art and Text* (Princeton, N.J.: Princeton University Press, 2007).

judgment. These themes reflect each of the five books of the *Adversus Haereses*. When he discusses these themes, Irenaeus's focus is always the same. He structures his argument with a simple goal: to help his readers understand themselves in the economy of salvation that the scriptures—when interpreted with the faith—recount. With all of this in mind, I will begin discussing Book One.

1 ☩ SILENCE

> I repeat the request I made of you when I was on my way to Macedonia, that you stay in Ephesus to instruct certain people not to teach false doctrines or to concern themselves with myths and endless genealogies, which promote speculations rather than the plan of God [οἰκονομίαν θεοῦ] that is to be received by faith.

> 1 TM 1:3—5

The structure of the *Adversus Haereses* is the argument of the *Adversus Haereses*, and the structure of the *Adversus Haereses* is the faith. The faith, of course, helps the reader of scripture to understand God's economy (οἰκονομία) of salvation. Without the faith, without the structure that it provides, one is left merely with speculations, rather than the economy, the plan of God.

Paul's first letter to Timothy warns of the dangers of false teaching and false teachers. Writing from Lyon more than one hundred years after Paul, Irenaeus also confronts false doctrines that concern themselves with myths and endless genealogies.[1] Paul does not specify what the false teaching is or who teaches it. Irenaeus, however, has a specific teacher and a specific teaching in mind. The teacher he confronts is Valentinus of Alexandria, and it seems that Valentinus's pupil Ptolemy has followers who teach in Irenaeus's Gaul. In his letter, Paul does not trace the counterfeit genealogies of the ersatz teachers. In Book One of the *Adversus Haereses*, Irenaeus aims to do just that. Paul does not argue against the false teachers he mentions. He only tells

---

1. The date and composition of 1 Tm need not concern us here. Irenaeus believed that the Apostle Paul wrote the first letter to Timothy.

Timothy that these teachers do not promote the *oikonomia* of God that ought to be received by faith. Throughout the *Adversus Haereses*, Irenaeus argues against the teachings of Valentinus and his forebears and successors.[2] Irenaeus argues against these teachers by arguing against how they understand the plan of God as it is laid out in scripture. Yet, in order to understand the plan itself, one needs a method for interpreting it. That is to say, because God's *oikonomia* is not self-evident, one needs principles for understanding how God presents this plan in scripture. Valentinus, so Irenaeus believes, had such principles, but these principles were foreign to the scriptures themselves. In order to show this, Irenaeus must first lay out what these principles are, and then he must show where they lead. He aims to do this in the first two books of his treatise. In rhetorical terms, Irenaeus lays out the *narratio* of the case he prosecutes. The *narratio* is "the biased description of the events of the deed before the court."[3] In this *narratio*, the key term, as we will see, is silence. His opponents' speculations are grounded in silence. Irenaeus's speech is grounded in the Word that announces and recapitulates the economy of salvation.

I should note here that Irenaeus does not give us a clear itinerary of his argument at the beginning of Book One. In the preface to the book, Irenaeus explains his goal. He wants to present his opponents' teaching so that "having learned of these mysteries yourself, you can make them clear to all your people and warn them to be on guard against this profundity of nonsense and blasphemy against God."[4] He then explains, "We are neither used to writing nor practiced in the art of words. But love prompts us to acquaint you and all of yours with the teachings. These teachings have been kept hidden, but now, thanks to the grace of God, have become manifest."[5] Irenaeus's disavowal of

---

2. In this chapter, I am less concerned about the content of Valentinus's writings and those of his school than I am in Irenaeus's *perceptions* of those writings. There is a large body of scholarship on Valentinus. One should start with Lampe, *From Paul to Valentinus*, and Markschies, *Valentinus Gnosticus?*

3. Lausberg, *Handbook of Literary Rhetoric*, §290.

4. Μαθὼν αὐτα πᾶσι τοῖς μετὰ σοῦ φανερὰ ποίησῃς καὶ παραινέσῃς αὐτοῖς φθλά-ξασθαι τὸν βυθὸν τῆς ἀνοίας καὶ τῆς εἰς τὸν Θεὸν βλασφημίας. 1.P.2.

5. Μήτε συγγράφειν εἰσθισμένοι μήτε λόγων τέχνην ἠσκηκότες ἀγαπης δὲ ἡμας προτρεπομένης σοί τε καὶ πᾶσι τοῖς μετὰ σοῦ μηνῦσαι τὰ μέχρι μὲν νῦν κεκρυμμένα ἤδη δὲ κατὰ τὴν χάριν τοῦ θεοῦ εἰς φανερὸν ἐληλυθότα.

rhetoric is itself a rhetorical move.[6] We should note, though, that love prompts Irenaeus's writings, and Irenaeus's words make what was hidden manifest, in good rhetorical fashion. Irenaeus reminds his reader, however, that he could not do this without God's grace. "To the best of my power I will report the teaching of these people who are passing down opinions. I speak of the disciples of Ptolemy, an offshoot of the school of Valentinus."[7] Irenaeus will also "offer suggestions, to the best of our limited capacity, for refuting this teaching, by showing how absurd, inconsistent, and incongruous with the truth their statements are."[8] I will argue that the "concise and clear report" lines up with Book One, whereas the "suggestions" for refuting Ptolemy seems to line up with Book Two. As we will see, though, Book One offers moments of refutation as well. Both books make up Irenaeus's *narratio*.

With Irenaeus's words in mind, we can now turn to Book One, which we can divide into three major sections.[9] The first nine chapters discuss Ptolemy's hermeneutical system. This system, however,

---

6. This disavowal of rhetorical ability is itself a mark of rhetorical ability. Socrates makes a similar disavowal in *Apology* 17b.

7. Καὶ, καθὼς δύναμις ἡμῖν, τήν τε γνώμην αὐτῶν τῶν νῦν παραδιδασκόντων, λέγω δὴ τῶν περὶ Πτολεμαῖον, ἀπάνθισμα οὖσαν τῆς Οὐαλεντίνου σχολῆς.

8. καὶ ἀφορμὰς δώσομεν κατὰ τὴν ἡμετέραν μετριότητα πρὸς τὸ ἀνατρέπειν αὐτήν, ἀλλόκοτα καὶ ἀσύστατα καὶ ἀνάρμοστα τῆι ἐπιδεικνύντες τὰ ὑπ᾽ αὐτῶν λεγόμενα (1.P.2).

9. There has been a robust discussion in the secondary literature on how Irenaeus structured Book One. See David H. Tripp, "The Original Sequence of Irenaeus Adversus Haereses I: A Suggestion," *Second Century: A Journal of Early Christian Studies* 8, no. 3 (1991): 157–62; Joel Kalvesmaki, "The Original Sequence of Irenaeus, against Heresies 1: Another Suggestion," *Journal of Early Christian Studies* 15, no. 3 (2007): 407–17. Tripp argues that the original sequence of Book One was a. 1–12; b. 23–31; c. 13–16.2; d. rest of text through 22. Kalvesmaki argues that the original sequence was a. 1–22.1 and then the last section of 32. He argues that 22.2 through 32.1 was inserted later and Irenaeus took this section from an earlier heresiological text, such as Justin Martyr's *Syntagma*; this text is attested in Justin Martyr, *The First and Second Apologies* (New York: Paulist Press, 1997), 1.28.8, and Eusebius Caesarea, *The Ecclesiastical History*, 4.1.10. See also Einar Thomassen, *The Spiritual Seed: The Church of the "Valentinians"* (Leiden; Boston: Brill, 2006), 10n4; Rowan A. Greer, "The Dog and the Mushrooms: Irenaeus's View of the Valentinians Assessed," in *Rediscovery of Gnosticism*, ed. Bentley Layton (Leiden: Brill, 1980), 1:146–75. I am largely persuaded by Kalvesmaki's analysis, which, as he notes, agrees with Thomassen's. As we shall see, Kalveskmaki's view of the "first edition" of Book One and his view of the final edition of Book One both fit with my argument about the structure of the book. Because Irenaeus's argument spirals, each section contains moments of the other two.

makes specific (and to Irenaeus, grossly wrongheaded) claims about who God is. Ptolemy and his followers misunderstand God because they misunderstand scripture and they misunderstand scripture because they misunderstand God. Chapters 11 through 21 discuss the many different interpretative principles of the teachers Irenaeus opposes. In this section Irenaeus spends considerable time discussing Marcus the Magician. In these chapters Irenaeus describes the *oikonomia*, or more specifically the lack of uniformity in the various teachers' views of God's economy. For Irenaeus, this is a sign of interpretative weakness, rather than strength. To discuss these various views of God's *oikonomia* is to discuss two things at once: their view of scripture and their view of creation. Irenaeus recapitulates his argument in chapters 23 through 31, which focus more specifically on the teaching of Valentinus. Valentinus is Irenaeus's main opponent in the *Adversus Haereses*, and thus it makes sense that Book One would build to him. Valentinus represents the arguments of all these teachers at their strongest and most persuasive.

Irenaeus confronts a basic problem when narrating views of his opponents. Unlike the Apostolic teaching, which he argues is clear for all to see, the teaching offered by Ptolemy, Valentinus, and the like is shrouded in silence and secrecy. This is one of the issues—perhaps the main issue—in his dispute with his opponents. Even in the brief overview of Book One that I have just offered, it is clear how central principles of scriptural interpretation are to Irenaeus's argument and his prosecution of his opponents' points. When I say that Irenaeus and his opponents disagreed about scriptural interpretation what I mean is that they disagreed on what scriptural verses to take literally and what scriptural verses to take metaphorically. They also disagreed on the rules that governed these readings. Irenaeus believes that his opponents have rules governing their scriptural interpretation. He just does not think that these rules come from scripture itself. Any good literary interpretation must help the reader come to a deeper understanding of the coherence of a text and what that text teaches. For Irenaeus, the Valentinian rules do not do this. They distort the coherence of the scriptural witness and, as a result, they distort what the scripture teaches about a whole panoply of topics, chief among them, the nature of God, the nature of Christ, the nature of the Spirit, the nature of creation, and the nature of human beings and human salvation. In Irenaeus's view, one chief problem of the rules for his opponents' exegesis (perhaps *the* chief problem of their exegesis) is that they draw their inspiration not from the Law and the prophets of Israel but from Greek philosophy and poetry. They distort the scriptural witness because instead of basing their interpretation on the clear words of scripture, they draw their interpretative inspiration from Greek philosophical and literary sources that themselves are shrouded in secrecy.

Probatio, 1.1–8: God

In the *Adversus Haereses* Irenaeus has set up two rival methods of scriptural interpretation. It is fair to say that in order to do so, he identifies rival traditions of teachings and teachers who pass down these methods. We could say, in fact, that by examining these teachers, Irenaeus makes an ethical argument. Showing how these men live and how they teach helps Irenaeus to build a case against them.[10] Ptolemy is the first teacher we encounter in the text. Irenaeus's presentation of Ptolemy's teaching itself comes under three headings: Ptolemy's view of God and creation (1.1–3), his view of Christ (1.4–5), and his view of human salvation (1.6–8). In setting up these three headings, Irenaeus's goal is to instruct (rather than delight or move) his audience; he relies on *logos* (rather than *ethos* or *pathos*).

The first disagreement between Irenaeus and Ptolemy is how Ptolemy brings together certain biblical texts to form a picture of God.[11] In these chapters, Irenaeus discusses how Ptolemy attempts to read the first chapter of Genesis together with the prologue to John's Gospel. Irenaeus does not object to such a pairing (he himself pairs these two texts), but he does object to the way Ptolemy makes his argument and

10. For a study of the Valentinian way of life, see Ismo Dunderberg, *Beyond Gnosticism: Myth, Lifestyle, and Society in the School of Valentinus* (New York: Columbia University Press, 2008).
11. For a good overview of the threat perceived by Irenaeus, see Terrance L. Tiessen, *Irenaeus on the Salvation of the Unevangelized* (Metuchen, N.J.: Scarecrow Press, 1993), 35–45; F. Sagnard, *La gnose Valentinienne et le témoignage de saint Irénée* (Paris: PUF, 1947), 140–98.

what his argument says.[12] Like the other teachers, Ptolemy's words are persuasive because they subtly parody the Apostolic interpretation of scripture's role of creation. For Irenaeus, creation manifests the goodness of God. For his opponents, the visible world is a pale shadow of the hidden depths of the universe. Let us look at Irenaeus's account of how Ptolemy reads Genesis. Unlike the belief of the Apostolic faith that holds that God the Father created the world through the Word, the students of Ptolemy believe "there are Aeons, which are perfect, in the invisible and unnarratable places."[13] The Aeons exist "in silence and great tranquility."[14] Aeons, on Ptolemy's account, are reified "ages" (αἰών) that emanate from the creator god to make the universe. These Aeons include Thought, Bythos, Nous, Silence, Wisdom, and others. In each of these, Ptolemy has taken a word from scripture and reified it. And so, according to his exegesis, the world begins when Thought, also known as Grace, sends forth Bythos, and Bythos impregnates Silence. The union of Bythos and Silence produce Nous "which is both similar to and equal to the one who sent it forth and alone capable of the greatness of the Father."[15] Nous is also called the Only-Begotten of the Father and the Beginning of all things. Truth is also sent out with Nous. These four—Bythos, Silence, Nous, and Truth—form the "Pythagorean Tetrad" which Ptolemy and his students call the "root of all things."[16] Nous and Truth then emit Logos and Zoe (Life), which, in turn, emit Anthropos (Human Being) and Ekklesia (Church). These four are added to the four of the Tetrad to produce the Ogdoad. The union of Logos and Zoe send forth ten more Aeons and the union of Anthropos and Ekklesia send forth twelve. All together, there are thir-

---

12. Three recent monographs have explored how Irenaeus responds to Valentinian interpretation of the Book of Genesis. See Thomas Holsinger-Friesen, *Irenaeus and Genesis: A Study of Competition in Early Christian Hermeneutics* (Winona Lake, Ind.: Eisenbraums, 2009); M. C. Steenberg, *Irenaeus on Creation: the Cosmic Christ and the Saga of Redemption* (Leiden: Brill, 2008); Stephen O. Presley, *The Intertextual Reception of Genesis 1–3 in Irenaeus of Lyons* (Leiden: Brill, 2015).

13. τινα εἶναι ἐν ἀοράτοις καὶ ἀκατονομάστοις ὑφώμασι τέλειον Αἰῶνα προόντα (1.1.1).

14. ἐν ἡσυχίᾳ καὶ ἠπερμίᾳ (1.1.1).

15. ὁνοιὸν τε καὶ ἴσον τῷ προβαλόντι καὶ μόνον χωροῦντα τὸ μέγεθος τοῦ Πατρός (1.1.1).

16. ῥίζαν τῶν πάντων (1.1.1).

ty Aeons, which constitute the foundation of the world and which are manifested through scripture "properly" interpreted. Of the Tetrad, Silence merits special mention. Irenaeus has said that error does not show itself. One reason for this is that silence is at the heart of the Tetrad, which itself is the basis for all things. The way to combat Silence, of course, is through speech: hence the task of the rhetor.

Here we begin to see the difficulty of Irenaeus's task. He confronts a method of interpretation that hides itself.[17] Obviously, if one reads the first chapter of Genesis and the first chapter of John's Gospel, one does not find talk of Aeons. One would search in vain for talk of Tetrads or Ogdoads. In order to have a debate, the two sides must agree on the terms of the debate. But it is not clear that Irenaeus and Ptolemy agree on that much. Now, to be sure, both Irenaeus and Ptolemy agree that words like Logos and Zoe are important to understanding who Jesus Christ is. But—and this is what Irenaeus is at pains to point out—the two interpreters use these words in such different contexts that it is almost as if they are dealing with different words.

There is a deeper issue at play here. According to Irenaeus, the truth shows itself. This is not to say that the truth is easy to discern, but it is to say that if one follows certain clear-cut rules, one can discover the truth. To borrow an image from the beginning of John's Gospel, the truth is the light that shines for all to see. Ptolemy begins his exegesis, according to Irenaeus, not in the light but in the depths of darkness. Ptolemy begins not with the Word, but with Silence. Ptolemy's radical revision of Genesis and John reads: In the beginning were Depth and Silence. Ptolemy's god hides in his silence. Irenaeus's God shows himself in and through his Word. As an interpreter of God's Word, Irenaeus proclaims the true Apostolic interpretation of scripture through his own speech. In these chapters, Irenaeus offers his *probatio* to instruct his audience about the terms of the debate before them.

Ptolemy makes claims about the nature of human beings as well

---

17. Irenaeus's method of argumentation has been the focus of much study. For two good pieces, see Barbara Aland, "Polemik bei Irenäus von Lyon: Strategie — Ertrag — Wirkung," in *Polemik in der frühchristlichen Literatur* (Berlin: De Gruyter, 2011), 579–602; and Ysabel de Andia, "L'hérésie et sa réfutation selon Irénée de Lyon," *Augustinianum* 25, no. 3 (1985): 609–44.

as about the nature of God. For Ptolemy, human beings are above all Nous, the rational principle that directs all human knowledge and action. Nous is itself one of the Aeons, and indeed it holds a certain pride of place among the Aeons. Nous "delights in seeing the Father and rejoices in considering the Father's great immensity."[18] Irenaeus's account thus far is telling for what Ptolemy leaves out as much as for what he includes. The Father is fundamentally incomprehensible, but Nous can comprehend him. It is a short step from this to saying that the way to approach the Father is through knowledge. But that knowledge, as we have already seen, must come to know a god who fundamentally remains silent in the depths. How then can the nous present in individual human beings reach this Aeon Nous?

One might think that Wisdom can play a role here, but for Ptolemy it is not that simple. Sophia is the farthest Aeon from the Father, and because of her distance she cannot comprehend the Father's greatness. As a result, she suffers. Because of the suffering from this desire, Sophia wandered from the other Aeons but has been "purified and consolidated and restored" to the union of the Aeons thanks to the Limit imposed by the Father.[19]

Irenaeus paints a fantastical picture of Ptolemy's cosmos. The Pleroma is the eternal world, and the created world is outside the Pleroma. The Aeons that make up the Pleroma are completed when the Only Begotten "emits another unity according to the foreknowledge of the Father- Christ and the Holy Spirit."[20] Christ "proclaims to them the knowledge of the Father so that they might know what is incapable and ungraspable and is not to be seen or heard except by the Only Begotten."[21] Christ breaks the silence, reaches into the depths, and brings knowledge that leads to salvation.

---

18. μόνος δὲ ὁ Νοῦς κατ' αὐτοὺς ἐτέρπετο θεωρῶν τὸν Πατέρα, καὶ τὸ μέγεθος τὸ ἀμέτρητον αὐτοῦ κατανοῶν ἠγάλλετο (1.2.1).

19. Διὰ δὲ τοῦ Ὅρου τούτου φασὶ κεκαθάρθαι καὶ ἐστηρίχθαι τὴν Σοφίαν, καὶ ἀποκατασταθῆναι τῇ συζυγίᾳ (1.2.4). To help navigate these frankly tricky waters, see Themistocles Adamopoulo, "Sophia, the Creator and the Created Cosmos: Early Christian Cosmogonic and Cosmological Polemics," *Phronema* 8 (1993): 33–48.

20. τὸν Μονογενῆ πάλιν ἑτέραν προβαλέσθαι συζυγίαν κατὰ προμήθειαν τοῦ Πατρός, ἵνα μὴ ὁμοίως ταύτῃ πάθῃ τις τῶν Αἰώνων, Χριστὸν καὶ Πνεῦμα ἅγιον (1.2.5).

21. Τὸν μὲν γὰρ Χριστὸν διδάξαι αὐτοὺς συζυγίας φύσιν, ἀγεννήτου κατάληψιν

Now it is worth stepping back here and considering what, thus far, Irenaeus finds objectionable. After all, what could be wrong with saying that Christ brings knowledge of the Father? The prologue of John's Gospel says just that. The problem is not so much with what Ptolemy and his students say as with what they do not say: the problem is the context within which they use their words. For example, Ptolemy has reified the words Bythos, Silence, Nous, and Truth by removing them from their proper context, which is the economy of salvation as it is recounted in scripture. This is a central theme in Irenaeus, and it is crucial that he begins his discussion and prosecution of Ptolemy's beliefs by discussing it. Here Irenaeus does not mince words. Ptolemy does "violence" to the words of scripture and he conforms the words to his "evil fabrications."[22] Ptolemy perverts the evangelists, the Apostles, the Law, and the prophets.

This perversion comes because Ptolemy is silent about the economy of salvation. Irenaeus's argument with his opponents ultimately rests on the shape of the biblical narrative and how this narrative manifests the history of salvation, the economy (*oikonomia, dispositio*) of God's grace. Christ is central to the economy of salvation, as both Ptolemy and Irenaeus recount it. In Irenaeus's presentation of Ptolemy's ideas, Jesus of Nazareth is only important because he can show forth the cosmic Christ. The material world, the economy of creation, is only good insofar as it can show forth the Pleroma.[23] Of course, I will continue to chart the importance of Christ in the interpretation of Irenaeus and his opponents. It is worth pointing out here, though, the close connection between each side's view of Christ and its view of reading scripture. For those who read the scriptures in the Valentinian

---

γινώσκοντας, ἱκανοὺς εἶναι, ἀναγορεῦσαί τε ἐν αὐτοῖς τὴν τοῦ πατρὸς ἐπίγνωσιν, ὅτι τε ἀχώρητός ἐστι καὶ ἀκατάληπτος, καὶ οὐκ ἔστιν οὔτε ἰδεῖν οὔτε ἀκοῦσαι αὐτόν· ἢ διὰ μόνου τοῦ Μονογενοῦς γινώσκεται (1.2.5).

22. δολίως ἐφαρμόζοντες (1.3.6).

23. The economy meant different things to Valentinian and Apostolic teaching. As Jeffrey Bingham has noted, "On the one hand, it conveys the spiritual arrangement, economy which exists above the Pleroma and Demiurge and of which the Pleroma is the image. On the other hand it conveys the orthodox conception of the designed nature of the created arrangement, economy of the Father, Creator of all things and only true God." D. Jeffrey Bingham, *Irenaeus' Use of Matthew's Gospel in Adversus Haereses* (Leuven: Peeters, 1998), 52.

tradition, it is fair to say that Jesus of Nazareth is merely a metaphor that points beyond himself to the heavenly Christ. For those who read the scriptures in the Apostolic tradition, however, the life of Jesus of Nazareth has significance because he is the literal Word made flesh. His body does not point beyond itself to the economy of salvation. In his body, the Father recapitulates the economy of salvation. Here, Irenaeus raises an important contrast between his teaching and that of his opponents. Irenaeus believes the economy of creation is meant to bring salvation to human beings through Christ.

In narrating Ptolemy's views, Irenaeus confronts the fact that Ptolemy's Jesus teaches in secret. For Irenaeus, this presents a host of difficulties. First, Ptolemy's god hides in the depths of silence. Second, one can only find this god by attending to secret interpretations of the scriptures that wrest words and meanings out of their context. Third, Ptolemy's Christ is not Jesus of Nazareth. He only joins with Jesus for a short time to bring knowledge for salvation. One way for Irenaeus to get around these difficulties, to bring Ptolemy's teaching out of the darkness and into the light, is to focus on the teachers who follow Ptolemy. (We should remember that Ptolemy himself follows Valentinus.) The teacher in Ptolemy's tradition claims to manifest the secret revelations taught to him; the teacher of the Apostolic succession claims to pass down the revelations manifested through the economy of God.

Thus, Irenaeus presents a debate between two types of teachers. One teacher urges his students to take the literal sense of scripture seriously because of what it explains about the economy of salvation. The other teacher urges his students to eschew the literal sense of scripture precisely because it does not address the economy of salvation. Irenaeus does not deny that there is a genealogy of his opponents' teaching. In fact, identifying this genealogy is a key component of his strategy for detecting and overthrowing their interpretation of scripture. And in discussing the issue of tradition and the teachers who pass on this tradition, we are returning to the issue of *ethos*. One of the main distinguishing characteristics separating the tradition of the church and the tradition of Irenaeus's opponents is whether teaching is written down. His opponents' hypothesis, "which neither the prophets announced, nor the Lord taught, nor the Apostles handed down" is known from "unwritten sources."[24] They make "a practice of twisting the sayings from cords of sand."[25]

Ptolemy's interpretation twists the biblical narrative to say things the Bible does not say. It silences the true voice of the prophets, the true teaching of Jesus, and the true tradition of the Apostles. Of course, this is precisely why Irenaeus needs to expose it in order to overthrow it. Irenaeus recognizes that the power of Ptolemy's exegesis comes from its ability to make the silencing of some texts and the weaving together of other texts sound so plausible. When Ptolemy and his followers reify terms in John's Gospel or misinterpret words in Paul's letters, they damage the truth because they transfer these words from their proper context "into their own hypothesis."[26]

Irenaeus's use of the word "hypothesis" here is suggestive. We think of "hypothesis" as a testable idea, and we usually associate it with the natural sciences. In the tradition of Greco-Roman rhetoric, however, the hypothesis was the plot of the drama.[27] Hypotheses, moreover, dealt with specific questions whereas theses dealt with general questions.[28] As Roos Meijering notes, the orator makes his hypothesis clear in the beginning of a speech.[29] What Irenaeus is really saying here, then, is that his opponents (in this case, the disciples of Ptolemy) have their own understanding of the plot of the scriptures and they fit certain scriptural passages to that plot. Further borrowing from literature, Irenaeus asks his reader to imagine the lines of Homer rearranged to make a new poem.[30] The words would be the same, but

24. Τοιαύτης δὲ τῆς ὑποθέσεως αὐτῶν οὔσης, ἣν οὔτε Προφῆται ἐκήρυξαν, οὔτε ὁ Κύριος ἐδίδαξεν, οὔτε Ἀπόστολοι παρέδωκαν, ἣν περὶ τῶν ὅλων αὐχοῦσι πλεῖον τῶν ἄλλων ἐγνωκέναι, ἐξ ἀγράφων ἀναγινώσκοντες (1.8.1).

25. καὶ τὸ δὴ λεγόμενον, ἐξ ἄμμου σχοινία πλέκειν ἐπιτηδεύοντες (1.8.1).

26. Εἰς τὴν ἰδίαν ὑπόθεσιν μετήνεγκαν (1.9.2).

27. Roos Meijering, *Literary and Rhetorical Theories in Greek Scholia* (Groningen: E. Forsten, 1987), 72.

28. Ibid., 115. Meijering notes *huptithesthai* is used in the sense of proposing a theme for a speech and its derivative *hypothesis*, "the theme of a literary text," a use which is "particularly frequent in rhetorical contexts." *Literary and Rhetorical Theories*, 107. For primary sources see Anaximenes, *Ars Rhetorica: Qvae Vvlgo Fertvr Aristotelis Ad Alexandrvm* (Berlin: De Gruyter, 2010), 1–2 and 29, and Aristotle, *Rhetoric* 1414b25–26.

29. Meijering, *Literary and Rhetorical Theories*, 109 (see also 107–11).

30. *AH* 1.9.4.

the plot, or the hypothesis, would be altered, and that variation in the hypothesis makes all the difference.[31]

Because Ptolemy's interpretation attempts to say things the scriptures do not say, it is ultimately unstable, but that does not mean that it fails to be persuasive. Because it is persuasive, it can easily lead people astray and cause them to misunderstand the revelation of God's love in Christ. As if to remind his reader about the stability of the Apostolic rule (and compare it favorably with the Ptolemaic rule), Irenaeus inserts in Book One the Apostolic faith and its power to interpret scripture. Unlike his opponents' rule, which is available only to spiritual human beings, believers in the Apostolic tradition receive the rule of truth at baptism.[32] Because of it, they know "the names from the Scriptures and the laws and the parables."[33] The Apostolic faith, in other words, is open for all to see because it is pronounced at baptism. The sound of the Apostolic faith confounds the silence of Ptolemy's hypothesis.

Excursus, 1.10 and 1.22: The Rule of Faith

The transition between the ninth and tenth chapters of Book One is important. Irenaeus has given his readers the hypothesis of the drama of the scriptures as he understands it from Ptolemy and his followers. Now Irenaeus must turn to the hypothesis of the scriptures that comes from the Apostles. Because not everything can be silent, Irenaeus must combat—or perhaps punctuate—Ptolemy's silence with words. And so, at two points in Book One, Irenaeus breaks from his *narratio* of his opponents' teaching and discusses the principles of interpretation that

31. For a detailed reading of this passage, see R. L. Wilken, "The Homeric Cento in Irenaeus' Adversus Haereses I,9,4," *VC* 21, no. 1 (1967): 25–33.

32. Dunderberg contests Irenaeus's account of Valentinian teaching here. See Dunderberg, *Beyond Gnosticism*, 134–46.

33. τὰ μὲν ἐκ τῶν γραφῶν ὀνόματα, καὶ τὰς λέξεις, καὶ τὰς παραβολὰς ἐπιγνώσετα (1.9.4). On the rule of truth in Book One, see Thomas C. K. Ferguson, "The Rule of Truth and Irenaean Rhetoric in Book 1 of Against Heresies," *VC* 55, no. 4 (2001): 356–75. On rhetoric in Book One more generally, see Pheme Perkins, "Irenaeus and the Gnostics. Rhetoric and Composition in Adversus Haereses Book One," *VC* 30, no. 3 (1976): 193–200.

come from the Apostles. These two sections come at chapters 10 and 22, which means that they bookend Irenaeus's *refutatio* in Book One. In these chapters, Irenaeus takes account of Apostolic teaching before he discusses another form of Valentinian teaching. He punctuates the silence of the Bythos with the sound of the Logos. When Irenaeus discusses the faith in Book One, he is also following good rhetorical practice. Quintilian writes, "It will be useful also to sow some seeds of the proofs, but in such a way that we may never forget that this is still the narrative and not the proof."[34] In every case, this is what Irenaeus's sections on what I call "theological methodology" do. He makes sure that his readers never forget his ultimate proof, which is the faith of the church. That is, the church guards the proper interpretation of the scriptures because the church lives out the faith. Indeed, the faith, the church, and the scriptures ultimately reinforce each other. Although Irenaeus is closely associated with the rule of faith, it is interesting that he does not use the term "rule of faith" when he lays out the rule in Book One. Instead, he simply discusses "the faith." The term "canon of faith" comes in 1.9.[35]

John Behr has helpfully explained the importance of terms like canon and hypothesis. A canon was originally a reed, but it came to be known as a straight line that was used for judging whether other lines were straight.[36] Both Plato and Aristotle were interested in discovering first principles that could then be used to judge other claims.[37] These principles, ultimately, were taken on faith. Irenaeus is keen to

34. "Ne illud quidem fuerit inutile, semina quaedam probationem spargere. Verum sic ut narrationem esse meminerimus, non probationem." Quintilian, *The Orator's Education* 4.2.54.

35. As one would expect, Irenaeus's discussion of the "rule of faith" has garnered much scholarly discussion. See Albert Ebneter, "Die 'Glaubensregel' Des Irenaeus Als Oekumenisches Regulativ," in *Unterwegs zur Einheit*, ed. Johannes Branchtschen, Heinrich Stirnimann, and Pietro Selvatico (Freiburg: Universitaetsverlag, 1980), 588–608; William Reuben Farmer, "Galatians and the 2d Century Development of the Regula Fidei," *Second Century: A Journal of Early Christian Studies* 4, no. 3 (1985): 143–70; Philip J. Hefner, "Saint Irenaeus and the Hypothesis of Faith," *Dialog* 2, no. 4 (1963): 300–306; Norbert Brox, "Irenaeus and the Bible," in *Handbook of Patristic Exegesis: The Bible in Ancient Christianity*, ed. Charles Kannengiesser (Boston: Brill, 2004), 483–506.

36. Aristotle, *De anima* 1141a5–7.

37. For a particularly helpful discussion of this, see Behr, *Irenaeus of Lyons*, 112–13.

stress the foundational role that the faith of the Apostles plays in his interpretation of scripture.

Irenaeus's presentation of the rule of faith has received much scholarly attention, but the exact contours of *how* Irenaeus presents the rule of faith has not. In 1.10, Irenaeus devotes three paragraphs to talking about the faith. Although Irenaeus did not make up the paragraph headings, it is important to note that he begins two of those three sections with discussions of the church. The importance of this is clear: one cannot talk about the faith, about the proper way to interpret the scriptures, without first talking about the church. It is the church, after all, who "received from the apostles and their disciples the faith."[38] This faith, in turn, is in the one God, the one Jesus Christ the Son of God enfleshed, our savior, and in the one Holy Spirit. These three, we might say, are the *probatio* of the faith. They are the first principles of any interpretation of scripture.[39] It is the Spirit, according to Irenaeus, that "announced through the prophets the economies and the coming and the being born from a virgin and the suffering and the rising from the dead and the enfleshed ascension into heaven of the beloved Christ Jesus our Lord."[40] If one understands the work of the Spirit properly, one understands the true economy of the scriptures. That is Irenaeus's *refutatio*, and Christ himself is the *recapitulatio*. The faith that the church receives holds that Christ came "to 'recapitulate all things' [Eph 1:10] and to save all human flesh in order that 'every knee should bend in heaven and on earth and under the earth and every tongue confess' [Phil 2:10–11] to Jesus Christ our Lord and God and Savior and King."[41] When Christ returns in glory he

38. παρά τε τῶν ἀποστόλων καὶ τῶν ἐκείνων μαθητῶν παραλαβοῦσα τὴν … πίστιν (1.10.1).

39. It is worth noting here that in the *Demonstration of the Apostolic Preaching*, Irenaeus explicitly links the faith of the Father, Son, and Holy Spirit, which is received at baptism, with the understanding of scripture. Paul M. Blowers, "The Regula Fidei and the Narrative Character of Early Christian Faith," *Pro Ecclesia* 6, no. 2 (1997): 190–228; Nathan MacDonald, "Israel and the Old Testament Story in Irenaeus's Presentation of the Rule of Faith," *Journal of Theological Interpretation* 3, no. 2 (2009): 281–98.

40. "qui per prophetas praedicavit dispositiones Dei et adventum et eam quae est ex Virgine generationem et passionem et resurrectionem a mortuis et in carne in caelos ascensionem dilecti Iesu Christi Domini nostri" (1.10.1).

41. «ἀνακεφαλαιώσασθαι τὰ παντα» καὶ ἀναστῆσαι πᾶσαν σάρκα πάσης

will justly judge the dead, leading the wicked into the eternal fire and granting incorruptible life and eternal glory to the just.[42] God, Spirit, Christ, *probatio, refutatio, recapitulatio*—this is the hypothesis, the plot of the scriptures. This hypothesis is spoken by God in the Holy Spirit and recapitulated by God in Jesus Christ. The structure of the *Adversus Haereses* is the argument of the *Adversus Haereses* because the structure of the text mirrors the structure of the faith, which tracks the hypothesis of the scriptures. Irenaeus's first theological excursus sets the groundwork for the four that will follow. If you do not have the plot of the scriptures correct, you do not have a grasp of the basic first principles, that is, the faith, and therefore you cannot make any arguments. Irenaeus responds to Ptolemy's silence with the *kerygma* of the faith of the church.

In 1.22, Irenaeus uses the term "rule of truth" (*regula veritatis*). This chapter comes after Irenaeus's *refutatio* in Book One (which will be my focus in a moment). Irenaeus does not feel the need to repeat verbatim what he said in 1.10. Here Irenaeus says, "We guard the rule of truth."[43] I take that "we" to be the church, and so once again, Irenaeus notes the communal aspect of the proper interpretation of the scriptures. This rule is that "there is one all-powerful God, who created all things through his Word. He 'prepared and made all things out of nothing,' just as Scripture says, 'By the word of the Lord the heavens were made firm and by the breath of his mouth all his host' [Ps 32:6]. And again, 'all things were made through him and without him nothing was made' [Jn 1:3]."[44] Irenaeus spends a few lines talking about

---

ἀνθρωπότητος, ἵνα χριστῷ ἰησοῦ τῷ κυρίῳ ἡμῶν καὶ θεῷ καὶ σωτῆρι καὶ βασιλεῖ (1.10.1).

42. Irenaeus quotes Rom 2:5 and Eph 6:12 here.

43. "Cum teneamus nos regulam veritatis" (1.22.1).

44. "Unus Deus omnipotens qui omnia condidit per Verbum suum et aptauit et fecit ex quod non era ad hoc ut sint omnia, quemadmodum Scriptura dicit. Verbo enim Domini caeli firmati sunt, et Spiritu oris eius Omnia virtus eorum, et iterum omnia per ipsum facta sunt, et sine ipso factum est nihil" (1.22.1). Irenaeus seems to be quoting the *Shepherd of Hermas* Mandate 1.1 as scripture here. See Charles E. Hill, "'The writing which says ...' The Shepherd of Hermas in the Writings of Irenaeus and the Shepherd of Hermas," *Studia Patristica* 65, no. 13 (2013): 127–38; M. C. Steenberg, "Irenaeus on Scripture, Graphe, and the Status of Hermas," *St. Vladimir's Theological Quarterly* 53, no. 1 (2009): 29–66. For similar scriptural passages see 2 Mc 7:28 and Wis 1:14. See also

God's creative powers, and these lines, no doubt, are meant to counter his opponents' ideas that creation occurred through lesser powers and not God himself. Although Irenaeus focuses on creation in this iteration of the rule, he is keen to stress that God the creator is the "God of Abraham, the God of Isaac, and the God of Jacob," which we can read as shorthand for the economy of the Old Covenant and the people of Israel. And as we would expect, Irenaeus reminds his readers that "This is the Father of our Lord Jesus Christ, as we will show you."[45] What is interesting here is Irenaeus's phrase "as we will show you." Presumably this means that he does not believe he has sufficiently shown that the God of Abraham, Isaac, and Jacob is the Father of Jesus Christ, nor would we expect him to have shown that yet. He is still in his *narratio*, laying out his opponents' teaching. Even in the *narratio*, though, Irenaeus wants his readers to know that those who "condemn the handiwork of God contradict their own salvation." When such people rise again, "they will not be numbered among the just because of their unbelief."[46] We can see the same pattern again. The *probatio* is the question of the creator, the *refutatio* is the economy of the scriptures, and the *recapitulatio* is the judgment that all will face. The structure of the faith is the argument of the *Adversus Haereses*.

Allow me to end this brief excursus on the same note with which I began it. In 1.1–9, Irenaeus attempts to lay out the terms of the debate that he finds himself in with Ptolemy and his followers. Immediately, though, he is in a bind: his opponents are not clear about what they want to say. Not only are they unclear about what their principles of interpretation are, but they also claim that these principles are shrouded in the depth of silence. Irenaeus, then, needs to present his principles of interpretation, the Apostolic faith, so that he can remind his readers where his dispute with his opponents lies.

St. Theophilus, *Ad Autolycum*, trans. Robert Grant, Oxford Early Christian Texts (Oxford: Clarendon Press, 1970), 1:4, 1:7, 2:10, 3:9.

45. "hic Pater Domini nostri Iesu Christi (cf Eph 1:3), quemadmodum ostendemus" (1.22.1).

46. "Plasma autem Dei contemnunt, contradicentes suae saluti … cum iustis autem non adnumerabuntur proper incredulitatem suam" (1.22.1).

Refutatio, 1.11–21: Scripture/Economy

The Word defeats silence. Truth defeats secrecy. Although Irenaeus follows good rhetorical precedent in laying out his opponents' arguments before refuting them, in an important sense for him to expose Ptolemy's teaching is already for him to defeat it. This is because, as we have seen, the very nature of Ptolemy's teaching is that it is shrouded in silence. As soon as he can show the instability of Ptolemy's rule of faith, for example, Irenaeus can let that rule show its own weakness.

Part of the rule's weakness comes from its silence about its own origins.[47] Ptolemy and his followers did not make clear their view of the hypothesis of the scriptures, so because Irenaeus has only the silence that Ptolemy offers, he can only trace the line of teachers that Ptolemy follows. For Irenaeus, this line of teachers extends back to Simon Magus from the Acts of the Apostles. By discussing this genealogy of teachers, Irenaeus can address the past, which is appropriate to the *refutatio*, and he can offer an epideictic of blame for those teachers. By doing this, he can delight his audience. For Irenaeus, how those teachers understand the ordering of God's salvific work is connected to the ordering of the teachers themselves.

If we look at 1.11–21 as a unit, a basic pattern emerges, one that can be found throughout the *Adversus Haereses*. In 1.11–12, Irenaeus lays out the basic interpretative principles of the teachers he will be discussing. These principles are, of course, exactly what the debate centers on. In 1.13–20, Irenaeus focuses on the teacher of Marcus the Magician, who, like Ptolemy, was a disciple of Valentinus. Irenaeus lays out Marcus's interpretative principles and some of his interpretations of scripture. In 1.21, Irenaeus turns his focus specifically to the issue of salvation, and in this chapter he recapitulates the themes he has argued since 1.11. Thus, even though I argue that these chapters form the *refutatio* of Book One, within that *refutatio* we find *probatio*, *refutatio*, and *recapitulatio*. Whenever Irenaeus presents his opponents' teaching, he offers a genealogy of this teaching, tracing it back to its origi-

47. For a good analysis of 1.11, see Anne M. McGuire, "Valentinus and the Gnōstikē Hairesis: Irenaeus, Haer I,XI,1 and the Evidence of Nag Hammadi," *Studia Patristica* 18, no. 1 (1985): 247–52.

nal proponent. He is especially concerned to show the interpretative principles that underlie the scriptural interpretation of that teacher.

So on the one hand, Ptolemy and those before him, like Marcus, claim that their teaching is rooted in the divine silence. On the other hand, Irenaeus argues that when this teaching does make a sound, the sound is cacophonous, and its meaning contradictory. Irenaeus begins 1.11 by writing, "Now let us look at the unstable doctrine of these men and how, since there are two of them, they do not say the same things about the same subject, but contradict themselves in regard to things and names."[48] Irenaeus's wording here suggests that he is starting a new section of his text. He wants to focus his attention on Marcus's unstable doctrine. This diversity is a weakness, not a strength, because it stems from a rule of interpretation that is not fixed. Just as each teacher understands himself to be the embodiment of the rule of truth, each has his own view of Christ. Because Irenaeus believes that Christ is the center and the summit of the economy of salvation, for Christians to disagree about Christ is for Christians to disagree about God's saving power and about the material constitution of human beings. For Irenaeus, a debate about the nature of God is already about the nature of Christ and *vice versa*. Irenaeus must constantly return to this point as he makes his case.

Irenaeus shows the silence and the cacophony by attending to the views of various teachers in his *narratio*. His opponents, as we have seen, do not have a clear hypothesis of the scriptures because they do not have a stable rule with which to interpret scripture. We should remember, of course, that neither Ptolemy nor Marcus is Irenaeus's main target—rather, he is attacking Valentinus. Without a stable transmission of teaching, Irenaeus cannot argue fully against his opponents. In a strange way, their cacophony ends up collapsing into silence. Irenaeus punctuates this cacophonous silence by offering a genealogy of teachers. He begins with Marcus the Magician, whom he classifies as a

48. Ἴδωμεν νῦν καὶ τὴν τούτων ἄστατον γνώμην, δύο που καὶ τριῶν ὄντων πῶς περὶ τῶν αὐτῶν οὐ τὰ αὐτὰ λέγουσιν, ἀλλὰ τοῖς πραγμασιν καὶ τοῖς ὀνόμασιν ἐναντία ἀποφαίνονται (1.11.1). For a helpful discussion of this chapter, see Unger's notes in *Against the Heresies: Book 1*, 190–94n1. See also McGuire, "Valentinus and the Gnōstikē Hairesis."

student of Ptolemy. Irenaeus is especially concerned with the way Marcus conducts what might best be called parodic Eucharistic rites and how he seems to abuse women during those rites. Women who came to Irenaeus told him that Marcus concocted "love potions and charms for some of them ... in order to insult even their bodies; and that they were violated in body by him."[49] Irenaeus's discussion of these Marcosian rites is more than just a discussion of Marcus's *ethos*, though that is important as well. Irenaeus closely links how one reads the scriptures with how one celebrates the Eucharist.[50] To misunderstand that the Eucharist is truly Christ is to misunderstand Christ's presence in scripture and *vice versa*. And if one misunderstands Christ's presence in scripture, one misunderstands the scriptures.

Thus the liturgical context is key for understanding Marcus, but in order to narrate Marcus's position fully, Irenaeus needs to do more than discuss the Marcosian Eucharistic rites.[51] He needs to lay out the full economy of Marcus's teaching and show how Marcus misunderstands the economy of salvation as it is recounted in scripture. Marcus, like John at Patmos, is a recounter of visions who, through his words, presents these visions to his audience. As in the case of his teacher Ptolemy, Marcus's teaching is shrouded in a complex numerology. According to Marcus, Jesus the man was part of the economy of salvation, but Christ descended into him from on high. God himself, then, was not part of the economy. Because of this teaching, Marcus has led "all those who are persuaded by him into the highest blasphemy and greatest impiety."[52] Of course, Irenaeus recognizes that even though he finds Marcus's rule to be blasphemous, it does have interpretative power. This power comes from the way Marcus maps his numerology onto an account of the Book of Genesis. The numerology even extends to the name "Jesus Christ." Marcus counts the letters in the name "Je-

49. ὅτι δὲ φίλτρα καὶ ἀγώγιμα πρὸς τὸ καὶ τοῖς σώμασιν αὐτῶν ἐνθβρίζειν ἐμποιεῖ (1.13.5).

50. We will see Irenaeus return to this theme in the first few chapters of Book Five.

51. For more on this see Nicola Denzey Lewis, "*Apolytrosis* as Ritual and Sacrament: Determining a Ritual Context for Death in Second-Century Marcosian Valentinianism," *Journal of Early Christian Studies* 17, no. 4 (2009): 525–61.

52. εἰς τὴν ἀνωτάτω βλασφημίαν καὶ μεγίστην ἀσέβειαν ἐμβέβληκας ἅπαντας τούς σοι πειθομένους (1.15.5).

sus Christ" and argues that this number shows forth the Duodecad (1.15.2). Irenaeus has to refute Marcus by showing that this numerology does not map onto the *oikonomia* of God's plan of salvation, which is the true hypothesis of scripture. Christ does not save human beings through a mathematical formula. God saves human beings in the fullness of time by recapitulating all things to himself in Christ (Eph 1:10).

Jesus Christ, the Word of God made flesh, who recapitulates the economy of salvation, stands at the center of Irenaeus's interpretation of scripture. For Irenaeus, Christ also says something about the nature of human beings. Irenaeus does not expose his opponents to make academic points, but wants to refute them because their silence about Christ conceals God's saving power in Christ. Irenaeus and Marcus agree that to talk about Christ is to talk about human beings. Even though his opponents' interpretation is parasitic on the Apostolic understanding of the hypothesis of scripture, it is precisely the closeness of the two that gives their interpretation its power. Thus Irenaeus must recount how Marcus understands the economy of creation and salvation. Irenaeus notes that, according to the Marcosian system, man "who has been fashioned according to the image of the power above, has in himself the power from one source."[53] The power is located "in the place of the brain."[54] Marcus, like other teachers, believed that the image of God in human beings was solely in the intellect and not in the body. As we will see, this is a key distinction between Irenaeus and his opponents. According to him, they distinguish among the three races of men on different days of creation. "Earthly man was fashioned on our sixth day and carnal man on the eighth."[55] His opponents also say, Irenaeus reports, "that the androgynous human being came about according to the image and likeness of God." This human being "is the spiritual man."[56] As we saw already with Ptolemy, Marcus brings together two pictures of humanity found in the scriptures. Ptolemy

53. Ἀλλὰ μὴν καὶ τὸν πλαστὸν ἄνθρωπον κατ' εἰκόνα τῆς ἄνω δυνάμεως ἔχειν ἐν αὑτῷ τὴν ἀπὸ τῆς μιᾶς πηγῆς δύναμιν (1.18.1).

54. Ἱδρῦσθαι δὲ ταῦτα ἐν τῷ κατὰ τὸν ἐγκέφαλον τόπῳ (1.18.2).

55. εἰ μὴ τὸν μὲν χοϊκὸν ἐν τῇ ἕκτῃ τῶν ἡμερῶν ἐροῦσι πεπλάσθαι, τὸν δὲ σαρκικὸν ἐν τῇ ὀγδόῃ (1.18.2).

56. Ἔνιοι δὲ ἄλλον θέλουσιτὸν κατ' εἰκόνα καὶ ὁμοίωσιν Θεοῦ γεγονότα ἀρσενόθηλυν ἄνθρωπον, καὶ τοῦτον εἶναι τὸν πνευματικόν (1.18.2).

combined Genesis and John's Gospel; here Marcus combines Genesis with Paul's first letter to the Corinthians.

If such a view of human beings has interpretative strength—and Irenaeus believes that it does—it is because this view (and in this case, more specifically the Marcosian view) of human beings is itself set into a broader context of scriptural interpretation. His opponents can set up this context because they offer persuasive interpretations, and this is why Irenaeus sees them as a danger. Both Irenaeus and his opponents interpret scripture in the light of their understanding of Christ, and their understanding of Christ in turn shapes their views of human salvation. Either you base your interpretation of the scriptures on the faith or you do not; if not, you will not understand God's plan of salvation, and will instead be left with mere speculations and endless genealogies.

The interpretations that Ptolemy and Marcus offer generally eschew the biblical narrative. This narrative, of course, leaves out many details about the lives of biblical protagonists and biblical scenes. When Ptolemy and Marcus fill in those details, their interpretation can be especially persuasive. Irenaeus knows this. Ptolemy, Marcus, and the rest interpret actual passages of the scriptures, and provide added details; pointing to their interpretative rule is not enough. Let us now examine one example of Marcus's interpretation, as Irenaeus presents it. Irenaeus focuses on how the Marcosians interpret the Book of Genesis. They believe that Moses showed forth the Tetrad of God, beginning, heaven, and earth when Moses wrote "In the beginning God made the heaven and the earth."[57] These teachers not only transform the words of the prophets to fit their interpretation, they also transform the words of Christ. When Christ addresses the Father and praises him for hiding these things from the wise and revealing them to children,[58] Irenaeus's opponents believe that Christ "most clearly reveals that before his coming no one clearly knew the Father of Truth." Irenaeus argues, though, that these interpreters "discover" this Father of Truth.[59] I will not address all of the misinterpretations

57. Ἐν ἀρχῇ ἐποίησεν ὁ Θεὸς τὸν οὐρανὸν καὶ τὴν γῆν (1.18.1).
58. Mt 11:25–27.
59. Ἐν τούτοις διαρρήδην φασὶ δεδειχέναι αὐτὸν, ὡς τὸν ὑπ' αὐτῶν παρεξευρημένον πατέρα ἀληθείας πρὸ τῆς παρουσίας αὐτοῦ μηδενὸς πώποτε ἐγνωκότος (1.20.3).

of scripture here, but it is enough to underscore the importance of getting the hypothesis of the scriptures right. My own argument about Irenaeus obviously focuses on the structure of his argument. But he pays close attention to the structure of his opponents' arguments, close attention, that is, to how they see the hypothesis of scripture. If the structure is incorrect, one ends up reifying certain words—"God," "beginning," "heaven," and "earth"—so that they no longer mean what they should mean. Irenaeus holds such teaching up to scorn, in the hopes of persuading his audience that it is the result of the misinterpretation of scripture. This scorn, in turn, serves a particular end for Irenaeus. It prepares his audience for the last section of Book One, where he wants them to see the results of such choices.

Recapitulatio, 1.23–31: Christ/Salvation

In the first section of Book One, Irenaeus set up his *probatio* about the power of God and used forensic rhetoric to expose how Ptolemy's interpretation of scripture limited God's power. In the second section, Irenaeus laid out his *refutatio* of his opponents' understanding of the economy of salvation and used epideictic rhetoric to blame these teachers, especially Marcus, for the way they misinterpreted the proper understanding of the economy of God's salvation. In this final section, Irenaeus sets up his *recapitulatio* and here his discussion focuses on human salvation and the saving power of Christ. Irenaeus's concern with the proper interpretation of scripture is part and parcel with his concern for the salvation of human beings. In the person of Christ, who according to the letter to the Ephesians, recapitulates all things to himself (Eph 1:10), the proper interpretation of scripture and the salvation of human beings come together. Thus we should not find it surprising that the final chapters of Book One recapitulate major themes found in the book, and that Irenaeus focuses his attention on his opponents' views of salvation. We should also not find it surprising that Irenaeus's recapitulation here is a bit odd. Instead of bringing all his points together, he shows, through an examination of the various teachers, that their views do *not* come together. In these final chapters of Book One, Irenaeus shifts to a more deliberative rhetoric. He presents the various views of his opponents, which will culminate in his discussion of Valentinus, to show his readers what they are choosing if they choose this method of interpretation. Because Valentinus misunderstands Christ, he misunderstands human salvation. And Valentinus's misunderstanding of Christ is closely linked to his misreading of what ought to be read literally and what ought to be read metaphorically in the scriptures.

In one sense, the problem here is simple. Because his opponents do not agree on a single principle of interpretation, a reader cannot always tell whence their interpretations arise. Irenaeus answers this problem at the end of 1.22, for example, where he writes, "Therefore, since the detection and overthrow of all the heretics is various and multiform and since it was proposed to us to give an answer to everyone according to his own character, we have judged it necessary first of all to refer to their source and root so that knowing their sublime Bythos, you may understand the tree from which such fruit comes."[60] The silence on this point is deafening. This silence also causes a problem for Irenaeus's own *narratio*. When he wants to talk about Marcosian views of redemption, he laments, "Concerning their redemption, this is what has come down to us. Because they all differ in their teaching and tradition, and since those who are acknowledged as newer teachers come up with something new every day which a person never imagined, it is difficult to describe their opinions."[61] Of course, a proper recapitulation should bring all the points together. But a proper recapitulation presupposes a properly ordered speech, which presupposes a properly thought-out plan. His opponents' teaching, as Irenae-

60. "Cum sit igitur adversus omnes haereticos detectio atque convictio varia et multifaria, et nobis propositum est omnibus his secundum ipsorum charactera contradicere, necessarium arbitrati sumus prius referre fontem et radicem eorum, uti sublimissimum ipsorum Bythum cognoscens, intellegas arborem de qua defluxerunt tales fructus" (1.22.2).

61. "καὶ περὶ μὲν τῆς ἀπολυτρώσεως αὐτῶν ταῦτα ἐστιν ὅσα εἰς ἡμᾶς ἐλήλυθεν. Cum autem discrepent ab inuincem et doctrina et traditione, et qui recentiores eorum agnoscuntur adfectant per singulos dies nouem aliquid adinuenire et fructificare quod numquam quisquam excogitauit, durum est omnia describere sententias" (1.24.5). On the question of Valentinian determinism, see Winrich A. Löhr, "Gnostic Determinism Reconsidered," *VC* 46, no. 4 (1992): 381–90.

us has tried to show, does not have a proper hypothesis or *oikonomia* that enables its adherents to interpret the scriptures properly. Simply put, it does not accord with the faith of the church on which Irenaeus has structured his argument. Thus Irenaeus's recapitulation here must end this way, not with a rousing discussion of Christ's salvation, but with a confusion about what Irenaeus's opponents are saying and why they are saying it.

To be sure, Irenaeus's recapitulation in Book One differs markedly from his recapitulations in the other books, especially Books Three through Five. One could argue, for example, that 1.23–30 simply continues the *oikonomia* found in 1.11–21. But here, I think, we should take Irenaeus's own words in 1.22 seriously. There he tells us that he wants to give an account of the source and root of Valentinus and his teaching. And so, in order to do that he discusses Simon the Magician (1.23), Saturninus and Basilides (1.24), Carpocrates and his followers (1.25), Cerinthus (1.26.1), the Ebionites and the Nicoletes (1.26.3–4), Cerdon and Marcion (1.27.1–4), and the remaining sects (1.28.1–2). Following these discussions, Irenaeus turns to the "Gnostics," a group that includes the Barbeliotes (1.29), the Ophites (1.30), and other diverse sects such as the Cainites (1.31).[62] Here I pay less attention to the differences among the various groups than Irenaeus does. I want to underscore, though, how Irenaeus argues that these schools agree on fundamental points about the nature of Christ and the nature of human salvation.

One of Irenaeus's main hermeneutical principles is that one should understand the least clear passages of scripture with the aid of the more clear passages. He does the same thing with the teachers he discusses. Ptolemy, Marcus, and the rest were the prelude to discussing Valentinus himself. By reading what Irenaeus has written, those Christians who are persuaded by his opponents' teaching will "learn well from us what has been taught badly" by his opponents.[63] Irenaeus wants to protect those Christians who have been taken up by the "false

62. See A. Le Boulluec, *La notion d'hérésie dans la littérature grec (IIe–IIIe siècle)* (Paris: Etudes augustiniennes, 1985), 136–57, for how Irenaeus develops the term "heresy" and how he understands the various schools of his opponents.

63. "sed a nobis bene discentes quae ab illis male docentur" (1.31.3).

SILENCE**47**

persuasion" of Valentinus.[64] He also wants the followers of Valentinus themselves to repent and be saved.

When Irenaeus talks about Valentinus's understanding of Christ, he also talks about creation and salvation, and brings together Genesis 1–3 with Paul's 1 Corinthians 15. When Irenaeus narrates Valentinus's teaching on human salvation, he says that Valentinus and his followers believe the creator gave man "intellect and thought and these were the things that saved him."[65] Indeed, in this chapter, Irenaeus narrates the economy of salvation as Valentinus understands it. In this picture, shared by all of Irenaeus's opponents, neither the human body nor the created world is worthy of or an aid to salvation. Obviously Irenaeus brings all of this up in order to refute it, but it is just as obvious that Irenaeus understands the subtlety in Valentinus's presentation. Irenaeus realizes that Valentinus's exegesis is persuasive and, given the interpretative principles that Valentinus uses, difficult to rebut. The difficulty comes in large part because of Valentinus's interpretative silence, or better, how Valentinus exploits the silences in the biblical narrative to import his own interpretative principles. That is why Irenaeus must build up to Valentinus and, in building up to him, show that the interpretative principles the teacher from Alexandria uses are not the interpretative principles that come from the Apostles. Irenaeus's argument against Valentinian understandings of Intellect and Thought, as well as the spiritual man, is an argument for everyday Christian life. This is especially important for Christians who can understand the *kerygma* as proclaimed in the life of the community simply because they are baptized, not because they are privy to esoteric scriptural interpretation.[66] It is an argument for those who receive the Word rather than those who are fascinated by scriptural silences. Irenaeus's interpretation of scripture honors the martyrs whose bodies and sufferings his opponents disregard, and his interpretation of scrip-

64. "reliqui autem iam non abstrahantur a prava quasi verisimili suasione eorum" (1.31.3).
65. "hominem autem inde habuisse nun et enthymesin, et haec esse quae salvantur dicunt" (1.30.6).
66. On baptism being all that is needed to interpret the scriptures correctly, see Irenaeus of Lyon, *On the Apostolic Preaching*, trans. John Behr (Crestwood, N.Y.: St. Vladimir's Seminary Press, 1997), §3 and §100. I will return to this in my conclusion.

ture stands against those who argue that scripture is only understood by those whose scriptural interpretation is underwritten by a view of the world that denigrates creation.

In the recapitulation in Book One, Irenaeus focuses specifically on Valentinian teaching because he sees this teaching as the most dangerous for the Apostolic tradition. He also sees in Valentinian teaching a recapitulation of all previous teachings he has narrated. According to Valentinus, the mistake that the disciples made was that "they thought he was resurrected in a worldly body, not knowing that 'flesh and blood will not inherit the kingdom of God' [1 Cor 15:50]."[67] Here is the central issue at stake between Irenaeus and Valentinian teaching. For Irenaeus, the fact that Christ died and rose in the flesh shows that all believers will die and rise in the flesh. For Valentinus, that fact that Christ did not die and rise in the flesh shows that his followers need to escape the body in order to be saved. This is the culmination of his opponents' teaching, in Irenaeus's view, and, that being said, it must be exposed and defeated. Having exposed this mistaken and blasphemous teaching about Christ and salvation, Irenaeus spends the rest of the *Adversus Haereses* defeating it on its own terms and in light of scriptural teaching.

At the end of Book One, Irenaeus tells his readers what he has done. "By such mothers and fathers and ancestors it was necessary to expose clearly the followers of Valentinus ... and to bring their teachings out in the open."[68] He hopes that this exposition will help them convert back to God. And he also hopes that this will stop others from being misled. "The manifestation of their teaching is victory against them."[69] At this point, Irenaeus writes, "there is no longer any need for many words to overthrow their teaching."[70] Irenaeus tells his readers

67. "Et hunc maximum errorem inter discipulos eius fuisse dicunt, quoniam putarent eum in corpore mundiali resurrexisse, ignorantes quoniam caro et sanguis regnum Dei non apprehendunt" (1.30.13). For a sober analysis of these issues, see Greer, "The Dog and the Mushrooms: Irenaeus's View of the Valentinians Assessed."

68. "A talibus matribus and patribus et proavis eos qui a Valentino sunt, sicut ipsae sententiae et regulae ostendunt eos, necessarium fuit manfeste arguer et in medium adferre dogmata ipsorum" (1.31.3).

69. "Detectio autem eorum haec est; sive adversus eos victoria est sententiae eorum manifesto" (1.31.3).

70. "Iam enim non multis opus erit sermonibus ad evertendum doctrinam ipsorum manifestum omnibus factam" (1.31.3).

that they "are now in a position to examine what has been said and to overthrow their wicked and unfitting teachings and to demonstrate the dogmas that do not harmonize with the truth."[71] He ends the Book by noting, "The account is long . . . . As we encounter all of them in the order in which they were narrated, we shall supply means for overthrowing them so that we may not merely expose the beast, but may also wound it from many sides."[72] Here Irenaeus reminds his readers of what he has accomplished and what he hopes to accomplish. It is worth noting here that Irenaeus uses the word *narratio* to discuss how he has laid out his opponents' positions.

Like Paul in his letter to Timothy, Irenaeus has encountered false doctrines. These false doctrines are grounded in a *mythos* about silence—rather than the Word—at the heart of God. Although Irenaeus cannot hear the silence of Valentinus and his followers, he can offer a genealogy of their teaching and their teachers. How one interprets scripture, how one interprets God's plan, is one of the ways—perhaps *the* main way—one identifies as a Christian. The structure of Irenaeus's argument in the *Adversus Haereses* is, so he believes, the structure of the economy of salvation. Christians need to understand this structure and their place in it, as it is the plan of God (οἰκονομίαν θεοῦ). In order to make his case persuasively, he must first show the vacuity of the speculation offered by his opponents.

71. "Adest enim et tibi et omnibus qui tecum sunt ad haec quae praedicta sunt exerceri et evertere namquam ipsorum doctrinas et inconditas et non apta veritati ostendere dogmata" (1.31.3).

72. "Cum igitur haec sic se habeant, quatemus promise secundum nostrum virtutem inferemus eversionem ipsorum omnibus eis contradicentes in sequenti libro—enarratio enim in longum persit, ut vides—et viatica quoque dabimus ad eversionem ipsorum occurentes omnibus sententiis secundum narrationis ordinam, ut simus non tantum ostendentes, sed et vulnerantes undique bestiam" (1.31.4).

2 ⊹ FICTION

> But immorality and all impurity or covetousness must not even
> be named among you, as is fitting among saints. Let there be no
> filthiness, nor silly talk, nor levity, which are not fitting; but in-
> stead let there be thanksgiving. Be sure of this, that no immoral
> or impure man, or one who is covetous (that is, an idolator), has
> any inheritance in the kingdom of Christ and of God. Let no one
> deceive you with empty words, for it is because of these things
> that the wrath of God comes upon the sons of disobedience.
>
> EPHESIANS 5:3–6

Irenaeus does not quote these lines from Paul's letter to the Ephesians,
but they sum up his advice to his audience about the teachers who
would lead Christians astray with their biblical interpretation. Leading Christians astray in this way compromises their Christian identity,
for if Christians do not interpret the Bible correctly, they cannot offer
proper thanks to God. This is impiety, and such impiety means that
one cannot have a share in God's kingdom. The teachers whom Irenaeus opposes think that God's creation and the human body are impure
and thus have no place in the kingdom of God. Irenaeus teaches, following Ephesians, that impiety comes not from what God has created
but from filthiness, silly talk, and levity. In Book Two, he attempts to
show how, on its own terms, his opponents' teaching is impure in this
sense.

If the operative word in chapter 1 was "silence," in chapter 2 it is
"fiction," or perhaps "fabrication." In the first chapter I discussed how
Irenaeus had to interpret the silences in his opponents' interpretation
of scripture. In this chapter I want to discuss one of the consequences

of those silences and indeed of couching one's interpretation in an ultimate silence. For Irenaeus, Jesus Christ, the Word of God enfleshed, is
the ultimate interpreter and interpretation of the scriptures. The Apostles have carried on the Word's interpretation such that it cannot truly
be called their own. Yet, precisely because they claim that silence is at
the heart of their interpretation, Valentinus and his followers fabricate
their own fictive interpretations. At one point in Book Two, Irenaeus
goes so far as to say that they fabricate another god.[1] Their interpretations are their own, and because of this they lack the unity that characterizes the truth.

Irenaeus first had to expose the silence so that he could counter the fiction. In Book Two, he is still narrating the views of his opponents, but now he tries to refute them on their own terms, which
span familiar territory. Irenaeus wants to counter his opponents on
the same three points of the faith: God, God's presence in economy,
and salvation. The first division has two parts that deal with the relationship between God and creation. In 2.1–11 Irenaeus lays out his
opponents' understanding of God. In 2.12–19, he discusses the Aeons,
which constitute the way, so his opponents argue, in which God has
emanated and related to the created order. The second major division
deals with scriptural exegesis, and it also has two parts. In 2.20–24,
Irenaeus discusses how his opponents interpret specific scriptural
passages, and in 2.25–28, Irenaeus attempts to lay out their principles
or rules of interpretation. Notice how the sequence of each division
mirrors the other: 2.12–19 and 2.25–28 both discuss *oikonomia*. And
in the last division, 2.29 to the beginning of 2.35, Irenaeus discusses
eschatology. At the very end of 2.35, Irenaeus discusses his plan for
Book Three.[2]

Book Two has a similar structure to Book One. Here we find the
characteristic rhetorical moments of *probatio, refutatio,* and *recapitu-*

---

1. 2.10.1. I will come back to this.
2. This structure largely follows the division of the text that Rousseau and Doutrea-
leau offer in the SC edition. Greer, however, has argued that it is "impossible to locate
these divisions in the text." Greer, "The Dog and the Mushrooms," 151 and 154. As we
shall see, I do think this basic structure works within the rhetorical structure that I have
argued is present throughout the *Adversus Haereses*. Please refer to the appendix for the
structure of Book Two.

latio. Although these moments correspond roughly to the themes of
God, creation, and salvation, Irenaeus's concern in Book Two largely focuses on three major issues: knowledge, testimony, and reason.
That is to say, the conditions for knowing about God; the proper way
to interpret the testimony about God and God's creation offered in
the scriptures; and the role that human reason plays in understanding
scripture. More specifically, Irenaeus discusses what the Old and New
Covenants say about the final destiny of human beings. Underlying
these three issues is the way one interprets. Irenaeus has argued in
Book One that all of his opponents' interpretations of scripture con-
form to certain (mistaken) principles of interpretation. In Book Two,
Irenaeus wants to show how those principles, when carried to their
logical conclusions, make nonsense of the scriptures.[3] For Irenaeus,
the faith does not float freely apart from the scriptural text that it helps
to interpret. Instead, the faith is a summary of that text, and it is taken
from it. Because the scriptures explain, in a way appropriate to human
reasoning, God, God's creation, and God's offer of salvation, the faith
should bear some similarity to these. Irenaeus's own argument—structured as it is on the faith—follows the same structure. Because there
is one God, there should be one clear principle. Insofar as there is one
economy of salvation recounted in all of the scriptures, that principle
should help *all* Christians understand *all* of those scriptures, without
recourse to another set of texts.

Probatio, 2.1–19: God

Of all the books of the *Adversus Haereses*, Book Two is the most
difficult in terms of structure and content.[4] Irenaeus is still in the

3. Of course, to say that their principles of interpretation make nonsense of the
scriptures is not to say that nothing else makes sense of them. When Irenaeus turns to a
full consideration of the Apostolic rule of faith, he will show how that rule makes sense
of the entire economy of scripture and creation.

4. Book Two has garnered much less scholarly attention than the rest of the *Adver-
sus Haereses*. An exemplary exception is Norris's work. Richard A. Norris, "Irenaeus'
Use of Paul in His Polemic against the Gnostics," in *Paul and the Legacies of Paul*, ed.
William S. Babcock (Dallas, Tex.: Southern Methodist University Press, 1990), 79–98;
"Theology and Language in Irenaeus of Lyon," *Anglican Theological Review* 76, no. 3

narratio of his argument, and so he is exposing his opponents' views and trying to refute them on their own terms. But if their views are incoherent, then organizing his argument is a challenge. Although the structure is similar to that found in Book One, it is fair to note that it is not as clear-cut as the organization in the other books. Even with Book Two, my general point about the structure of the *Adversus Haereses* being the argument of the *Adversus Haereses* still stands. The problem Irenaeus faces in Book Two is that he has to refute his opponents' positions on their own terms. And so, the structure comes from them, not from him. Irenaeus writes, "In this book, we will build up our own system as far as we are able and as time will permit, and we shall overturn their entire rule [*regula*] by main principles [*capitula*]. And so, because this work is an exposition and refutation of their opinions, I have titled it such."[5] Once again, we see Irenaeus focus on the rule of his opponents and that he wants to overturn their rule on *their* principles, not his.

In the previous chapter I discussed how Irenaeus's argument rests in part on showing how the scriptural interpretations that he opposes confuse what ought to be read literally with what ought to be read metaphorically. In Book Two, Irenaeus lays out the logical consequence of this confusion. To show this, Irenaeus must begin, as he always does, with how not to speak about God. He argues, "it is necessary ... that we begin with the first and greatest heading, with the Creator God, who made heaven and earth and all things in them."[6] Once again,

(1994): 285–95; "The Insufficiency of Scripture: Adversus Haereses 2 and the Role of Scripture in Irenaeus's Anti-Gnostic Polemic," in *Reading in Christian Communities: Essays on Interpretation in the Early Church*, ed. Charles A. Bobertz and David Brakke (Notre Dame, Ind.: University of Notre Dame Press, 2002), 63–79; "The Transcendence and Freedom of God: Irenaeus, the Greek Tradition and Gnosticism," in *Early Christian Literature and the Classical Intellectual Tradition,* ed. William Schoedel and Robert Louis Wilken (Paris: Editions Beauchesne, 1979), 87–100; "Irenaeus and Plotinus Answer the Gnostics: A Note on the Relation between Christian Thought and Platonism," *Union Seminary Quarterly Review* 36, no. 1 (1980): 13–24; "Who Is the Demiurge? Irenaeus' Picture of God in Adversus Haereses 2," in *God in Early Christian Thought*, ed. Andrew McGowan, Brian E. Daley, SJ, and Timothy J. Gaden (Leiden: Brill, 2009), 9–36.

5. "In hoc autem libro instruemus quae nobis apta sunt et quae permittit tempus, et evertemus per magna capitula omnem ipsorum regulam. Quapropter quod sit et detection et eversio sententiae ipsorum, opus huius conscriptionem ita tituavimus" (2.1.1).

6. "Bene igitur habet a primo et maximo capitulo inchoare nos, a Demiurgo Deo,

we see the faith structure Irenaeus's argument. His *probatio* is God. To put this another way, the putative claim of Irenaeus's opponents is that their scriptural interpretations lead Christians to a closer union with God. But if their interpretations confuse literal and metaphorical meaning, then they cannot lead Christians closer to God, and for a simple reason. Irenaeus's opponents base their knowledge on their own imagination, not the created order as such. Their interpretations do lead readers to a closer relationship with the origins of these interpretations, but the origins are the teachers themselves, not Christ or God. In fact, as we will see, Irenaeus ultimately connects those interpretations to Satan.

Before I get to Satan, however, let us first address this idea of fiction or fabrication. Irenaeus agrees with many philosophical schools of his time in believing that knowledge is only possible when there are clear foundations for one's knowledge.[7] By definition, in fact, his opponents' teaching cannot understand God properly because the Valentinian teachers have usurped one of the main characteristics of God, his stability as the creator. These foundations of knowledge about God cannot come from human beings, but can only come from God. If the rules or canons of knowledge were made by humans, they would be as variable as the human who made them, and therefore would lack stability. In order to overturn his opponents' reading of scripture, Irenaeus must show that it does not produce knowledge of God or lead readers closer to God. True knowledge does bring the knower into closer contact with the known. But because Irenaeus's opponents fabricate their stories about God, they end up bringing their students to *themselves* and not to God. In creating their own god, they end up creating their own students. Neither teacher nor student has grounded the teaching in God, but merely in another human being.

What is even more strange in this account, is that according to

---

qui fecit caelum et terram et omnia quae in eis sunt" (2.1.1). Importantly, *capitulo* here as a rhetorical valence. The "headings" would be the major points of a speech.

7. Needless to say, the epistemology of Hellenistic philosophy is well beyond the scope of my argument. I have found Boys-Stones, *Post-Hellenistic Philosophy*, and A. A. Long, *Hellenistic Philosophy; Stoics, Epicureans, Sceptics, Classical Life and Letters* (New York: Scribner, 1974), helpful in navigating this terrain.

Irenaeus's opponents, the creator god's work proceeds without knowledge. Although the teachers Irenaeus opposes claim to impart knowledge, the knowledge that they attribute to God is contradictory. God left the Pleroma either "out of zeal or ignorance."[8] Irenaeus continually points to the instability of his opponents' rule, but of course, he would argue that this is only so-called knowledge. In order to be knowledge truly, knowledge must be of something that is itself true. Otherwise, it is mere opinion. As we have already seen, Irenaeus believes that his opponents rely on opinion and not knowledge because their interpretation of scripture does not understand God the right way. Ultimately these teachers themselves are the creators, not God.

If the interpreters are the creators, and thus not truly interpreters, something curious follows. In the interpretation Irenaeus refutes, God, because he is created, is subject to necessity as all created things are. Only the uncreated is free of necessity, and this issue of necessity interests Irenaeus in two ways. First, by following his opponents' belief to its inevitable conclusions, Irenaeus can point out its absurdity. Second, Irenaeus argues that for the Valentinian teacher, "necessity" takes priority over the love of God found in the economy of salvation and the life of Christ. An example of Irenaeus's first concern comes in his refutation of Ptolemaic teaching about Christ. We saw this in the previous chapter. Although Irenaeus does not use this language, his concern about this second case of necessity would be that "necessity" functions for the Valentinian teachers in the same way that "fate" functions for Greek tragedy. That is, the god of these teachers is subject to necessity in the same way that the gods of Greek tragedy are subject to the fates. Their god is little more than the gods of Greek literature. Irenaeus even compares this god to Zeus.[9] In 2.6–8, Irenaeus continues to discuss the logical impossibilities of ignorant Aeons that have no connection to their creator.

We should remember here that in these opening sections of Book Two, Irenaeus's mode is forensic rhetoric, the goal of which is to instruct. Irenaeus discusses these issues at the beginning of Book Two,

8. "et informe hoc, utrum praesciente Propatore quae in eo futura erant, ex studio sic reliquisse an ignorante" (2.3.1).

9. 2.5.4.

remember, because the creator god's knowledge and the creator god's relationship to necessity are precisely the issues under discussion in Irenaeus's *probatio*. By addressing these issues at the beginning of the book, Irenaeus sets up the terms of his debate with his opponents, and ultimately this debate concerns how one ought to read the scriptures to understand the nature of God. Of course, the faith plays a central role in this discussion. For Irenaeus, the church is marked as an interpretative community insofar as it hands down the faith found in the Law, the prophets, the life and passion of Christ, and the teaching of the Apostles. The faith, like God the creator of the world, "stands firm even to those who in many ways contradict him and confess him, calling him Maker and saying that he is an angel."[10] Irenaeus states the faith numerous times throughout the *Adversus Haereses*, and each time he does so he discusses in some way God, creation, and salvation. We should note here that Irenaeus's discussion of the Apostolic faith in Book Two comes at almost exactly the same place as his discussion of it in Book One. As we have seen in Book One, the faith itself is handed down through tradition. This tradition begins in the scriptures of the Old Testament, in the Law and the prophets. The Lord teaches this tradition and brings it to fulfillment in himself. Then, the Apostles continue it, and the church accepts the tradition from the Apostles.[11] With the faith, those entrusted to interpret the scriptures have a clear guide for that interpretation.

Ireneaus's opponents lack such a clear guide because they are the creators of the god they discuss. These teachers "go in search of one who does not exist, but is supposed to be above [God], and who has never been proclaimed by anyone." These teachers "wish to explain ambiguous Scriptural passages" so they "fabricated another God."[12] Of course, this is the key issue. For Irenaeus, the issue is not that he and his opponents are interpreting the same God differently, but that

10. "constat et ipsi qui multis modis contradicunt ei et confitentur eum, Fabricatorem eum uocantes et Angelum dicentes" (2.9.1).

11. 2.9.1.

12. "Perquam itaque irrationale est, praetermittentes eum qui uere est Deus et qui ab omnibus habet testimonium, quaerere si est super eum is qui non est et qui a nemine umquam adnuntiatus est... velint ambiguas exsoluere Scripturas... alterum Deum fabricaverunt" (2.10.1).

they are interpreting different gods. Because of the increasingly elaborate allegories that his opponents construct,[13] they get further and further away from the text of scripture. And, as the text recedes from their view, they go further and further away from the true knowledge of God that comes from interpreting scripture along with the faith. Irenaeus argues that the faith that has been passed down by the Apostles adheres closely to the witness about God recounted in the scriptures, though that witness and those scriptures are not always easy to understand. The point, however, is that Irenaeus believes the scriptures do not need anything beyond themselves to make sense of them. Everything needed to understand God is found there.

The fundamental disagreement between Irenaeus and his opponents results, in Irenaeus's view, from their misinterpretation of scripture. These teachers are bad theologians because they are bad readers. Therefore they (and Irenaeus's audience) face a choice: they either will or will not "see their arguments dissolve and they will return to the truth, humbling themselves and give up their manifold phantasms. They will appease God in regard to the blasphemies they uttered against him and be saved."[14] Ultimately, Irenaeus is not interested in these interpretative disagreements on an academic level, but rather on a pastoral level. Perhaps it is better to say that the only reason Irenaeus is interested in their interpretative system is because he is concerned for their salvation.

Because his opponents fabricate their own fictive god, who is subject to necessity, this god's relationship to the rest of creation must be flawed. As we saw at points in Book One, the fact that Irenaeus's argument does not line up precisely—and indeed seems to diverge greatly—from rhetorical precedent actually says more about Irenaeus's categorization of his opponents than it does about his own thinking. That is to say, because his opponents, for example, are confused about God and the Aeons, Irenaeus does not try to fit their discussion into

13. See Scott D. Moringiello, "Allegory and Typology in Irenaeus of Lyon," *Studia Patristica* 93, no. 19 (2017): 255–64.

14. "dissolutam suam uidentes argumentationem, aut reuertentes ad ueritatem et semetipsos humilitantes et cessantes a multifaria sua phantasia, placantes Deum de his quae aduersus eum blasphemauerunt, saluentur" (2.11.2).

a coherent system. In order to refute his opponents' claims, he must structure his refutation on their lines, not his. Irenaeus begins his discussion with the Aeons in 2.12, which form the basis for his opponents' scriptural interpretation. The Aeons, according to this teaching, are the emanations that come from God the Father, which result in the created world. In all, there are thirty Aeons, and they form what Irenaeus calls the Triacontad. Although Irenaeus does not say this explicitly, we can argue that the thirty Aeons are simply reified concepts or emotions.[15] Precisely because his opponents have reified these concepts or emotions, their discussion of them does not make sense, nor does their interpretation of biblical text show that these Aeons exist in the first place. When we come to a fuller discussion of the faith, we shall see that Irenaeus believes the faith not only helps interpret the scriptures, but it does so because it comes from the scriptures themselves and is a summary of them.

The scriptures came from the creator God, and the Apostolic faith comes from the scriptures. Because of this, Irenaeus sees both the scriptures and the faith as stable, because neither is created by human beings. According to Irenaeus, the rule his opponents follow, such as it is, comes from Greek literature and philosophy.[16] This, I would argue, is one of Irenaeus's central points in Book Two. For Irenaeus, the idea that his opponents take their cues from Greek literature and philosophy shows that they impart an alien methodology on their in-

15. This is the argument developed in Hans Jonas, *The Gnostic Religion: The Message of the Alien God and the Beginnings of Christianity* (Boston: Beacon Press, 1963).

16. Irenaeus's own knowledge of Greek philosophy has garnered much discussion in the secondary literature. See Schoedel, "Philosophy and Rhetoric." Schoedel builds on earlier studies, especially Grant, "Irenaeus and Hellenistic Culture." Grant tried to correct earlier articles, including Reynders, "Paradosis"; Morton Scott Enslin, "Irenaeus: Mostly Prolegomena," *Harvard Theological Review* 40, no. 3 (1947): 137–65; Th.-André Audet, "Orientations théologiques chez saint Irénée: le contexte mental d'une gnōsis alēthēs," *Traditio* 1, no. 1 (1943): 15–54. These scholars argued that Irenaeus had little formation in the Hellenistic culture of his time. Philip Hefner focuses on the importance of the hypothesis of scripture or the rule of faith in Irenaeus's theological method. Hefner does not address broader cultural issues in his article. See Philip J. Hefner, "Theological Methodology and St Irenaeus," *Journal of Religion* 44, no. 4 (1964): 294–309. See also Anthony Briggman, "Revisiting Irenaeus's Philosophical Acumen," *VC* 65, no. 2 (2011): 115–24, and Michel Rene Barnes, "Irenaeus's Trinitarian Theology," *Nova et Vetera* 7, no. 1 (2009): 67–106. Barnes argues that Irenaeus borrowed from Stoicism.

terpretation of scripture. Irenaeus views Greek philosophy as essentially a product of human fabrication. The fact that Greek philosophers disagreed meant that they were not building on a stable rule. Their systems did not come from God, but from themselves. That is, unlike some other early Christian authors who see philosophy as a way to truth (however inchoate), Irenaeus sees it as a road to irreligion. Unlike Justin Martyr or Clement of Alexandria, Irenaeus is not interested in showing Greek philosophical antecedents to Christian belief. His opponents also try to pass off these literary and philosophical beliefs as their own, without acknowledging their debt to others. They take their ignorance and irreligion from Aristophanes, Thales, Homer, Anaximander, Anaxagoras, Democritus, Epicurus, Plato, and Hesiod. The problem, of course, is that these thinkers disagree with one another, and so to borrow from each of them leads to confusion. If Greek philosophy were true, Irenaeus wants to say, the philosophers would not disagree with one another. His opponents do not even align themselves with *one* philosophy, though even that would provide a degree of unity. Instead, his opponents "style ignorance about true knowledge. Well did Paul speak of 'novelties of words of the false knowledge' [1 Tm 6:20]. For their knowledge is found to be false."[17] Notice how Irenaeus contrasts his opponents' use of Greek literature with his own use of Apostolic writing. Irenaeus finds himself in the same position as Paul, because both understand themselves as working within a tradition, and both see their opponents subverting that tradition. This subversion occurs because Irenaeus's opponents *manufacture* their tradition; they do not inherit it. This, then, is the problem with their understanding of the Aeons: there is no tradition of interpreting the Book of Genesis or the Gospel of John that makes use of the Aeons. His opponents use familiar words from the scriptures to attract people to their teaching about the Aeons, "but since emissions from these have no plausibility or proof, they have fabricated all things out of all sorts of things."[18]

17. "Secundum antiphrasin ergo ueritatis ignorantiam agnitionem uocant, et bene Paulus ait, uocum nouitates falsae agnitionis: uere enim falsa agnitio ipsorum inuenta est" (2.14.7).
18. "quae autem ex his non iam uerisimiliter et sine ostensione omnia ex omnibus mentiti sunt" (2.14.8).

When Irenaeus talks about creation, he argues that it is well-ordered because it was the work of the creator God. Yet because his opponents fabricate their own god, they are not able to talk about the appropriate cause prior to creation and as a result they "fall into a great aporia."[19] Notice again that because his opponents cannot interpret the scriptures correctly, they cannot understand creation correctly. All of their talk has "plunged them and all who believe them into the greatest impiety."[20] Of course, this, Irenaeus would believe, is the same impiety that the letter to the Ephesians warns against. Such impiety blinds a person to the power and love of God revealed in the scriptures, and although Irenaeus does not say it explicitly here, being blind to the power and love of God will lead to judgment.

Refutatio, 2.20–28: Scripture/Economy

In 2.1–19, then, Irenaeus has laid out his opponents' basic position on God and the Aeons. The Aeons, as we have seen, occupy a liminal space between God and the created order. It is not quite right to say that God created the Aeons, but instead we should say that they emanated from him. The Aeons are important for my study, however, because of the role they play in scriptural interpretation. If 2.1–19 served as Irenaeus's *probatio*, stating the case for his opponents' view of God and the Aeons, 2.20–28 are Irenaeus's *refutatio*, in which he shows the implausibility of the Aeons for scriptural interpretation. Thus we can now turn to this second major section in Book Two and further divide it into two groups. First, in 2.20–24, Irenaeus refutes specific interpretations that claim to show the Aeons. Second, in 2.25–28, Irenaeus steps back and offers what can best be described as a theological methodology for approaching scripture and setting the proper boundaries on theological inquiry. In both cases, Irenaeus's refutation concerns what scripture says about the *oikonomia* of God's creation. In this sec-

---

19. "illos autem propriam causam de his quae anteriora sunt et semetipsos perfecta non habentes enuntiare in summam aporiam incidere necesse est" (2.15.2).

20. "Quis enim sustinebit reliquum eorum uaniloquium, quod astute parabolis adaptare conantes, et se et eos qui sibi credunt in maximam conuerterunt impietatem?" (2.19.9).

ond section, Irenaeus shifts to epideictic rhetoric where he blames his
opponents' view of creation. As befits epideictic rhetoric, Irenaeus's
goal here is to delight his audience, but he aims to do this through his
mockery of the opposing side.

Both Irenaeus and his opponents see Christ as the key to interpreting the scriptures. Irenaeus, as we shall see, links Christ's "parables and
deeds" to the witness of the Law and the prophets. His opponents, by
contrast, interpret Christ's parables and deeds in light of their Aeon-
inspired numerology. In this way, Irenaeus's opponents subject Christ
to their own fabrications. Christ, on this account, must be understood
in light of what the Valentinians themselves have created. Jesus Christ
is central to Irenaeus and his opponents. And both sides believe they
pass on Jesus' own interpretation of the scriptures. This interpretation,
in turn, helps each side understand God's economy of creation. Irenaeus argues that only he interprets Christ properly.

Because Irenaeus is in his *refutatio*, he argues that his opponents
fabricate Christ to interpret a fabricated economy. Irenaeus begins
2.20 by noting, "We have shown that they apply both the parables and
the deeds of the Lord to their fabrication improperly and illogical-
ly."[21] For example, to counter the claim that Judas was the type of the
twelfth Aeon, Irenaeus asks, "how can Judas be compared according
to likeness [with her] since he was thrown out of the number of the
Twelve and never restored to his place? For the Aeon, whose type [*typum*] they claim Judas is, was restored after her Intention had been
separated."[22] Irenaeus's use of *typum* here is significant. He will argue,
especially in his *refutatio* in Book Four, that the proper—and only—
typum (form or imprint) for Christ is found in the Old Covenant. The
types found in the Old Covenant are important *precisely because* they
are not human fabrications.

The best way for Irenaeus to offer his *refutatio* is to show that the

---

21. "Quoniam et parabolas et actus Domini improprie et inconsequenter inferunt
figmento suo, ita ostendimus" (2.20.1).
22. "Hoc ergo quod dicunt duodecimi Aeonis passionem per Iudam demonstrari,
quomodo potest in similitudinem comparari Iudas, qui eiectus est de numero duodec-
imo, neque restitutus est in locum suum? Aeon enim cuius typum Iudam dicunt esse,
separate eius Enthymesi, restitute est siue reuocata" (2.20.2).

principles his opponents use do not work for interpreting any individual passage, and that they do not work for systematically interpreting the scriptures. In his opponents' scheme, Paul—certainly an Apostle one needs to include if one is to offer a persuasive interpretation of the scriptures—has no place. As Irenaeus writes, "We must not be silent about Paul. We must demand from them in what Aeon the Apostle is handed down to us as a type [*typum*]."[23] Irenaeus even mocks his opponents by saying that Hesiod described Pandora as the type for Paul.[24] Ultimately, Irenaeus traces his interpretation back to people while his opponents trace their interpretation back to theories. This too is appropriate in a *refutatio*. Irenaeus's argument trades on *ethos*. He has disparaged the character of his opponents and shown his own line of trustworthy teachers.

There is a strange irony here. Irenaeus argues that the Apostolic faith comes from the scriptures and thus from God himself. The interpretative principles of his opponents come from the fabrications of those teachers. Yet the fabrications lead to a complex numerology that supposedly justifies the interpretations. Irenaeus's stable Apostolic faith can be traced back to people, to individual teachers connected to Christ himself, while his opponents' rule, created as it was by human beings, traces itself back to inert numbers. The idea that Irenaeus's interpretation of scripture derives from the Apostles themselves plays a central role in Irenaeus's argument in Book Three. In Book Four, Irenaeus will place the genealogy of interpretation even further back. Here, though, Irenaeus stresses that his interpretation goes back to those people who lived when Jesus lived. His opponents, by contrast, rely not on eyewitnesses, but "they attempt to adduce proofs at times from numbers, at times from syllables of names, at times from letters of syllables, at times by numbers that are represented by the Greek letters."[25] For Irenaeus, this "demonstrates their machination and unsta-

23. "Sed nec de Paulo quidem tacendum est, sed exigendum ab his in cuius Aeonis typum Apostolus traditus est" (2.21.2).

24. 2.21.2.

25. "etiam hoc ipsum quod per numeros aliquando quidem et per syllabas nominum, aliquando uero et per numeros qui secundum Graecos in litteris continentur, temptant inferre probationes" (2.24.1).

ble fabrication [*figmentum*] to be false."[26] Again we see Irenaeus use "fabrication" pejoratively. Instead of following the economy of God's creation as it is recounted in the scriptures and understood with the faith, Irenaeus's opponents create their own view of creation and their own interpretative lens to understand that view. Irenaeus goes on to show how his opponents attempt to link their complex numerology to scriptural interpretation.

Excursus, 2.25–28: Theological Method

Irenaeus's discussion in 2.25–28 has received sustained attention in secondary scholarship. In fact, I borrow the term "theological method" from William Schoedel, who characterizes these chapters in precisely this way.[27] Recent scholarship has rightly argued that Irenaeus was far more philosophically sophisticated that he has been given credit for.[28] Although I have argued—and will continue to argue—that Irenaeus draws from the rhetorical tradition and views with suspicion interpretative moves that might come from certain philosophical schools, I do not want to set "philosophy" in opposition to "rhetoric." Doing so would set up a binary that simply did not exist in Irenaeus's time. Although the scholarship on this section of Irenaeus's text has paid attention to the supposed opposition between philosophy and rhetoric, it has paid considerably less attention to where this section falls in Irenaeus's argument and how it relates to those other sections of Irenaeus's argument, where I think he is also making a point about theological methodology.

In Book One, Irenaeus laid out the faith. The structure of Irenaeus's presentation of the faith, I argued, mirrored Irenaeus's argument itself. In Book Two, Irenaeus does not lay out the faith of his opponents, but is clear about their interpretative principles and the genesis

---

26. "Adhuc autem et falsum demonstrat commentum eorum et instabile figmentum eorum" (2.24.1).

27. William R. Schoedel, "Theological Method in Irenaeus (Adversus Haereses 2:25–28)," *Journal of Theological Studies* (hereafter, *JTS*) 35, no. 1 (1984): 31–49.

28. The scholarship here is long and growing. One could begin with the work of Richard Norris listed in note 4.

of those interpretative principles. We might more appropriately call these sections guides to interpreting the scriptures rather than theological methodology. Just as in Book One, where 1.10 and 1.22 closed Irenaeus's *refutatio*, 2.25–28 come at the end of his *refutatio* in Book Two. The placement of these chapters is important. Irenaeus has just refuted his opponents on their own terms and now he wants to remind his readers of the key points in his opponents' arguments. As such, the main point in this part of Irenaeus's argument is the fiction of his opponents' god.

These four chapters (2.25–28) clearly form a unit, because at the beginning of 2.25 Irenaeus discusses names and at the end of 2.28 he says that this is enough talk about what Valentinians do to numbers and names.[29] For Irenaeus, the "main principles" of Valentinian exegesis rely on a numerology, inspired by Pythagoras, that stands as a rule behind any act of interpretation and especially the interpretations of Jesus' parables. The faith, which is itself a summary of the scriptures, ought to govern the reading of any scriptural passage. Scripture trumps Pythagorean numerology when it comes to interpreting the scriptures themselves. Therefore when there is a choice between following human rules and following God's rule, one must follow the faith that ultimately comes from God himself. Readers of scripture must guard their knowledge and they should not "go beyond God himself; for no one can go beyond him." The key to Irenaeus's theological method and the key to his refutation of Valentinian exegesis is clear: do not "go in search of what is above the Creator; you will not find it, for your Artificer is without limits."[30] As we have seen, the Valentinian artificer certainly has limits, and those limits include the interpreter himself, who fabricates his interpretation. Irenaeus's opponents are not content with the literal sense of scripture and must create ever more elaborate metaphors to justify their interpretations. Nor are they content with the creator as the ground for all their interpretations of scripture, and

29. See 2.25.1 and 2.28.9. Irenaeus often bookmarks his arguments in this way. See, for example, 4.33.1 and 4.33.15.

30. "Ordinem ergo serua tuae scientiae et ne ut bonorum ignarus supertranscendas ipsum Deum, non enim est transibilis, neque super Demiurgum requiras quid sit, non enim inuenies: indeterminabilis est enim Artifex tuus" (2.25.4).

so they create their own creator. Irenaeus wants to stress there are no philosophical shortcuts to attaining God-like knowledge.

It is important to distinguish between God-like knowledge and knowledge about God. Irenaeus emphatically argues that knowledge about God is possible. Building on Paul's admonishment that knowledge puffs up but love builds up (1 Cor 8:1), Irenaeus argues that knowledge of God must come not from human reasoning, but from divine love. It is "better and more useful" to "know very little and come near to God through love" than to think you "know much and have much experience" and then be found "among the blasphemers" "by having fabricated another God the Father."[31] Irenaeus's concern is "arrogant knowledge."[32] One who has arrogant knowledge presupposes that "he is greater and more perfect than he who made and formed and gave the breath of life and gave being itself."[33] We could even say that human beings need to fabricate their own god when they do not accept the love of the God and Father of Jesus Christ.

Irenaeus makes an even more substantive point, which he will develop especially in Book Four, that "knowledge" of God does not come through the type of discursive reasoning his opponents attempt to employ, but instead through sharing in the love of God offered in Christ. Thus at the center of Irenaeus's theological methodology is an epideictic of praise for God's love, a love offered in Christ and a love that allows human beings to understand the words of scripture correctly. This love can only be understood in light of the economy of salvation recounted in the Old and New Covenants. Irenaeus's rhetoric cannot produce the love that enables human beings to understand God's economy, but it can praise that love. According to Irenaeus, it is better

31. "Melius est ergo et utilius idiotas et parum scientes exsistere et per caritatem proximum fieri Deo, quam putare multum scire et multa expertos in suum Dominum blasphemos inueniri, alterum Deum Patrem fabricantes" (2.26.1). For a thorough account of Irenaeus's understanding of this distinction, see D. Jeffrey Bingham, "Knowledge and Love in Irenaeus of Lyons," *Studia Patristica* 36 (2000): 184–99, and Scott D. Moringiello, "Teaching the Rule of Faith in Love: Irenaeus on 1 Cor 8:1," in *Irenaeus and Paul*, ed. Todd Still and Davie Wilhite (Waco, Tex.: Baylor University Press, forthcoming).

32. "scientiam supercilium" (2.26.1).

33. "opinetur quis se meliorem et perfectiorem esse eo qui fecerit et plasmauerit et spiramen uitae dederit et hoc ipsum esse praestiterit" (2.26.1).

"not to go in search of knowledge about about anything other than 'Jesus Christ the Son of God, who was crucified for us,' or through subtle questions and hairsplitting falling into impiety."[34] Whatever else Irenaeus's theological method entails, it first of all entails a knowledge of God based on the crucified Christ.[35]

This love of God in Christ is, for Irenaeus, the true fullness. His opponents have reified "pleroma," and because of this they do not offer fullness but lack. They offer not the Word but Silence. They do not discuss God's creation but their own fabrication, and base their method on Pythagorean numerology. Scriptural interpretation, backed up by the rule of truth, is not difficult. The faith makes the lessons of scripture easy to see. "There are these things which occur before our eyes and are positioned in Scripture openly and without ambiguity."[36] The contrast here is with the "unstable" figments of his opponents' imaginations. Thanks to the faith, the readers of scripture can see the heavenly visions that scripture displays. The reader who interprets dangerously, however, is the one who refuses to see. He interprets "those things which are not said openly nor placed before the eyes" and are "put together by the interpretation of parables."[37] Interpreting this way "each one finds as he wishes." As a result, there is "no rule of truth"

34. "neque aliud inquirere ad scientiam nisi Iesum Christum Filium Dei qui pro nobis crucifixus est, aut per quaestionum subtilitates et minutiloquium in impietatem cadere" (2.26.1). Here Irenaeus quotes 1 Cor 2:2.

35. Interestingly, neither Schoedel nor Norris discuss this. Schoedel is clear that he neglects the primacy of scriptural interpretation in his argument. He writes: "The one difficulty with this approach to the passage is that fact that Irenaeus is concerned about the interpretation of parables and at times seems to have no more in mind than degrees of exegetical difficulty. Yet this displeasure with the Gnostic interpretation of the parables is intimately linked with his fear of speculation." He also notes the limits of his comparison between Irenaeus and skepticism: "The eschatological element in Irenaeus' thought introduces a problematic for which there is no parallel in the Empiric tradition. For the Empiricists kept their eyes fixed resolutely on this world" (35–36). Yet to deny the eschatological aspect of the *Adversus Haereses* is to miss quite a lot. For example, *AH* 5.25–26, the final section of the work, deals explicitly with eschatological themes.

36. "Sunt autem haec quae ante oculos nostros occurrunt et quaecumque aperte et sine ambiguo ipsis dictionibus posita sunt in Scripturis." Reynders is helpful on how Irenaeus understands the manifestation of the truth in the scriptures in "Paradosis," 17.

37. "sic enim et qui absoluit sine periculo absoluit, et parabolae ab omnibus similiter absolutionem accipient."

among such people who "seem to endeavor truths against themselves and to make contrary teachings and question just as the pagan philosophers."[38] Such people cannot tell what passages to interpret literally and what passages to interpret metaphorically. Even though his opponents have created their own god, their own view of creation, and thus their own scripture, they are not able to interpret god or creation or scripture, because such human fabrications lack the stability that is necessary for true knowledge.

Irenaeus draws a further contrast between the Apostolic faith and the various rules of his opponents. Contrary to the interpretative free-for-all that Irenaeus finds in his opponents' beliefs, the faith among Apostolic Christians provides a "discipline of finding."[39] What marks Irenaeus's Apostolic reading of the scriptures is its adherence to the faith. Such an adherence is the only *reasonable* way to read the scriptures, because it is the only method that accounts for the hypothesis of the economy of salvation that the scriptures recount. The pagan philosophers do not have a clear identity because their questions are at war with each other. Indeed, as Irenaeus notes, according to that kind of reasoning "man would always be in search without ever finding, because he rejected the very method of investigation."[40] Their methods are difficult to discern and are often contradictory. The faith of the Christian scriptures, however, is clear and unambiguous. One symptom of his opponents' irrationality is their pride in creating a myth that serves as an interpretative principle for the scriptures.[41]

---

38. "Sed quae non aperte dicta sunt neque ante oculos posita copulare absolutionibus parabolarum, quas unusquisque prout uult adinuenit: sic enim apud nullum erit regula ueritatis, sed, quanti fuerint qui absoluent parabolas, tantae uidebuntur ueritates pugnantes semet inuicem et contraria sibimet dogmata statuentes, sicut et gentilium philosophorum quaestiones" (2.27.1).

39. "eo quod ipsam inuentionis abiecerit disciplinam" (2.27.2).

40. "Itaque secundum hanc rationem homo quidem semper inquiret, numquam autem inueniet" (2.27.2).

41. See 1.9.5, where Irenaeus describes the Valentinian interpretative principle this way. Although I cannot address the issue at length here, I would argue that Irenaeus uses "myth" in a way similar to Aelius Aristides. For Aristides, Suzanne Saïd writes, a myth is "a cryptic discourse that prevents the uninitiated from understanding a sacred truth." See Suzanne Saïd, "Aristides' Uses of Myths," in *Aelius Aristides between Greece, Rome, and the Gods*, ed. William V. Harris and Brooke Holmes (Leiden: Brill, 2008), 52.

This myth lacks epistemological modesty. It aims to say things about
God that God, in the scriptures, did not say about himself. This is Irenaeus's problem with allegory, as he defines it: allegories go beyond the
hypothesis of scripture. Allegories, for Irenaeus, are ultimately human
fabrications of humanly fabricated scripture.

In contrast to his opponents' interpretation, which is available only
to the philosophically trained, the rule of truth, "our testimony about
God, is placed in the open."[42] The faith itself provides the basis for
arguing with his opponents. Although the faith is a sure guide, it is not
able to provide answers to all questions. Here we see the limits to the
rule itself and to a dependence on rhetorical categories more generally. The nature of God, the nature of human beings, and the nature of
scripture are such that there are some things in scripture that "we can
interpret thanks to the grace of God, [and] others which we commend
to God not only in this age but also in the future."[43] Even the greatest
rhetor, the greatest interpreter of scripture, can see only the visions
that scripture provides, because God himself has offered these visions.
The faith guides the reading of scripture. And this faith, which always
remains firm, reminds "us that there is only one true God, and so that
we love him always, that he alone is Father."[44] Although the faith does
not provide the answer to every question, it helps the reader of scripture to see what scripture teaches. Irenaeus recognizes, of course, that
there are passages in scripture that are difficult to interpret. Yet the
best way to interpret these difficult passages is not to resort to endless myths that come from outside the scriptures, but to attend to the
scriptures themselves and use easier passages to interpret more difficult ones. For Irenaeus human knowledge is essential, but it is essential
to remember it has its limits. Irenaeus distinguishes his theological
method from his opponents' on the issue of God's creation. For Irenaeus, God's creation, as recounted in the scriptures, does not need a

42. "Habentes itaque regulam ipsam ueritatem et in aperto positum de Deo testimonium" (2.28.1).

43. "quaedam quidem absoluimus secundum gratiam Dei, quaedam autem com-
mendamus Deo, et non solum in hoc saeculo, sed et in future" (2.28.3).

44. "Semper enim fides quae est ad magistrum nostrum permanet firma, adseuer-
ans nobis quoniam solus uere Deus, et ut diligamus eum semper, quoniam ipse solus
Pater" (2.28.3).

theoretical frame from outside those scriptures to understand it. To argue that it does, Irenaeus might say, is to say that there is something lacking in creation and in scripture itself. It might also imply that creation is not worthy of redemption.

Recapitulatio, 2.29–35: Christ/Salvation

At the end of Book Two, Irenaeus's rhetoric is deliberative: it looks to the future and urges his audience to make a choice. In this way, Irenaeus ends Book Two in the same way that he ends Book One, by discussing eschatology. Irenaeus fears that Christians who are swayed by his opponents risk misunderstanding scripture and the person of Christ. And because they misunderstand these, they risk their very salvation. In his description of their eschatology, Irenaeus is clear that he is returning "to the remaining points of their argument."[45] If Irenaeus's opponents misread Paul's first letter to the Corinthians and believe that there are three classes of human souls and that one class automatically is saved, then there is no reason for Christ to come in the first place.[46] They interpret Paul's words literally instead of metaphorically, and this confusion, Irenaeus would argue, comes from the philosophically-inspired rules of interpretation that his opponents follow. What is more, these "spiritual" human beings believe that they can ascend beyond the creator in their union with the Father of Christ. They believe this, again, because of a misinterpretation of scripture.

45. "Reuertamur autem nos ad reliqua quae sunt eorum argumentationis" (2.29.1).
46. Of course, the "gnostic" exegesis of Paul is vast, and different teachers focus on different aspects of Paul's teaching. My focus here is not on how well Irenaeus understood these various exegeses of Paul, but instead on Irenaeus's own presentation. For an introduction to gnostic readings of Paul see Pagels, *The Gnostic Paul*. There has also been a robust discussion in the secondary literature about Irenaeus's characterization of Valentinian eschatology, starting with Pagels, "Conflicting Versions of Valentinian Eschatology: Irenaeus' Treatise vs the Excerpts from Theodotus," *Harvard Theological Review* 67, no. 1 (1974): 35–53. There were responses from James F. McCue, "Conflicting Versions of Valentinianism: Irenaeus and the Excerpta Ex Theodoto," in *Rediscovery of Gnosticism* (ed. Layton), 1:404–16; Roland Bergmeier, "'Koniglosigkeit' als nachvalentinianisches Heilspradikat," *Novum Testamentum* 24, no. 4 (1982): 316–39; and Daniel L. Hoffman, "Irenaeus, Pagels, and the Christianity of the Gnostics," in *Light of Discovery*, ed. John Wineland (Eugene, Ore.: Pickwick, 2007), 65–82.

They understand the injunction "Seek and you will find" (Mt 7:7) to mean that "they may find themselves above the Demiurge, calling themselves greater and better than God."[47] Of course, Irenaeus thinks they have simply created their own creator.

As with Book One, Irenaeus ends by directing his refutation in Book Two primarily against the teaching of Valentinus. In 2.31 he says, "since we have disproven the followers of Valentinus, the entire crowd of heretics is refuted."[48] Everything he has written "can equally be applied to the followers of Marcion and Simon and Menander, or anyone else who, in like manner, separates our creator from the Father."[49] These teachers and their followers, Irenaeus says, claim to work miracles but they do not perform their works "through God's power or in truth, or for the benefit of humankind but through magical deceptions and total fraud."[50] Here Irenaeus strikes at his opponents' *ethos*, and he shows that neither they—nor their interpretations—are trustworthy. In fact, Irenaeus makes an eschatological point when he argues that "inasmuch as they are filled completely with all deceitfulness and rebellious inspiration and demoniac energy and illusory vision of idolatry [2 Thes 2:4], they are indeed precursors of the dragon that, because of such an illusory vision, will with its tail make a third of the stars rebel and hurl them to the earth [Rv 12:4]."[51] Again, we see how high the stakes of a proper recapitulation are. Irenaeus will fill this picture out in Book Five, but it is clear that he equates his opponents with the Antichrist. Here Irenaeus employs *pathos*. His audience surely does not want to be compared to the dragon of the Book of Revelation.

Irenaeus contrasts the loose morals of his opponents with the stern

47. "uti super Demiurgum semetipsos adinueniant, maiores et meliores uocantes semetipsos quam Deum" (2.30.2).
48. "Destructis itaque his qui a Valentino sunt, omnis haereticorum euersa est multitudo" (2.31.1).
49. "et aduersus eos qui sunt a Marcione et Simone et Menandro, uel quicumque alii sunt qui similiter diuidunt eam quae secundum nos est conditionem a Patre" (2.31.1).
50. "Non in virtute Dei neque in veritate neque ut benefici hominibus ea faciunt, sed in perniciem et in errorem, per magicas elusiones ey universa fraude" (2.31.2).
51. "et operatione daemoniaca et phantasmate idolatriae per omnia repleti, praecursores uere draconis eius qui per huiusmodi phantasiam abscedere faciet in cauda tertiam partem stellarum et deiciet eas in terram" (2.31.3).

ethical teachings of Jesus. They "boast" Christ "as their teacher and claim he has a much better and stronger soul than the rest."[52] This boast, though, like the Christ it boasts about, is a fiction. Christ actually "commanded that certain things must be done with great care, inasmuch as they are good and excellent, but that one must abstain not only from certain actions but also from the thoughts that lead to these actions, as something evil and harmful and wicked."[53] Christ's work, Irenaeus argues, continues to be performed by the church. "In this she neither misleads [her members] nor accepts bribes from them. For just as she has received freely from God, so she ministers freely" (2.32.4).[54] In this way, we can see how the economy of salvation, which centers on and is recapitulated in Christ, stretches from the Law and the prophets to the church of Irenaeus's own day.

Although Irenaeus is interested in refuting his opponents logically, his use of *logos* is always at the service of the proper interpretation of scripture. Reason helps readers of scripture to understand what ought to be read literally and what ought to be read metaphorically. In this instance, Irenaeus's point is clear: human decisions matter and there are consequences for human action. Indeed, "by the will of God the Creator" souls "continue to exist and extend themselves afterward."[55] Thus befitting deliberative discourse, Irenaeus ends Book Two leaving the choice between Apostolic and Valentinian interpretation—and the consequences of that choice—up to the reader.

The last chapter of Book Two comes, perhaps, as a bit of a disappointment. Instead of a rousing recapitulation of all the points he has made, Irenaeus rehearses minor points about his opponents' scriptural exegesis. He addresses, for example, the numerology of Basilides and how some other teachers misuse the Hebrew language in their inter-

---

52. "isti magistrum gloriantur, et eum multo meliorem et fortiorem reliquis animam habuisse dicunt" (2.32.3).

53. "Cum magna diligentia quaedam quidem fieri isuuit quasi bona et egregia, sed etiam his cogitationibus quae ad opera ducunt, quasi malis et nocivis et nequam" (2.32.4).

54. μήτε ἐξαπατῶσά τινα μήτε εξαργυριζομένη ὡς γὰρ δωρεὰν εἴληφεν παρὰ θεοῦ δωρεὰν καὶ διακονεῖ (2.32.4).

55. "perseuerant autem et extenduntur in longitudinem saeculorum secundum uoluntatem Factoris Dei: ita ut sic initio fierent, et postea ut sint eis donat" (2.34.2).

pretation. In a sense, though, the fact that the opponents' teaching does not come together is precisely Irenaeus's point. The only kind of speech that can have a rousing recapitulation is a well-organized speech whose *oikonomia* has no contradictions and that follows logically from point to point. Irenaeus has been at pains in Books One and Two to show that his opponents' understanding of the *oikonomia* does no such thing, and cannot, because their *oikonomia* does not track the true God's plan of creation and redemption. Instead of the true orator who recapitulates all things in and through his Word, these teachers have fabricated an ersatz god and an ersatz economy.

At the end of 2.35, Irenaeus writes, "We believe that we have sufficiently proved that the preaching of the apostles, the teaching of the Lord, the announcement of the prophets, the spoken messages of the apostles, and the service of the law all harmonize with what we have said and prove that there is one and the same Father, God of all things."[56] In this way, he has, it seems, refuted his opponents. Irenaeus goes on to say, "Lest we seem to be avoiding the proof from the Lord's Scriptures, since the Scriptures themselves preach this very teaching much more obviously and clearly ... we will supply a special book, which will use these Scriptures, and so, for all who love the truth, we will bring into clear light proofs from the divine Scriptures."[57] For Irenaeus, without a true love of the truth, one cannot learn from the scriptures. And the lessons of the scriptures are clear for those who love the truth and read the scriptures with the faith of the church.

I return to the language from the letter to the Ephesians with which I began the chapter. We have seen Irenaeus try to stop the deception of those with empty words, who have fashioned their own god and are, therefore, disobedient. Irenaeus is now ready to turn his attention to his positive account of the faith.

---

56. "Quoniam autem dictis nostris consonat praedictio apostolorum et Domini magisterium et prophetarum adnuntiatio et apostolorum dictatio et legislationibus ministratio unum eundemque omnium Deum Patrem" (2.35.4).

57. "Sed ne putemur fugere illam quae ex Scripturis dominicis est probationem, ipsis Scripturis multo manifestius et clarius hoc ipsum praedicantibus his tamen qui non prave intendant eis, proprium librum qui sequitur has Scripturas reddentes ex Scripturis divinis probationes apponemus in medio omnibus amantibus veritatem" (2.35.4).

3 ✠ MANIFESTATION

John testified to him and cried out, saying, "This was he of whom
I said, 'The one who is coming after me ranks ahead of me because he existed before me.'" From his fullness we have all received, grace in place of grace, because while the law was given
through Moses, grace and truth came through Jesus Christ. No
one has ever seen God. The only Son, God, who is at the Father's
side, has revealed him.

JOHN 1:15–18

I do not intend to offer an exegesis of the prologue of John's Gospel
here, but instead I want to point to three themes we find in this passage
that we also find in Book Three of the *Adversus Haereses*. The prologue
stresses John the Baptist's testimony, the relationship between Moses
and Christ, and the revelation of the Father that the Son offers. For Irenaeus, testimony can only be understood in light of a tradition of teachers. Just as he offered a genealogy of teachers in Book One, he will offer
a genealogy of Apostolic Christianity in Book Three. This genealogy will
stand as rhetorical proof for the scriptural interpretation that Irenaeus
offers. In order for this interpretation to be true to Christ's teaching, it
must discuss the relationship between the Law that was given through
Moses, and the grace and truth that came through Jesus Christ. That
is to say, it must show how Christ brings the New Covenant that was
promised in the Old Covenant. Finally, Irenaeus's interpretation must
show how Christ reveals the Father. This revelation occurs, as we shall
see, both in what Christ teaches and in who Christ is. Irenaeus will not
exhaust these topics in Book Three, as he will save his strongest argument about the relationship between Moses and Christ for Book Four.

I have probed the themes of silence and fabrication in chapters 1 and 2. With chapter 3, and Book Three of the *Adversus Haereses*, we come to a new theme: manifestation. In the previous two books, Irenaeus argued that his opponents' confused teaching stemmed from a confused lineage of teachers. This teaching announced Silence instead of the Word, and produced a fabrication of the teachers' own making. In Book Three, Irenaeus shows how the scriptures manifest God's love in Christ. This manifestation occurs in a few different ways. First, Irenaeus will argue that the Apostolic teaching manifests itself in the genealogy of Apostolic teachers. Once he has established the proper genealogy of teachers, Irenaeus can then discuss the proper interpretation of the scriptures those teachers endorse. The proper interpretation of the scriptures turns on how the visions presented by scripture manifest themselves.

It is worth reflecting a bit on Irenaeus's overall aim. Obviously, I am discussing Irenaeus in an academic context. This book is aimed at other academics who study Irenaeus, second-century Christianity, or early Christianity more broadly. Irenaeus did not write for an academic audience. Nor did he specifically use terms like "silence," "fabrication," or "manifestation" to frame his argument. We must remember that Ireaneus wrote because he believed members of his community were being led astray by other Christian teachers. In fact, Irenaeus does not even think that this opposing teaching truly qualifies as Christian. The lessons that these other teachers offer prohibit their students from seeing the visions that scripture provides. These lessons do not honor the martyrs whose deaths were witnessed by Irenaeus's community.

I have already argued that the *Adversus Haereses* roughly fits the pattern of a forensic speech as Quintilian understands it. Within that pattern, Quintilian allows for instances of *epideixis*, or praise. As one would expect, in Book Three, Irenaeus offers such praise to Christ himself. Irenaeus also praises the community of the church because the church has guarded the tradition of interpretation of scripture that praises Christ. Indeed, were it not for the church there would be no scriptures nor any interpretation of them. Irenaeus's *probatio*, or proof, is also his *epideixis*. He cannot point to Christ without praising him. The themes of *epideixis*, the past, and identity figure in Irenaeus's discourse, and in Book Three, we again find them. When I say "identity" here, I mean who Christ is in relation to the Father and in relation to the tradition of the Old Covenant. Irenaeus believes that he and his opponents differ profoundly on this question. And the "past" here refers to the tradition of the church, which began with the prophets of the Old Covenant and continued through Christ and the Apostles. Thus, the identity of Christ can be understood only through a discussion of Christ's relationship to the Old Covenant, which Irenaeus sees as the Christian church's proper past. The identity of Christ can be secured only through the testimony of the properly identified community of believers. Thus, the genealogy of teachers and scriptural exegetes that Irenaeus presents is crucial.

The genealogy is crucial not in itself, but because of what it represents. The teachers that Irenaeus praises in Book Three all interpreted scripture correctly both in the interpretations of texts they offered and in the ways of life they lived. In other words, Irenaeus relies on their *ethos* in making an argument. They did not import alien philosophical reasoning into their interpretation, and they allowed scripture itself to provide the rules for its own interpretation. That is to say, the teachers with whom he aligns himself knew the proper limits of metaphor. While they understood the need for typological language in understanding the relationship between the Old Covenant and the New, they also understood that that typology must be governed by the *oikonomia* of God's salvific plan, by the true hypothesis of scripture. How Irenaeus understands all of this is the argument that I will make in this chapter and the two that follow it. In order to make that argument, let us first examine the basic organization of Book Three.

We can divide Book Three into three major sections. From the prologue through 3.8, Irenaeus lays out the importance of tradition. Here he focuses on the role the Apostles and their chosen followers played in establishing the faith. In 3.9–15, Irenaeus discusses the Gospels, the Acts of the Apostles, and the letters of Paul and shows how these ought to be read with the faith in mind. Finally, in 3.19–25, Irenaeus discusses Christ and how the scriptures of the Old Covenant prophesy Christ's work on earth. Once again, we have three major sections that map onto the three major rhetorical moments that I have discussed.

Irenaeus's discussion of tradition in 3.1–8 is actually a discussion of the rules with which one can speak properly about God. This section serves as the *probatio* and the forensic mode of the book. His discussion of scriptures in 3.9–15 is a discussion of how, given the rules of speech provided by tradition, Christians ought to understand God's economy of salvation as it is recounted in the writings of the New Covenant.[1] This section serves as the *refutatio* and the epideictic mode of the book. The discussion of the prophets 3.19–25 not only recapitulates Irenaeus's own argument about the unity of God's economy, but also addresses how Christ's own recapitulation effects the salvation of humankind.[2] This section serves as the *recapitulatio* and the deliberative moment of the book. Just as we saw in Books One and Two, Irenaeus has a section on theological methodology in Book Three (3.16–18). By offering principles of interpretation focusing on the life of Christ, these chapters also serve as an *epideixis* of praise of Christ himself. The proper interpretation of scripture comes from a proper understanding of Christ as truly God and truly man. Once this is understood, the only proper response to Christ is praise. Thus, we could say that Book Three deals generally with the manifestation of Christ in scripture.

If Book Three functions as the *probatio*, the proof, of Irenaeus's speech, we should consider how the rhetorical tradition understands proof. Aristotle distinguishes between syllogisms and enthymemes. Syllogisms are arguments where conclusions necessarily follow from premises. Rhetoric, however, deals with the realm of human action, and human actions rarely follow necessarily from premises. Human action, therefore, is the domain of enthymemes.[3] An enthymeme is a like a syllogism, but it lacks a stated premise. According to Aristotle, there are two kinds of proof: those that involve skill and those that do not. Proofs that do not involve skill include witnesses, torture, and contracts. Proofs that do involve skill are those that the rhetor

---

1. On Irenaeus as a scriptural theologian see Lawson, *The Biblical Theology of St. Irenaeus*; D. Fakasfalvy, "Theology of Scripture in St. Irenaeus," *Revue Bénédictine* 78, nos. 3–4 (1968): 319–33; A. Faivre, "Irénée, premier théologien 'systématique'?," *Recherches de science religieuse*, 65, no. 1 (1991): 11–32.

2. Irenaeus will spell out this connection between the prophets of the Old Covenant and the unity of the economy of salvation at great length in the next chapter.

3. See Aristotle, *Rhetoric* 1357a.

furnishes himself and which we have seen before: *ethos, pathos,* and *logos.*[4] As Kennedy points out, it is often the case that logical proofs justify a decision that was made on the basis of *ethos* or *pathos.*[5] In his interpretation of scripture, Irenaeus does not offer irrefutable syllogisms. Although "logical" proofs play a central role in his argument, Irenaeus must ultimately rely on his ability to persuade his audience, on his ability to use enthymemes. This rhetorical mode of argument, though, fits the scriptural text well. Much of scripture presents visions to behold. As we have seen, Irenaeus, like Plutarch and like Aristotle, wants to paint a picture that will convince his audience.

Nowhere is this more clear than in the prologue to John's Gospel, which ends with these words: "No one has ever seen God, but the only begotten of God who is at the bosom of the Father, this one interprets [*exêgêsato*] God" (Jn 1:18). The Revised Standard Version translates *exêgêsato* as "made him known"; the New American Bible, as "revealed." The Word (the Logos of Jn 1:1) interprets, makes known, reveals the God who is not seen. Every subsequent interpretation imitates that first interpretation offered by the Word as it manifests a light that shines in the darkness. Of course, the Johannine corpus is replete with the language of manifestation. The opening passage of the Book of Revelation is the *locus classicus*: "The revelation [*apocalypsis*] of Jesus Christ, which God gave to him to show [*deixai*] to his servants what must happen soon. He showed [*esêmamen*] the messages through his angel to his servant John, who witnessed [*emarturêsen*] the Word of God and who saw the witness [*martyrian*] of Jesus Christ." Just as Irenaeus imitates Paul when he searches out the genealogies of falsely so-called knowledge and refutes them, so too does he imitate John in bearing witness to the Word. John reported what Christ revealed to him and Irenaeus has revealed his opponents' teaching and follows John—and Christ—in the interpretation (*exêgêsis*) of God's word.[6] Indeed, for Irenaeus, following John here, the *revelation* of Christ brings with it the *interpretation* of God's message.

---

4. Aristotle, *Rhetoric* 1355b.

5. Kennedy continues, "The same is almost always the case in religious discourse" (*New Testament Interpretation through Rhetorical Criticism*, 17).

6. See Wingren, *Man and the Incarnation*, 88.

For Irenaeus, as a rhetor, words can help to recreate the visions John beheld.[7] Here Irenaeus agrees with Cicero that an explanation should be, as it were, placed in front of the eyes of the listener.[8] Obviously Irenaeus's images are based on faith in the risen Christ who appears to his followers, but we can find the language of vision in the rhetorical tradition as well. Indeed, in Plutarch's text *On the Glory of the Athenians*, this slightly older contemporary of Irenaeus says that Thucydides was such a great orator that he "made his listeners seers."[9] Quintilian too speaks of images being seen and narrations being beheld by the eyes of the mind.[10] For Quintilian, the heart or the emotions play a role in this seeing. These emotions are the key part of *pathos*. To talk about the emotions is to talk about the interplay between the speaker and his audience. The speaker has his own methods and the audience is motivated in a particular way. Moreover, the audience must have enough faith in the speaker to find his arguments believable.[11] In Book Three, Irenaeus draws on the tradition of

7. This theme of vision, especially in its Johannine manifestation, is a central theme in Hans Urs von Balthasar's interpretation of Irenaeus. He writes, "Theology begins by seeing what is.... To see. The two words *videre* and *ostendere* fall constantly from Irenaeus's pen." *The Glory of the Lord: A Theological Aesthetics*, vol. 2: *Studies in Theological Style: Clerical Styles*, trans. John Kenneth Riches (Edinburgh: T and T Clark, 1986), 45. Kevin Mongrain has argued that Irenaeus's theology is key to understanding the theology of Balthasar. See Kevin Mongrain, *The Systematic Thought of Hans Urs Von Balthasar: An Irenaean Retrieval* (New York: Crossroad, 2002).

8. "Nam et commoratio una in re permultam movet et inlustris explanatio rerumque, quasi geruntur, sub aspectum paene subiecto; quae et in exponenda re plurimum valet et ad inlustrandum id, quod exponitur et ad amplificandum; ut eis, qui audient, illud, quod augebimus, quantum efficere oratrio poterit, tantum esse videatur." Marcus Tullius Cicero, *De Oratore I–III*, ed. Augustus S. Wilkins (London: Bristol Classical Press, 2002), 3.202.

9. Plutarch, *De Gloria Atheniensium* 347a.

10. "Magna virtus res de quibus loquimur clare atque ut cerni videantur enuntiare. Non enim satis efficit neque, ut debet, plene dominatur oratio si usque ad aures valet atque ea sibi iudex de quibus cognoscit narrari credit, non exprimi et oculis mentis ostendi." Quintilian, *The Orator's Education* 8.3.62.

11. "Quare capiendae sunt illae de quibus dixi rerum imagines quas vocari fantasias indicavimus, omniaque de quibus dicturi erimus, personae, questiones, spes, metus, habenda in oculis, in adfectus recipienda: pectus est enim quod disertos facit et vis mentis." Quintilian, *The Orator's Education* 10.7.15. For more on processes and techniques of persuasion, see Kinneavy, *Greek Rhetorical Origins of Christian Faith*, 22. Note also where Kinneavy writes, "faith (*pistis*) meant the faith one could have in the personal

using *ekphrasis* in speeches. *Ekphrasis* is the vivid, verbal description of a work of art. The goal of *ekphrasis* is to make the audience feel as though they are in the middle of the action being described.[12] Although this technique might sound foreign to us today, Ruth Webb has argued that "ancient audiences were more consciously attuned to visual effects and did 'see' the subject of poems and speeches in their mind's eye."[13]

In Book Three, Irenaeus shifts from the forensic discourse necessary in Books One and Two to epideictic discourse. Instead of prosecuting his opponents' interpretation, Irenaeus praises Apostolic interpretation. In Books Three and Four, Irenaeus presents the content of the Apostolic faith and articulates an interpretation of the texts written by the teachers of that faith. For a writer who presents the Apostolic faith in the language of images, the epideictic moment is perfectly appropriate.[14] Of course, epideictic refers specifically to speeches, but for a writer schooled in Greco-Roman rhetoric, there would be little, if any, distinction between interpreting texts and giving speeches.[15]

At the beginning of Book Three, Irenaeus implies that for the purpose of overturning heresies, Books One and Two are sufficient. The fact that Irenaeus wrote the remaining books suggests that he wanted to do more than that.[16] He also wanted to present Apostolic teaching

---

credibility of a political speaking addressing the council; it meant the faith one could give to the promises or threats of a speaker before the city assembly; it meant the faith one could put in the seemingly logical arguments of a person in the law courts; it meant the faith one could put in a witness in a legal case" (*Greek Rhetorical Origins of Christian Faith*, 79).

12. Ruth Webb, *Ekphrasis, Imagination and Persuasion in Ancient Rhetorical Theory and Practice* (Burlington, Vt.: Ashgate, 2009), 10.

13. Ibid., 24.

14. For a treatment of oratory as display see Christopher Carey, "Epideictic Oratory," in *Companion to Greek Rhetoric*, ed. Ian Worthington (London: Blackwell, 2007), 237–40.

15. "Throughout the Greco-Roman period there is no clear difference between literary criticism and rhetorical theory." Kennedy, *A New History of Classical Rhetoric*, 159. See also Pernot who notes, "The intellectual resemblance and precise contact points between Aristotle's *Poetics* and *Rhetoric* reveal the bridges existing in antiquity between rhetoric and poetics, and more broadly between rhetoric and literary criticism." Pernot, *Rhetoric in Antiquity*, 135–36.

16. I should note here that Irenaeus's original intention in composing the *Adversus*

on its own account. Irenaeus consciously writes for those who will interpret the scriptures in the community and consciously evokes teachers in his writing. Christ is the interpreter *par excellence*, but the task of Christian scriptural interpretation was given to the Apostles and their successors. The love of God in Christ is the ultimate proof, and all that Irenaeus, as the rhetor, can do is interpret the scriptures in the light of that love through the teaching of the Apostles to whom the love was offered. Love, as we shall see, is the ultimate arbiter of which passages of scripture ought to be taken literally and which ought be to be taken metaphorically. This love, moreover, is found in Jesus Christ.

Irenaeus's praise of Christ, based on interpreting the New Testament with the Apostolic faith, is also, in an important sense, a praise of interpretation itself. This is another way of saying that Irenaeus praises the church because, as we have seen, there is no proper interpretation of scripture without the faith that the church guards. The revelation of Christ and the preaching of the Apostles are made manifest through the interpretation of scripture.[17]

Love, in Irenaeus's account, allows for the proper manifestation and interpretation of scripture. Irenaeus counters silence and fabrication with manifestation. Whereas silence and fabrication easily confuse the reader of scripture and encourage him to read literally what ought to be read metaphorically and *vice versa*, the manifestation of God's love can occur because Irenaeus allows his readers to see the visions that scripture recounts. While Irenaeus's *epideixis* in Book Three

---

Haereses is not my concern. He may well have originally intended to have what we now know as the *Demonstration of the Apostolic Preaching* as the conclusion of the work. My argument is that given the text we have, the rhetorical framework and the concerns of ancient rhetors make the most sense of the text. Furthermore, this would be a framework that would have made sense to Irenaeus himself. I am largely persuaded by John Behr's argument for the chronology of Irenaeus's writing in his *Irenaeus of Lyons: Identifying Christianity*, 69. Behr builds on Charles E. Hill, *From the Lost Teaching of Polycarp: Identifying Irenaeus' Apostolic Presbyter and the Author of Ad Diognetum* (Tübingen: Mohr Siebeck, 2006), 77–80. But, as I note, I am interested in the text as we have it now.

17. Olson points out that there are three principles of Irenaeus's interpretation. First, there is the rule of truth. Second, less obscure passages should be used to interpret more obscure passages. And third, the interpreter "must demonstrate humility, love of God, and a Spirit-led, ethical manner of living" (*Irenaeus, the Valentinian Gnostics, and the Kingdom of God*, 64).

praises the love of God offered in Christ, his main argument is that this love can only be understood thanks to the Apostolic tradition that preserves it. This Apostolic tradition passes on a method of reading scripture that allows God's love to be revealed. Without the proper exegetical lens, the scriptures can easily be misread. In fact, this is exactly what Irenaeus's opponents have done. They have misinterpreted scripture to focus on knowledge instead of love.

As with the previous chapter, I shall organize my discussion of Book Three under three main headings: God, the economy of salvation, and recapitulation in and through Christ. These three headings align with the rhetorical moments of *probatio*, *refutatio*, and *recapitulatio*.

Probatio, 3.1–8: God

I began my analyses of Books One and Two by discussing how Irenaeus's opponents understand God. This proved to be the key for their understanding of scripture, which I discussed in the second part of my analyses. In turn, the discussion of God and scripture sets the stage for the discussion of salvation. For Irenaeus's opponents, a discussion of God (or the Aeons) was always separated from a discussion of Jesus Christ, who was himself divided between the human Jesus and the divine Christ. In contrast to his opponents' separation of God and Christ, Irenaeus's discussion of God is centered on Christ, the Word made flesh, the subject of Irenaeus's own *probatio*. Even Irenaeus's positive account of the Christian *kerygma* is shaped by an opposition to his opponents' teaching. The forensic mood of the *Adversus Haereses* shapes its epideictic moments. Irenaeus's preface to Book Three is quite short. He recounts what he did in Books One and Two, and then says, "in this third book we will bring in proofs from the Scriptures, that we may not fall short with any of the things you had ordered us to do; and so that, over and above what you awaited, you may have from us the means for exposing and refuting all those who in any way propose wicked teaching. For the love [*caritas*] that is in God is rich and without envy. It gives more than is asked of it."[18] Once again we

18. "In hoc autem tertio ex Scripturis inferemus ostensiones, ut nihil tibi ex his quae praeceperas desit a nobis, sed et, praeterquam opinabaris ad arguendum et evertendum

see how central love—*caritas, agapē*—is to Irenaeus's understanding of what he does. He wants his speech to communicate God's love to those who hear it, and he knows he can only communicate that love thanks to God's grace.

The question, of course, is how one gains access to Christ, through whom one gains access to the Father. Christ has appeared on earth and will appear again at the end times (which Irenaeus believes are imminent). Christ also appears in the scriptures.[19] Irenaeus spends the bulk of his discussion in Book Three showing how a proper interpretation of scripture shows that God is one and that Jesus Christ is both God and man.[20] In order to do this, he goes through the Gospels twice. Following the testimony of the disciples means showing how the Gospels of Matthew, Mark, Luke, and John connect Jesus to the prophets of the Old Testament.[21] It also means demonstrating what the Gospels truly say about Christ.[22] Irenaeus probes the question under what conditions love of God manifests itself in the proper interpretation of scripture.

Perhaps the most important condition needed to understand or recognize this manifestation is the proper teacher in the proper community. And so, even though he begins Book Three by promising to bring evidence from scripture, Irenaeus starts with a discussion of

---

eos qui quolibet modo male docent occasiones a nobis accipias: quae enim est in Deo caritas, dives et sine invidia exsistens, plura donat quam postulat quis ab ea" (3.P).

19. Gerhard Richter argues that Irenaeus's theology is thoroughly Christocentric in his *Oikonomia: Der Gebrauch des Wortes Oikonomia im neuen Testament, bei den Kirkenvätern und in der theologischen Literatur dis ins 20. Jahrhundert* (Berlin: Walter de Gruyter, 2005), 125.

20. As Behr argues, the *Adversus Haereses* "while polemical, is also exegetical rather than analytical: it demonstrates, from Scripture, that there is but one God, one Christ, one Spirit, and one human race in which the economy is enacted, as unfolded in Scripture, rather than analyzing the human condition in static, philosophical terms" (*Asceticism and Anthropology in Irenaeus and Clement*, 86).

21. Bingham notes the different orderings of Gospels in Irenaeus. Irenaeus believes that the chronology of the writing of the Gospels is Matthew, Mark, Luke, and John. The ordering of the Gospels in terms of the events they describe is John, Luke, Matthew, and Mark. And the order of books in Irenaeus's bible is Matthew, Luke, Mark, and John. Bingham, *Irenaeus' Use of Matthew's Gospel*, 89.

22. For Irenaeus's use of the term "Gospel," see Yves Marie Blanchard, *Aux sources du canon, le témoignage d'Irénée* (Paris: Cerf, 1993), 151–64.

Apostles and the bishops. This is directly related to the faith, for Irenaeus cannot bring evidence from the scriptures about Christ unless he has already established the tradition of teaching that enables him to read scripture correctly. Irenaeus traces the genealogy of Apostolic teaching back to the Apostles themselves. Peter, Paul, Stephen, and John are the pillars of the church that Irenaeus praises, the sure exegetes of the *probatio* of God's love offered in Christ, the Word made flesh. Each of them, through his life and in his words, makes this truth manifest. Irenaeus recognizes, however, that each author had a different audience. As Irenaeus understands it, a common critique of Christian teaching was that the Apostles—and Jesus—tailored their teaching to their audience. It is possible to make an analogy with a good rhetor here. Christ and the Apostles taught not what their audience wanted to hear, but what it needed to hear.

We must remember that Irenaeus sees himself in competition with other interpreters of scripture. This competition turns on how the scriptures show themselves and what they show. Scripture reveals God's love for creation, but his opponents "turn those Scriptures into an accusation."[23] The truth is "not able to be found" by those who "do not know the tradition."[24] These teachers, in effect, have set up a rival tradition, which is not "handed down through letters but through a living voice."[25] They justify this rival tradition through Paul's words: "We speak wisdom among the perfect, a wisdom not of this world" (1 Cor 2:6).[26] This "wisdom" found outside this tradition passed on through a living voice, one that someone "finds by himself," is a "fiction."[27] Even though it is a fiction, this rival tradition thinks the truth can be found at times in Valentinus, at other times in Marcion or Cerinthus or Basilides.[28] Even though this teacher creates his fiction all

---

23. "in accusationem conuertuntur ipsarum Scripturarum" (3.2.1).

24. "quia non possit ex his inveniri veritas ab his qui nesciant traditionem" (3.2.1).

25. "Non enim per litteras traditam illam sed per uiuam uocem" (3.2.1).

26. "ob quam causam et Paulum dixisse: Sapientiam autem loquimur inter perfectos, sapientiam autem non mundi huius" (3.2.1).

27. "Et hanc sapientiam unusquisque eorum esse dicit quam a semetipso adinuenerit, fictionem uidelicet" (3.2.1).

28. "ut digne secundum eos sit veritas aliquando quidem in Valentino, aliquando autem in Marcione, aliquando in Cerintho, postea deinde in Basilide fuit" (3.2.1).

by himself, this fiction can attain the status of tradition once he hands it down. This ersatz tradition allows those teachers to circumvent the Apostolic tradition. Irenaeus combats their falsehood by showing forth Christian truth. These teachers rely on their own authority to anchor them to truth, while Irenaeus relies on the authority of the Apostles. These, then, are the terms Irenaeus has set up. The Apostles, whom he follows, have set up four Gospels and have set up a tradition of teachers whose task it is to interpret those scriptures correctly.

Before we turn to what Irenaeus says about the beginnings of the Apostolic tradition of teachers, let us step back for a minute and consider what the rhetorical tradition says about authority, as authority plays a central role in the first part of Book Three. For Quintilian, authority does not just mean the current word of a witness, but also "opinions which can be attributed to nations, peoples, wise men, distinguished citizens or famous poets."[29] Irenaeus evokes Peter, Paul, Stephen, and John precisely because they are wise men not enmeshed in his own disputes (even though he will argue that they faced similar challenges). By placing himself in their line of teaching, Irenaeus draws on them as proof for his interpretation of scripture.

It is important to note that Irenaeus sees himself not only in line with the teaching of the Apostles, but in an *unbroken* line of Apostolic teaching. The language of vision, of ekphrastic description, permeates Irenaeus's text. The Apostles make "manifest in all the world" the tradition that "is in the whole Church for all who wish to see it" (3.3.1).[30] Thus, the site for the proper manifestation of scripture comes from the bishops. It is worth pointing out here that whereas Irenaeus spends a great deal of time noting all of his opponents, he spends comparatively little time discussing "Apostolic" teachers. That is, although the Apostolic teachers help interpret the manifestation of God's love, they are not to be identified with God's love in the way that his opponents are

29. See Quintilian, *The Orator's Education* 5.11.36.
30. "Traditionem itaque apostolorum in toto mundo manifestatam in omni Ecclesia adest perspicere omnibus qui uera uelint uidere." For a comparison to the Apostles, see Ignatius, *ad Phil.* 5.1–2; Blanchard, *Aux sources du canon*, 10. For Clement on succession, see Fantino, *La théologie d'Irénée*, 42; and 1 Clement 42 and 44.1–2. For these texts see Michael W. Holmes, *The Apostolic Fathers: Greek Texts and English Translations* (Grand Rapids, Mich.: Baker Books, 1999), 33–131.

to be identified with their teaching. This is because, as we saw in the previous two chapters, each of those teachers creates his own fiction and voices his own silence, unlike the bishops who hand down Apostolic teaching.

The bishop of Rome plays a normative role for Irenaeus.[31] In such a work as the *Adversus Haereses*, Irenaeus notes, it would be difficult "to number the successions of all the churches."[32] By saying this, Irenaeus suggests that if he had the time and space he would offer such a number, including the churches, perhaps, of Jerusalem, Antioch, and Alexandria. The importance of Rome as a city, therefore, has nothing to do with its status as an imperial seat and obviously has no direct connection to the person or work of Christ. Instead, it is a result of the work of Peter and Paul there. Given Irenaeus's interest, we can assume the importance of their martyrdom. This tradition is conserved in the life and actions of the members of the church. Of course, this goes far beyond sitting together and offering interpretations of scripture. The early Christians knew each other personally and offered the liturgy together. The encountered each other in person and not only through texts.[33]

31. Perhaps unsurprisingly, Irenaeus's remarks about the bishop of Rome have taken up a lot of scholarly attention. See Luise Abramowski, "Irenaeus Adv. Haer. Iii.3.2: Ecclesia Romana and Omnis Ecclesia and Ibid. 3.3. Anacletus of Rome," *JTS* 28, no. 1 (1977): 101–4; H. S. Benjamins, "Die Apostolizität der kirchlichen Verkündigung bei Irenäus von Lyon," in *Apostolic Age in Patristic Thought*, ed. A. Hilhorst (Leiden: Brill, 2004), 115–29; Paul Galtier, "Ab his qui sunt undique Irénée, Adv Haer, Iii, 3,2," *Revue d'histoire ecclésiastique* 44, nos. 3–4 (1949): 411–28; R. Kereszty, "The Unity of the Church in the Theology of Irenaeus," *Second Century* 4, no. 2 (1984): 202–18; Emmanuel Lanne, ""'Église de Rome' a gloriosissimis duobus apostolis Petro Et Paulo Romae fundatae et constitutae ecclesiae' (Adv Haer iii 3:2)," *Irénikon* 49, no. 3 (1976): 275–322; Willy Rordorf, "Was Heisst; Petrus und Paulus Haben die Kirche in Rom 'Gegruendet': zu Irenaeus Adv Haer iii,1,1;3,2,3," in *Unterwegs Zur Einheit* (ed. Branchtschen), 609–16.

32. "Sed quoniam ualde longum est in hoc tali uolumine omnium Ecclesiarum enumerare successiones" (3.3.2).

33. Quintilian notes the following about the living voice of a teacher, a living voice that Irenaeus would have encountered. "Ipse aliquid, immo multa cotidie dicat quae secum auditores referant. Licet enim satis exemplorum ad imitandum ex lectione suppeditet, tamen uiua illa, ut diciture, vox alit plenius, parecipueque praeceptoris quem discipuli, si modo recte sunt instituti, et amant et velentur." Quintilian, *The Orator's Education* 2.2.8. Reynders notes how Irenaeus saw the scriptures as a living voice. "Paradosis. Le progrès et l'idée de tradition jusqu'à saint Irénée," *Recherches de théologie*

Irenaeus wants to bring his audience into a scene where the living voice of the Apostles gets passed down. Irenaeus notes that Clement, the bishop of Rome, "saw the blessed Apostles themselves and conversed with them." Clement "had the preaching of the Apostles fresh in his memory and the tradition before his eyes."[34] The tradition stands before his eyes because it is embodied in the Apostles, in what they teach and how they live. The tradition of the Apostles is handed down personally and liturgically. Irenaeus stresses that the tradition of which he is a part and the truth that it proclaims "comes to us from the order and succession of the Apostles, and this demonstration is most true."[35] The faith that is handed down is "life giving" and is "conserved and handed down in truth" until Irenaeus's own day.[36] Irenaeus stresses the ancient nature of Christian truth, a truth that traces its lineage back to the Law and prophets. This tradition is Irenaeus's *probatio*. Although Irenaeus does not say the succession of bishops offers the visionary experience he finds in the scriptures, it is clear from his account that without the bishops and the tradition and liturgy they embody, there would not be a steady faith by which to interpret scripture, and thus no manifestation to interpret.

The *probationes* of the Apostles only serve to highlight their teaching about Christ. These *probationes* offer themselves as sure guides to understanding the manifestation of the scriptures. Irenaeus believes he has established the authority of the Apostles and their successors, the bishops, because there are "such great proofs," "which can be obtained easily from the Church" that there is no need to look outside

---

ancienne et medieval 5, no. 2 (1935): 174. Elaine Pagels has noted the importance of ritual in Irenaeus's polemic. See Elaine H. Pagels, "Irenaeus, the 'Canon of Truth,' and the Gospel of John: 'Making a Difference' through Hermeneutics and Ritual," *VC* 56, no. 3 (2002): 339–71.

34. "Post eum tertio loco ab apostolis episcopatum sortitur Clemens, qui et uidit apostolos ipsos, et contulit cum eis et cum adhuc insonantem praedicationem apostolorum et traditionem ante oculos haberet, non solus: adhuc enim multi supererant tunc ab apostolis docti" (3.3.3).

35. "Hac ordinatione et successione ea quae est ab apostolis in Ecclesia traditio et ueritatis praeconatio peruenit usque ad nos" (3.3.3).

36. "Et est plenissima haec ostensio, unam et eandem uiuificatricem fidem esse quae in Ecclesia ab apostolis usque nunc sit conseruata et tradita in ueritate" (3.3.3).

the church for answers to questions of scriptural interpretation.[37] The Apostles taught that the Father sent Christ "on account of the super-abundance of his love for his creation."[38]

God loves creation. Christ teaches that love. Love leads to knowl-edge. In fact, Christ's entire mission and ministry manifests God's love for creation and especially human beings. *This*, Irenaeus wants to say, is the difference between himself and his opponents. The structure of the *Adversus Haereses*, grounded in the faith in the Father, Son, and Holy Spirit, is based on this love. Irenaeus sees himself as carrying on a tradition of reading that manifests the love of God in Christ, while his opponents fashion a knowledge hidden in secret. Irenaeus reminds his reader that "the Lord gave knowledge to his disciples," and this teaching comes from Christ himself. The Lord's teaching, especially as that teaching interprets the Law and the prophets, forms the basis of the Apostolic tradition of teaching.[39] Christ has handed this down to the Apostles, and the teaching remains in the church.[40] The Apos-tles, through their teaching, show what is in the scriptures.[41] Irenae-us's implication is clear: salvation comes from accepting the teaching of scripture, which can only be understood in its fullness when the distinction between literal and metaphorical language is understood properly. This distinction, moreover, can only be understood by ad-hering to the unbroken line of Apostolic interpretation of scripture. The successors of the Apostles carry on Christ's salvific work by open-ing up the scriptures to all people. God is not separated from creation

37. "Tantae igitur ostensiones cum sint, non opertet adhuc quaerer apud alios uer-itatem quam facile est ab Ecclesia sumere" (3.4.1).

38. "qui propter eminentissimam erga figmentum suum dilectionem" (3.4.2).

39. Bingham notes: "As the Apostles make explicit in their writings what is implicit in the Prophets, Irenaeus makes explicit in his polemic what is implicit in the Apostles" (*Irenaeus' Use of Matthew's Gospel*, 139).

40. "Traditione igitur quae est ab apostolis sic se habente in Ecclesia et permanen-te apud nos" (3.5.1). See Fantino, *La théologie d'Irénée*, 39, for the theme of succession διαδοχή in philosophical schools and an analogy to Apostolic and Valentinian schools. Fantino mentions Galen's *On the Natural Faculties* 1.12. See also Reynders for different understandings of tradition. Reynders, "Paradosis," 174.

41. As Reynders argues, for the Apostles everything about Jesus is part of the tra-dition ("Paradosis," 156). Blanchard notes that tradition for Irenaeus is not just about the content, but about preserving a message about unity and identity (*Aux sources du canon*, 167).

through the emanation of the Aeons. God is present in creation and will judge that creation at the end of time.

After he establishes the Apostolic tradition as the only sure guide for biblical interpretation, Irenaeus ends the first section of Book Three by addressing some scriptural texts that are difficult to interpret. For example, in 3.6, Irenaeus discusses passages in the Old Covenant that seem to suggest a plurality of gods. In 3.7, Irenaeus shifts from the Old Covenant to a problematic passage in Paul: "In their case, the God of this world has blinded the minds of unbelievers" (2 Cor 4:4). Paul is not distinguishing the God of this world from the God and Father of Jesus Christ. Irenaeus argues that Paul makes use of transposition here and the true sense of the passage is: "God has blinded the minds of the unbelievers." As we might expect, after Irenaeus discusses the prophets and then moves to Paul, he comes to the words of Christ. Irenaeus uses Christ's clear words about rendering to God and Caesar (Mt 22:21) to interpret Christ's words about serving God and mammon (Mt 6:24). Christ, Irenaeus says, "teaches the disciples who serve God not to be subject to mammon nor be dominated by it."[42] Thus, Irenaeus argues that when Christ says, "You cannot serve God and mammon" (Mt 6:24), he is not referring to different gods. Notice that in both cases Irenaeus interprets the scriptural texts just as a rhetor would interpret any text. Irenaeus's rhetorical moves are always within the context of the economy of salvation. His interpretations draw their inspiration from the faith. The structure of the faith is the structure of the argument.

In each of these cases, Irenaeus shows the fruits of the Apostolic interpretation of scripture. These are, if you like, test cases to show how the interpretative scheme he has outlined in 3.1–5 works out in practice. Irenaeus's order of presentation is important. He begins with a problematic passage in the Old Covenant, and after he solves that he moves on to a discussion of Paul. Following his discussion of Paul, he turns to Christ's own words. Here Irenaeus builds up to his strongest authority. Each case has to do with God's identity. Although Irenaeus is refuting his opponents' claims here, he is more specifically estab-

---

42. "sed discipulos docet seruientes Deo non subici Mammonae neque dominari ab eo" (3.8.1).

lishing the proper grammar with which to talk about the Father. This grammar, then, allows people to understand the manifestation of God in the scriptures. If the scriptures are not properly interpreted, the vision of God offered in the scriptures cannot be seen. These chapters serve as a bridge from his *probatio*, the faith as it is handed down by the church, to his *refutatio*, in which he turns to a fuller explanation of the rule of faith at work in the New Testament.

Refutatio, 3.9–15: Scripture/Economy

In 3.1–8, Irenaeus established that the only proper knowledge of God can come from the tradition of the Apostles. Just as his opponents furnished their students with principles of interpretation with which to understand scripture, Irenaeus has done the same. Yet to provide his audience with principles of interpretation is not the same as to interpret. In the second part of Book Three, Irenaeus lays out how the Gospels, the Acts of the Apostles, and the letters of Paul ought to be read with the Apostolic principles of interpretation, the faith, in mind. Only when this occurs can one truly see the *oikonomia* of God's salvation that is recounted in scripture. Thus, we come to the *refutatio* of Book Three. As with the *refutationes* of Books One and Two, Irenaeus's focus here is on scripture, specifically how the four Gospels, Acts, and the writings of Paul recount the *oikonomia* of God's salvation. This *oikonomia* is the fullness of the manifestation of God's love, and so it is crucial for Irenaeus to trace its contours. As we have already seen and will see again, the faith is essential for understanding the *oikonomia*.

Irenaeus is clear about the shift in his argument. He writes, "Therefore, it has been clearly demonstrated ... that neither the prophets nor the apostles nor Christ the Lord in His own name confessed any other as Lord or God but the one who is preeminently God and Lord." He then says, "The Lord Himself handed down to the disciples [that] the Father alone is God and Lord, who is alone God and Sovereign of all things. So, if we are truly their disciples, we must follow their testimonies."[43] Irenaeus relies on the testimony of others. His *ethos* is tied to

43. "Et adhuc ostendetur manifestius, neminem alterum Dominum vel Deum neque prophetas neque apostolos neque Dominum Christum confessum esse ex sua

theirs. And their *ethos* ultimately depends on how they act and write in accordance with the faith.

Central to Irenaeus's *refutatio* is the concept that the entire body of the scriptures contains and must be interpreted by the faith. The faith itself, as I have noted, is a part of that "living voice" of the tradition that comes from the Apostles. Irenaeus is trying to persuade his audience that the proper interpretation of scripture, the proper view of God and Christ, and the proper understanding of creation and salvation hinge on following the Apostolic faith. In order for this to work, his audience needs to follow the Apostles' testimony and not the testimony of Valentinus and his followers.

The testimony of the Apostles is recounted in the writings of the New Testament.[44] Irenaeus devotes three chapters to discussing how Matthew (3.9), Luke and Mark (3.10), and John (3.11) all acknowledge one and the same God and Father. God's "salvation, that is, his Word, he made visible to all flesh, himself becoming incarnate in order that their king might become manifest in all things."[45] In this, his *refutatio*, Irenaeus is careful to show how Christ fulfills the prophecies of the Old Covenant. Likewise, Irenaeus links Luke's and Mark's Gospels to the Law and the prophets. The best way to refute his opponents' claim, specifically that Jesus spoke of another Father who was not the creator of the universe, is to show that the only way to make sense of the Gospels is to understand them in light of the Old Covenant. That is, the only way to make sense of the story of the scriptures is to attend to the true hypothesis of that story. As we have seen, the faith from the Apostles is that true hypothesis of scripture. This faith not only structures the *oikonomia* of the scriptures; it structures Irenaeus's own argument.

Irenaeus stresses that there are four and only four Gospels. All four

---

persona sed praecipue Deum et Dominum.... et ipso Domino Patrem tantum Deum et Dominum eum qui solus Deus est et dominatur omnium tradente discipulis: sequi non oportet, si quem illorum sumus discipuli, testimonium illorum ita se habentia" (3.9.1).

44. On Irenaeus and the New Testament, see Hans Campenhausen, "Irenäus und das Neue Testament," *Theologische Literaturzeitung* 90, no. 1 (1965): 1–8; Jordan Daniel May, "The Four Pillars: The Fourfold Gospel before the Time of Irenaeus," *Trinity Journal* 30, no. 1 (2009): 67–79.

45. "Salutarem suum, hoc est Verbum suum, visibile effecit omni fieri carni, incarnatum et ipsum, ut in omnibus manifestus fieret Rex eorum" (3.9.1).

Gospels accord with the tradition of the Apostles and not vice versa. Thus, we can properly say that the faith has priority over the scriptures because the writings of the New Covenant were written in accordance with the faith. Seen in this light, Irenaeus's arguments in 3.6–8 take on a new importance. Remember, Irenaeus's *probatio* was the tradition, the faith, and his *refutatio* includes the Gospels.

If the tradition that hands down the teaching about God's love presented in Christ is Irenaeus's *probatio*, and if Irenaeus, as a rhetor, is primarily an exegete of scripture, it follows that Irenaeus would pay particular attention to the Acts of the Apostles in his *epideixis* of the Christian *kerygma*. Acts recounts the beginnings of the tradition after Christ's resurrection and pays particular attention to the early church's relationship with Jews and Gentiles. In this book of scripture we learn about two things at the heart of Irenaeus's project: the birth of the church and the teaching of the Apostles. We can divide Irenaeus's discussion into three major themes: the mission of Peter to the Jews; the mission of Paul to the Gentiles; and finally, the martyrdom of Stephen. Each of these themes deals with the question of how to offer a persuasive interpretation of the scriptures and each testifies to the presence of the Holy Spirit in the nascent church. In good rhetorical fashion, Irenaeus's argument builds from Peter to Paul to Stephen. Irenaeus concludes his discussion with Stephen so that he can show how Stephen combines the teaching of Peter and Paul. Significantly, Stephen's testimony in Acts coincides with his martyrdom.

Thus far we have seen that the way to behold the manifestation of God in the scriptures is to follow the teaching of the Apostles. The tradition of the Apostles is based on the teaching of Christ, and the teaching of Christ is itself a confirmation of the Law and the prophets. Irenaeus establishes the truth of the Apostolic tradition by showing how ancient it is and how it has built on what came before. In contrast to the sand of his opponents' teaching,[46] Apostolic teaching is founded upon the rock of Peter, who connects the Old Covenant testimony with the *kerygma* of the New Covenant. Peter's mission was to preach to the Jews that "God has made this Jesus, whom you crucified, Lord

46. See 1.8.1.

and Christ" (Acts 2:30–36). Christ "was raised up to the right hand
of God, accepting the promise of the Holy Spirit from the Father. He
poured out this gift which you now see and hear" (Acts 2:30–36). The
Jews who were present with Peter received visions from God. These visions could persuade them that Peter preached the truth, and Irenaeus
calls on these visions to persuade his audience that his own teaching
follows Peter's. Peter explained from his teaching of the prophets that
Jesus was "the Christ whom God promised to send."[47] This is Irenaeus's central argument. He can only refute his opponents by showing
that the *probationes* of scripture interpret Christ in light of the Old
Covenant. When he describes an episode from Acts 3 where Peter
cures a crippled man, Irenaeus notes that Peter used "clear preaching" (*phareon to kerygma*).[48] Peter's discourse makes the word of God
manifest, and the voice with which Peter preached is one of the voices
of the church.

Irenaeus presents Peter's interpretation of scripture in Acts to show
that the God of the Old Covenant and the God of Jesus Christ are the
same. Irenaeus then presents Paul's interpretation of scripture from
the same book to show that in Christ God's covenant extends beyond
the Jews. Paul "confessed one and the same preaching of all of those
who saw the Lord after the resurrection of the dead."[49] For "God is
not so poor that he has only one apostle who knows the economy
of his Son."[50] Paul's importance comes from the fact that he was the
Apostle to the Gentiles and, as such, spoke in an idiom the Gentiles
could understand. Irenaeus presents both Peter and Paul as interpreters of scripture, whose preaching allowed others to view the economy
of God's salvation.

Irenaeus stresses that Peter and Paul preach the same God. Paul's

---

47. "et ex prophetis cohortabantur eos quoniam eum quem promisit se Deus mis-
surum Christum, misit Iesum, quem ipsi crucifixerunt, quem Deus excitauit" (3.12.2).

48. 3.12.3.

49. "Unam et eandem praedicationem confitens omnium eorum qui Dominum
vidernunt post resurrectionem a mortuis" (3.13.1).

50. "Ipsius ergo Dei Petrus erat apostolus cuius et Paulus; et quem Petrus in cir-
cumcisione adnuntiabat Deum et Dei Filium, hunc et Paulus in gentes. Neque enim
Paulum solum venit salvare Dominus noster; nec sic pauper Deus ut unum solum haberet apostolum qui dispositionem Filii sui cognosceret" (3.13.1).

teaching accords with each of the four Gospels that Irenaeus addressed in his *probatio*. The fact that Irenaeus spends so much time defending the truth of Paul's preaching suggests that he recognizes that there are some who do not believe Paul is an Apostle or that Paul's teaching does not accord with the rest of the New Testament. Here indeed lies Irenaeus's point of contention with his opponents' various readings of Paul, but Irenaeus extends his argument even further.

As God's chosen Apostles to the Jews and the Gentiles, Peter and Paul warrant special attention, but Irenaeus continues to build his argument by moving to Stephen. It is obvious that Irenaeus praises Peter, Paul, and Stephen in an epideictic mode. His goal here is to delight his audience so that they will want to imitate these Apostles and their interpretation of the scriptures. Like Peter and Paul, Stephen died for his faith in Christ, but Irenaeus singles out Stephen's death, and says when Stephen was stoned, "he fulfilled the perfect teaching, imitating the teacher of martyrdom in all things and praying for all who killed him." *Ethos* shone in his death.[51] The *imitatio Christi* is a condition for perfection but so is the knowledge of Christ's teaching because the *imitatio Christi* is first an foremost an imitation of God's *love*. Stephen's death and the death of all martyrs is the ultimate *probatio* of God's love in Christ. Those who have been martyred are unable to "speak to men according to unstable opinions" and they "preach contrary things to those who do not assent to the truth."[52] The martyrs are a composite of Peter and Paul, for it is clear that they do not abandon the truth, but preach it to "Jews and Greeks with all faith."[53] Again we see that the martyrs do not teach by conveying information, but rather by manifesting God's love in the way they live their lives. Like Christ, they have

51. "Et haec dixit et lapidatus est, et sic perfectam doctrinam adimplevit, per omnia martyrii magistrum imitans et postulans pro eis qui se interficiebant et dicens: Domine, ne statuas eis peccatum hoc" (3.12.13).

52. "Quod ipsum si fecissent, non paterentur; sed quoniam contraria his qui non adsentiebant veritati praedicabant, ideo et passi sunt" (3.12.13).

53. "Manifestum est ergo quoniam non derelinquebant veritatem, sed cum omni fiduciae Iudaeis et Graecis praedicabant, Iudaeis quidem Iesum eum qui ab ipsis crucifixus est esse Filium Dei, Iudicem vivorum et mortuorum, a Patre accepisse aeternum regnum in Israel, quemadmodum ostendimus, Graecis vero unum Deum qui omnia fecit et huius Filium Iesum Christum adnuntiantes" (3.12.13).

lived out God's love and like Christ they ought to be praised. Indeed, their lives help others to praise Christ.

If we think of Irenaeus's social context, the praise of the martyrs is even more profound. We should remember that he is writing in the wake of a mass slaughter of Christians in Lyon and Vienne. We cannot know for sure, but it is likely that Irenaeus's audience could have witnessed some of the killing. They almost certainly would have known about the martyrdoms in their own land. These martyrdoms stand in stark contrasts to the fictions of Valentinus and his followers. And these martyrdoms all occurred in imitation of the martyr who died on the cross.

For Irenaeus, the *epideixis* of Christ is found in all of the writings of the New Covenant, not just the Gospels. In the Acts of the Apostles, for example, the Ethiopian eunuch discovers that it is "Jesus who fulfilled the Scripture in himself."[54] Some of the most important discussions about Christ in the New Testament are found in the letters of Paul. According to Irenaeus, in the letter to the Galatians, Paul "signifies clearly one God, who made a promise about the Son through the prophets and one Jesus Christ, who was born from the seed of David, from Mary."[55] To put it succinctly: Peter, Paul, Stephen, and the evangelists interpret scripture according to the faith. They understand the fatherhood of God, the economy of creation and salvation, and the recapitulation of all things in Christ.

At the end of the first section of Book Three, Irenaeus turns to specific issues in the interpretation of scripture, and does the same thing at the end of the second section. In 3.14–15, Irenaeus discusses those teachers who have "mutilated" the writings of Luke and Paul. There is a particular emphasis in these chapters on the judgment that awaits such people. Irenaeus links Marcion with Valentinus (itself a kind of recapitulation) and notes that if the disciples of Marcion discard Luke's Gospel, then they do not have the Gospel.[56] In 3.15, Irenaeus offers a

---

54. "Hunc esse Iesum et impletam esse in eo Scripturam" (3.12.8).

55. "manifeste significans unum quidem Deum qui per prophetas promissionem de Filio fecerit, unum autem Iesum Christum Dominum nostrum qui de semine David secundum eam generationem quae est ex Maria, hunc destinatum Filium Dei Iesum Christum" (3.12.8).

56. 3.14.4.

brief summary of Valentinian ideas on redemption. Irenaeus mocks a person who would follow the Valentinian interpretation of scripture and who thinks he has attained "redemption." Such a person is "puffed up [1 Cor 8:1] for he thinks he is neither in heaven nor on earth but he enters into the Pleroma and embraces his own angel."[57] By mutilating the scriptures, Marcion, Valentinus, and the rest have cut themselves and their followers off from God's manifestation. As the allusion to 1 Corinthians 8:1 suggests, these false teachers have chosen their own knowledge that puffs up over the manifestation of God's love that builds up.

The way Irenaeus ends this chapter shows that he is ready to move to a new section in his argument. He tells his readers, "Let us return to the treatise at hand." And after repeating that the Apostles only knew the one Lord God, creator of all, he writes, "The thought [*sententia*], therefore, both of the apostles and of their disciples about God, has been made manifest."[58] With this, Irenaeus is ready to turn to the section of theological methodology in Book Three, where he will focus on the proper understanding of Christ.

Excursus, 3.16–18: Theological Method

I began this chapter with a brief discussion of the prologue to John's Gospel. This prologue is one of the clearest discussions in the New Testament of the manifestation of God in and through Jesus Christ, the Word made flesh. I have argued throughout this chapter that Book Three is Irenaeus's main *probatio* or proof for his forensic speech, meant to lay out and prosecute his opponents' teaching. Irenaeus's theological methodology can be found in 3.16–18. That is, in these chapters Irenaeus offers his readers a method for interpreting the scriptures so that a reader can recognize the manifestation of God and learn what ought to be interpreted literally and what ought to be in-

57. "Si autem aliquis quasi paruam ouum deditum semetipsum ipsis praebeat, et inflatus iste talis, neque in caelo neque in terra putat se esse, sed intra Pleroma introisse et complexum iam angelum suum" (3.15.2).
58. "Nos autem revertamur ad eundem tractatum.... Manifesta igitur et apostolarum et discentium eorum ex verbis ipsorum de Deo facta est sententia" (3.15.3).

terpreted metaphorically. After arguing that his opponents' teachings were based in silence, and then that their interpretations were ultimately fabrications, Irenaeus can show how the Apostolic interpretation manifests the true teaching of the scriptures.

It should come as no surprise that Irenaeus shapes his positive teaching in accordance with the faith. In my discussion of 1.9–10 and 22, I argued that the structure of the faith was also the structure of the *Adversus Haereses*. That structure is the identity of God, the work of the Spirit in the economy, and the salvation in and through Christ. Or, to put it in terms familiar to us by now: *probatio*, *refutatio*, and *recapitulatio*. We see in 3.16 that Irenaeus offers scriptural proof that Christ is the Word of God. In 3.17, Irenaeus turns to prove that the same Spirit who descended on Christ in the Jordan was present with the Israelites throughout their history. Additionally, in 3.18, Irenaeus discusses Christ's passion in light of the redemption of human beings.

Jesus Christ is the manifestation of God, but we miss Irenaeus's point if we think that one could have unmediated access to this manifestation. To praise Christ and to understand the scriptures through him, one must also praise the Spirit that Christ offers. If to praise Christ is to praise the Spirit, then to praise the Spirit is also to praise the church. Of course, as we have seen in 1.10, the church guards the faith. The church is the proper community of interpreters, the proper site for recognizing the manifestation of God, because through the church believers come to participate in the life of God in the Father and through the Son and the Holy Spirit. This participation occurs as an entire way of life in the community. Conversely, those who have cut themselves off from the church and its teaching also cut themselves off from God. Therefore, they cannot participate in the ascent to God. The church offers these steps of ascent to God in the tradition of ritual and scriptural interpretation that is passed down through the work of the Son and the Spirit.

Christ is the focus of the church's interpretation, and so Irenaeus spends these chapters offering praise of Christ. Christ can only be praised properly if the scriptures are properly interpreted, and as we have seen time and again, the scriptures can only be interpreted properly, and Christ can only be understood properly, if the interpreter keeps the faith of the Apostles in mind when he interprets. This faith recognizes Christ as God, recognizes the Spirit of God at work in the economy of salvation as it in encountered in the scriptures, and recognizes that Christ will come in judgment.

Irenaeus needs to state the case before him. In this instance, the case is the identity of Christ. We can see the structure of 3.16–18 already in the first sentence of 3.16. "There are, however, those who say that Jesus was the vessel of Christ, upon whom Christ descended as a dove from on high."[59] Here is the *probatio*, focusing on the nature of Christ. Then comes the focus on the economy: "and when he had pointed out the unnamable Father."[60] Finally, recapitulation: "he entered into the fullness in an incomprehensible and invisible manner."[61] After he discusses the followers of Valentinus specifically, Irenaeus writes:

> For this is their rule, as we have said before: They assert that Christ, who was sent forth by the Only-Begotten for the correction of the Fullness is one being, but that Savior who was sent for the glorification of the Father is another being; still another being, moreover, is the Savior who was made for the economy, who gave support to Christ, who, they say, also suffered and returned to the Fullness.[62]

Notice how the structure of the Valentinian rule parodies the structure of the Apostolic faith. In order to refute this false rule, Irenaeus "consider[s] it necessary to make use of the entire teaching of the apostles concerning our Lord Jesus Christ, and to show that they ... did not think anything of the kind about him."[63] Just as importantly, though, Irenaeus believes that "through the Holy Spirit" the

59. "Quoniam autem sunt qui dicunt Iesum quidem receptaculum Christi fuisse, in quem desuper quasi columbam descendisse Christum" (3.16.1).

60. "et cum indicasset innominabilem Patrem" (3.16.1).

61. "incomprehensibiliter et invisibilier intrasse in Pleroma" (3.16.1).

62. "etenim haec est ipsorum regula, quemadmodum praediximus, ut alterum quidem Christum fuisse dicant qui ab Unigenito ad correctionem Plentituinis praemissus est, alterum vero Salvatorem esse in gloricationem Patris emissum, alterum vero ex dispositione quem et passum dicunt, recurrente in Pleroma Salvatore qui in Christum portabat" (3.16.1).

63. "necesse habemus universam apostolorum de Domino nostro Iesu Christo sententiam adhibere, et ostendere eos non solum nihil tale senisse de eo" (3.16.1).

Apostles "pointed out that the one who would teach such things in the future, was instigated by Satan to overthrow the faith of some and draw them away from life."[64] Irenaeus does not only repeat the teaching of the Apostles, but also engages in the same work they engaged in. Christian identity is not founded on mere repetition. It is founded on immersing oneself in the very structure of the faith, in seeing oneself as part of the economy of creation and redemption that Christ lived, taught, and accomplished. Irenaeus believes that the Apostles foresaw Satan's work in people like Valentinus. It is Irenaeus's task, then, to refute Valentinus and his ilk just as the Apostles refuted Simon the Magician, Cerdo, and their ilk.

Irenaeus's argument spirals, and we constantly see a repetition of *probatio*, *refutatio*, and *recapitulatio*—God, the economy, and Christ—in each section of the *Adversus Haereses*, and 3.16–18 are no different in this regard. I have repeatedly stressed that the structure of the *Adversus Haereses* is the argument of the *Adversus Haereses*. In 3.16, Irenaeus weaves a web of scriptural texts[65] that show this sequential argument: that there is "one and the same Word of God and that this was the Only-Begotten, and that he was the one who became incarnate for our salvation, Jesus Christ, our Lord."[66]

But Irenaeus knows it is not enough to say that there is one and the same Word of God. In order to refute his opponents' claims, he must show how Christ is foretold in the Law and the prophets. He recognizes that the Apostles "had it in their power" to proclaim the false narrative of his opponents "to declare that Christ descended on Jesus, or that the Savior from on high descended on the one of the economy, or that he who is from the invisible regions descended on him who is from the Demiurge."[67] But he argues that they did not. Instead the Apostles "told us what actually happened, namely the Spirit of God

64. "per Spiritum sanctum qui inciperent talia docere, sunmissi a Satana uti quorundam fidem everterent et abstraherent eos a vita" (3.16.1).

65. Mt 1:1, 1:18, 1:20–23; Is 7:14.

66. "unum et eundem novit Verbum Dei, et hunc esse Unigenitum, et hunc incarnatum esse pro salute nostra, Jesum Christum Dominum nostrum" (3.16.2).

67. "Etenim poterunt dicere apostoli Christum descendisse in Iesum, aut illum superiorem Salvatorum in eum qui sit dispositionis, et illum qui est ab invisibilibus in eum qui est Demiurgi" (3.17.1).

descended on him as a dove."[68] This Spirit "descended on the Son of
God, made the Son of man, becoming accustomed with him [Christ]
to dwell in the human race, and to rest among human beings, and to
dwell in God's handiwork, thus fulfilling the Father's will in them, and
renewing them from their old selves for the newness of Christ."[69] We
would expect Irenaeus to draw on passages from the Old Covenant
in this chapter, and that is exactly what we find. We also find a particular emphasis on the economy. Irenaeus's point is clear: "the Spirit
descended because of the preordained economy." But Irenaeus's point
in writing is even more clear: it is "incumbent on you, in fact, on all
who read this writing and are solicitous about their salvation, not to
succumb readily to the discourse of these men." The danger, Irenaeus notes, is that when the disciples of Valentinus "speak words that
sound like those of the believers, they understand not only different
doctrines, but even contrary ones."[70]

Having given his *probatio* on God and his *refutatio* on the Spirit
in the economy, Irenaeus turns to his *recapitulatio* on Christ's salvific
work in 3.18. When Jesus "became incarnate and was made man, He
recapitulated [*recapitulavit*] in Himself the long exposition of humankind, presenting salvation to us by way of compendium."[71] Because
human beings, who were under the curse of sin, could not receive
salvation, the Son of God "came down from the Father and [became]

68. "Quod autem erat, hoc et dixerunt, Spiritum Dei sicut columbam descendiesse
in eum" (3.17.1).
69. "unde et in Filium Dei Filium hominis factum descendit, cum ipso adsuescens
habitere in genere humano et requiescere in hominibus et habitare in plasmate Dei, voluntatem Patris operans in ipsis et renovans eos a vetustate in novitatem Christi" (3.17.1).
70. "τοῦ Πνεύματος οὖν κατελθόντος διὰ τὴν προωρισμένην οἰκονομίαν. Unde
oportebit et te et omnes qui intendunt huic Scripturae et solliciti sunt pro sua salute
non cum audiunt forinsecus eorum semones sponte succumbere ... non solem dissi-
milia sapiunt, sed et contaria et per plena blashpemiis, per quae interficiunt eos per
quae interficiunt eos qui per similtudinem verborum dissimile adfectionis eorum in se
adtrahunt venerum" (3.17.4).
71. "sed quando incarnatus et homo factus, longam hominum expositionem in
seipso recapitulauit, in compendio nobis salutem praestans" (3.18.1). Because I am focusing here on the shape of Irenaeus's argument and the role that Christ plays in it, I
shall not address the important Christological issues at work in these paragraphs. For a
good overview, see Steenberg's discussion in *St. Irenaeus of Lyons: Against the Heresies
(Book 3)*, 170n3.

incarnate and [descended] even to death, and [brought] the economy [*dispositionem*] of salvation to completion."[72] Thus we see the terms *recapitulatio* (Greek: *anakephalaiosis*) and *dispositio* (Greek: *oikonomia*) in Irenaeus's description of Christ's salvific work. Irenaeus makes his theological point about the salvation of human beings in rhetorical terms. Christ recapitulates a long exposition in an abridged form, just as a rhetor would do in concluding a speech. But the goal of the speech of the Word is not to sway a political decision, but to secure the salvation of humanity.

Indeed, the salvation of humanity is the center of Irenaeus's *cur deus homo* in this chapter. When his opponents misunderstand what ought to be read literally with what to be read metaphorically, they crucially misunderstand who Christ is and how Christ saves. Christ suffered just as human beings suffered and continue to suffer, and the deaths of the martyrs show the extent of that suffering. Jesus Christ can save human beings because he is both God and man, and as a human being, Jesus Christ truly suffers. After Peter tells Jesus that he is "the Christ, the Son of the living God," Jesus tells his disciples "that he must go to Jerusalem and suffer many things from ... the priests ... and be rejected ... and crucified, and on the third day be raised."[73] Christ was not speaking metaphorically here. Human beings can partake in the incorruptibility that God offers because God became a human being in Jesus Christ. The same Word of God present in the scriptures becomes flesh and offers the definitive interpretation of those scriptures. Any interpretation that Irenaeus offers must be in line with Christ's own interpretation. The whole point of these chapters is to show that Irenaeus aligns himself with Christ.

Given my discussion of these chapters, it might seem odd to classify them in terms of "theological methodology." How, exactly, do they differ from the others in Book Three? Part of the answer comes if we let go of our modern conception of methodology. For Irenaeus,

---

72. "utraque operatus est Filius, Verbum Dei exsistens, a Patre descendens et incarnatus et usque ad mortem a descendens et dispensationem consummans salutis nostrae" (3.18.2).

73. "Oportet illum Hierosolymam ire et multa pati a sacerdotibus et reprobari et crucifigi et tertia die resurgere" (3.18.4). See Mt 16:21, Mk 8:31, and Lk 9:22.

"method" is not a free-floating set of theories that can be applied to the scriptural text. Instead, the method for understanding the scriptures comes from the faith that undergirds those scriptures—the faith, more specifically, that the Apostles passed down. This faith has a particular content and a particular structure. Indeed, the content cannot be separated from the structure just as the scriptures cannot be separated from the faith. Without both parts, neither part makes any sense.

Recapitulatio, 3.19–25: Christ/Salvation

Irenaeus writes out of a pastoral concern. He is not concerned with damning heretics, nor does he worry about Christian identity formation as a sociological study. Instead, he worries that Christians are being led astray by incoherent interpretations of scripture. In order to combat those misguided interpretations, Irenaeus must paint a picture and offer a vision of the scriptures properly interpreted. As I have argued, the scriptures come into view when they are interpreted with the structure and the argument of the faith. This faith proclaims who God is, the economy of God's creation through the Spirit, and the recapitulation and salvation of that economy in Christ. The first chapters of Book Three offered a grammar for discussing the faith with reference to Christ. Irenaeus's focus on Christ in 3.16–18 leads directly to the final section of Book Three. In these last six chapters, Irenaeus—here recapitulating his argument for the book—aims to *move* his audience by presenting before them the question of salvation.

These chapters of Book Three are both the recapitulation of Irenaeus's argument in the previous chapters and the height of his *epideixis* of praise for Christ. Christ is most praiseworthy because of the salvation he offers human beings, but human beings can only understand this salvation if they understand that Jesus Christ is both God and man. Irenaeus must show how the proper interpretation of the scriptures shows Christ's humanity and divinity. Understanding the distinction between Christ's humanity and divinity is as important as understanding the distinction between what to understand literally and what to understand metaphorically in the scriptures. In fact, these things go together. Thus, Irenaeus marshals scriptural evidence to show that Joseph is not Jesus' biological father (3.19), that the messiah was to be born of a virgin (3.20–21), and that Jesus truly took flesh from Mary (3.22). Irenaeus stresses Christ's humanity in these chapters because Christ saves human beings as a human being who is also God. If Christ were not both, he could not effect human salvation. Christ's flesh casts out the metaphorical meaning of flesh as sin and renews the original, literal meaning of flesh as God's creation. Through Christ's flesh, sinful human beings are reconciled to God.

There is a history of scriptural interpretation just as there is a history of salvation. In fact, insofar as the history of interpretation implies a history of the community reading scripture through the lens of the faith, the history of interpretation *is* the history of salvation. Thanks to the faith, the history of interpretation has remained stable, and this stability proves its veracity. While one might expect Irenaeus to refer to the interpretations of scripture within scripture, he also locates traditions of interpretation in past Jewish communities. Irenaeus sees himself as bringing the customs of the Jews forward to his own day. For example, he describes the translation of the Septuagint and the reconstitution of the Hebrew scriptures after the Babylonian exile by Ezra (3.21.2). He can then say with confidence that "these Scriptures had been interpreted by truth and the grace of God" and that "God prepared and preformed our faith that is in his Son."[74] As always, Irenaeus stresses God's grace rather than any interpreter's ability. Irenaeus's task is to hand down the interpretation that has been handed down to him. This interpretation, however, always originates with the Son's revelation and interpretation of the Father.[75]

The Son's interpretation of the Father, as recorded in the Apostolic faith, predates his opponents' interpretation; it also predates Christian interpretation because it comes not from human beings (as do the rules of Irenaeus's opponents), but from God. The interpretation to which Irenaeus refers "was made before our Lord descended and before Christians were shown this interpretation."[76] To say this is to

---

74. "Cum tanta igitur ueritate et gratia Dei interpretatae sint Scripturae ex quibus praeparauit et praeformauit Deus fidem nostram quae in Filium eius est" (3.21.3).

75. See Holsinger-Friesen, *Irenaeus and Genesis*, 14.

76. "et haec earum Scripturarum interpretatio priusquam Dominus noster descenderet facta sit et antequam christiani ostenderentur" (3.21.3).

recognize that Christ does not come up with teachings divorced from the Jewish community. Jesus' teachings confirm the Law, the prophets, and the faith. This is why Irenaeus proclaims that the faith of the Christian church "has a clear display from the Scriptures which are interpreted" in the proper way.[77] Christ himself is the manifestation, the embodiment of the faith and of scripture interpreted correctly. The Apostles, of course, preach this interpretation.[78] If scripture is not interpreted properly, Christ is not properly praised. Here Ireaneus has shifted from an epideictic discourse focused on praise to a deliberative discourse focused on his audience choosing to follow the Apostolic discourse. If Christ is not praised properly, then one's salvation is at stake. This is why the audience's deliberation is so important, and why Irenaeus must *move* his audience to make the right decision. He wants his readers, who might be persuaded by the Valentinian interpretation, to know that Valentinus's interpretation leads to perdition because it does not truthfully preach who Christ is.

Christ can save because Christ is both Word and flesh. This is the same flesh as Adam.[79] Simply stated, if Christ "does not accept the substance of the flesh from man, he was not made man nor the Son of Man."[80] By becoming man, the Word of God "recapitulat[es] his creation in himself" because human beings "are a body, accepted from the earth, and a spirit accepted the Spirit from God."[81] Adhering to the

77. "Firma est autem et non fincta et sola uera quae secundum nos est fides, manifestam ostensionem habens ex his Scripturis quae interpretatae sunt illo modo quo praediximus, et Ecclesiae adnuntiatio sine interpolatione" (3.21.3). Mutschler argues that Irenaues does not usually concern himself with entire biblical books. Instead he focuses on passages within particular books. Bernhard Mutschler, *Irenäus als johanneischer Theologe: Studien zur Schriftauslegung bei Irenäus von Lyon* (Tübingen: Mohr Siebeck, 2004), 106. Irenaeus weaves these passages together to give a vision of the entire economy of salvation.

78. "etenim apostoli, cum sint his omnibus uetustiores, consonant praedictae interpretationi, et interpretatio consonat apostolorum traditioni" (3.21.3).

79. On the humanity of Christ from two very different perspectives, see Benjamin Dunning, "Virgin Earth, Virgin Birth: Creation, Sexual Difference, and Recapitulation in Irenaeus of Lyons," *Journal of Religion* 89, no. 1 (2009): 57–88; A. Houssiau, *La Christologie de Saint Irénée* (Louvain: Publications Universitaires de Louvain, 1955).

80. "Si enim non accepit ab homine substantiam carnis, neque homo factus est neque Filius hominis" (3.22.1).

81. "Hoc itaque factum est Verbum Dei, suum plasma in semetipsum recapitulans … nos autem quoniam corpus sumus de terra acceptum et anima accipiens a Deo Spiritum"

Apostolic faith means understanding that Jesus' divinity is not a metaphor. Christ can only save because he is truly God and truly man. In his recapitulation, Irenaeus urges his audience to choose the method of scriptural interpretation that recognizes this. Notice again that the structure of Irenaeus's argument is his argument here. When Irenaeus recapitulates his points on Christ's own recapitulation, he brings the question of salvation before the eyes of his audience.

Irenaeus has stressed Christ's humanity and reminded his readers that Christ's flesh, which comes from Mary, is human flesh that, united with the Word, saves human beings. Adam's salvation is important for Irenaeus because his opponents do not believe that Adam receives salvation. Because Irenaeus's "speech" here is now in a deliberative mood, he wants to be sure that his audience understands the choice before them. For example, Tatian, Irenaeus tells his readers, was the first to argue that Adam was not saved.[82] Such people "exclude themselves from life forever because they do not believe that the sheep that had been lost was found" (see Lk 15:4–7, Mt 18:12–13).[83] In fact, Irenaeus goes so far as to compare such people with the serpent who "gained nothing by persuading humanity, except that this showed him to be a transgressor, since he had humanity as the beginning and object of his rebellion."[84] Irenaeus has set up the contrast between his exegesis and his opponents' exegesis as a contrast between Christ and Satan. He will use this contrast again in Book Five.

The final two chapters of Book Three offer a summary of Irenaeus's argument. He places a particular emphasis on the role of the church here, and so returns to the theme with which he began the book. Irenaeus praises the church because it safeguards the faith. He also con-

---

(3.22.1). As we will see when we come to our discussion of Book Five, Irenaeus sees the human body and Christ's body in particular as a site of contestation with his opponents.

82. Irenaeus mentions Tatian three times in *AH*, at 1.28.1, 3.23.8, and 4.15.2–3. Irenaeus claims that Tatian was not truly a student of Justin because, unlike Justin, Tatian did not follow the rule of faith.

83. "Mentiuntur ergo omnes qui contradicunt eius saluti, semper seipsos excludentes a uita in eo quod non credant inuentam ouem quae perierat" (3.23.8).

84. "Quemadmodum et serpens nihil profecit dissuadens homini nisi illud quod eum transgressorem ostendit, initium et materiam apostasiae suae habens hominem" (3.23.8).

trasts the truth guarded in the church with those who are "alienated from the truth." As he tries to move his audience, Irenaeus underscores that his opponents never have "a stable teaching because they wish to be sophists of words rather than disciples of the truth."[85] This is why these people "create many gods," but "they can never find them."[86] Again, the contrast Irenaeus draws here is crucial. He does not simply contrast two methods of interpretation as if they were two academic options of reading a text, but highlights a fundamental difference regarding the very nature of the manifestation of God in the world. Does God manifest himself in the love offered in Christ and lived out in the community of the church? Or does God manifest himself in secret and through the knowledge offered to a select few? These are the terms Irenaeus has set up. Irenaeus contrasts a method of interpretation that tries to understand the manifestation it encounters and a method that fabricates its own stories. This is the contrast between Book Two and Book Three.

Irenaeus concludes Book Three with a meditation on God's providence. Because of his providence, God "gives counsel, and by giving counsel he assists those who have a case for morals."[87] Irenaeus's goal, of course, is to offer such counsel. Here at the end of Book Three, his tone is deliberative. His aim is neither to instruct nor delight, but to move. He wants his audience to know the consequences of following each competing rule of interpretation. God will "judge those who have received his goodness equally but have not lived lives according to the dignity of their gift."[88] Irenaeus hopes that those who have been led astray will change their ways. Employing *pathos*, he appeals to his audience. He cannot make the choice for them. He wants them to choose to be formed by Christ. It is Christ, after all, who brings "grace

85. "Alienati vero a veritate, digne in omni voluntantur errore, fluctuate ab eo, aliter atque aliter per tempora de isdem sentientes et numquam sententiam stabliem habentes, sophistae verborum magis volentes esse quam discipuli veritatis" (3.24.2).

86. "Propter hoc et multos deos fingunt. Et quaerere quidem semper in excusatione habent, caecutiunt enim invenire vero numquam possunt (cf. Eph. 3:19)" (3.24.2).

87. "Providentiam autem habet Deus omnium, propter hoc et consilium dat; consilium autem dans adest his qui morum providentiam habet" (3.25.1).

88. "iudicabit eos qui ex aequo benignitatem eius percipientes, non similter secundum dignitationem munerationis eius conversatis sunt" (3.25.4).

and truth," who has "revealed" God. This revelation of God comes in and through the church's interpretation of the scriptures. The end of that interpretation, of course, is God's love. Irenaeus ends Book Three where he started it: reminding his readers of God's love for them and praying for those who have separated themselves from God's church. "We pray for these things for them, loving them more than they think they love themselves. For our love, since it is true, is salvific for them— if they will accept it."[89] God's love is salvific. The reader can only understand this by reading the scriptures in the light of the faith. Only the faith, handed down by the Apostles, is the true hypothesis of the scriptures.

We ought to remember that Irenaeus writes his *Adversus Haereses* because he wants to help those Christians whose reading of the scripture has put their salvation at stake. The elaborate structure of the work and the lengths Irenaeus goes to lay out the proper interpretative lens for scripture are always at the service of a pastoral goal. For all his focus on the importance of tradition, on the witness of scripture that Christ is true God and true man, and on Christ's salvific work, Irenaeus has not yet focused on Christ's own interpretation of scripture. He says that he has "deferred treating the words of the Lord until the following book." Christ's words themselves form the strongest refutation of his opponents' interpretation. He hopes that "by convincing some of these by means of the very teaching of Christ," he can persuade them to give up their errors.[90] That is the task that Irenaeus sets for himself in Book Four, and to that book we now turn our attention.

89. "Haec precamur de illis, utilus eos diligentes quam ipsi semetipsos putant diligere. Quae enim est a nobis dilectio, cum sit vera, salutaris est si quidem eam recipient" (3.25.7).

90. "Prorogavimus autem super haec quae dicta sunt in sequenti libro Domini sermons inferre, si quos ex his per ipsam Christi doctrinam convincentes suadere possimus cessare ab eiusmodi errore et absistere ab ea blasphemia" (3.25.4).

4 ✠ PROPHECY

> In all wisdom and insight he has made known to us the mystery
> of his will in accord with his favor that he set forth in him as a
> plan for the fullness of times, to sum up all things in Christ, in
> heaven and on earth.

EPHESIANS 1:8–10

God's manifestation occurs in history. Jesus Christ, the Word made
flesh, lived in a particular time and in a particular place. The Gospels
of Matthew and Luke both show that Jesus not only had a history, but
he had a *Jewish* history. This might all seem pedestrian and more than
a touch pedantic, but for Irenaeus history turns out to be a key argument in his refutation of his opponents. The fabrications that come
from their silence occur in no place and at no time. As a result, there
is no connection between the fictive god of his opponents and that
god's fabricated cosmos, and between the loving creator God of the
Old Covenant and his creation.

This is why the passage from the letter to the Ephesians is so important. God, with wisdom and insight, has made the mystery of his
will known. He has done this through a plan—an *oikonomia*—for the
fullness (*pleroma*) of time. For Irenaeus, this fullness of time is inside,
not outside, historical time. The essence of the dispute between Irenaeus and his opponents is how God's plan is manifested, though a related question, of course, asks who God is. Irenaeus and his opponents
agree that the scriptures have something to say about that manifestation, but as we have seen, they disagree profoundly about how to interpret those scriptures. For his opponents, God's *oikonomia* can only

be understood by considering the emanation of the Aeons from the Pleroma. Christ can only be understood as the one who comes forth from the Pleroma to bring salvific knowledge. Irenaeus, by contrast, argues that God's *oikonomia* is present in the Law and the prophets found in the Old Covenant, and that Christ, as man and God, fulfills the prophecies of the Old Covenant. In Book Four, Irenaeus sets out to prove that the God and Father of Jesus Christ is the God of history: of the Law and the prophets.

This proof can be persuasive only if Irenaeus offers an interpretation of the New Covenant that shows its dependence on the Old Covenant. This interpretation will be even more compelling if Irenaeus provides rules for interpreting the New Covenant that show how *any* interpretation of the New Covenant needs to be dependent on the Old Covenant in order for that interpretation to cohere with others. In other words, Irenaeus needs to show how the faith offers interpretative stability. This stability comes when it is anchored in history and governs the relationship between the covenants. It also should regulate the metaphors and typologies that underlie this relationship.

This is what Irenaeus sets out to do in Book Four, the section of his argument that stands as his *refutatio* and that also ends up being his rhetorical *tour de force*. In the *refutatio*, which according to Quintilian was the most difficult part of the speech, the rhetor would refute the claims of his opponents and back up his proof.[1] Irenaeus confirms his own propositions by interpreting scripture itself.[2] This refuta-

---

1. Quintilian writes, "Refutatio dupliciter accipi potest: nam et pars defensoris tota est posita in refutatione, et quae dicta sunt ex diverso debent utrimque dissolvi. Et hoc est proprie cui in cuaesis quartus adsignatur locus, sed utrisque similis condicio est" (*The Orator's Education* 5.13.1). Quintilian also refers to this as the confirmation: "Ordine ipso narrationem sequitur confirmatio: probanda sunt enim quae propter hoc exposuimus" (4.3.1). On the difficulty of the refutation, see 5.13.53.

2. We should note here that Irenaeus intends his use of scripture to be a "logical proof." As Kinneavy points out, "Unlike the pathetic appeal, which is usually quite easy to discern, the logical appeal can take forms that are not immediately what the twentieth-century reader would call 'logical.' These forms are frequently inferences from Scriptural interpretations, Midrashic applications of the Old Testament, or they are reports of signs and miracles performed by Jesus or one of the Apostles. Or they are a sustained attempt to generalize from examples or parables. Or they are applications made of an assumed principle." Kinneavy, *Greek Rhetorical Origins of Christian Faith*, 127.

tion through scriptural interpretation occurs in three steps. In 4.1–20, Irenaeus shows the unity of the Old and New Covenants through the words of Christ. Then, in 4.21–35, he demonstrates how the Old Covenant prophesies the New. Finally, in 4.36–41, Irenaeus discusses how the parables of Christ refer to the God of the Old Covenant, who is also the God of the New Covenant.[3] This basic structure mirrors the structure of the *Adversus Haereses* as a whole. We can think of 4.1–20 as the *probatio*, 4.21–35 as the *refutatio*, and 4.36–41 as the *recapitulatio*. In this way, 4.1–20 confirms Irenaeus's point, and 4.21–41 refutes his opponents. This structure also mirrors the structure we have seen in Books One through Three. By showing the unity of the Old and New Covenants through the words of Christ, Irenaeus argues that the God of both covenants is one and the same. By showing how the Old Covenant prophesies the new, Irenaeus proves through the interpretation of scripture the unity of God's *oikonomia* of creation and salvation. The parables that Irenaeus discusses deal with the salvation of human beings. By showing how these parables ought to be understood in light of the Old Covenant, Irenaeus both recapitulates his argument about the unity of the scriptures and reiterates how Christ himself recapitulates all things through his interpretation of the scriptures. Once again: the structure of the *Adversus Haereses* is the argument of the *Adversus Haereses*. And that structure is based on the faith.

As with the previous books, in Book Four we find a section on Irenaeus's method. This section, as in Book Three, is an instance of epideictic rhetoric. Whereas Irenaeus's theological method in Book Three focused on an *epideixis* of Christ as the key to the proper interpretation of scripture, Irenaeus's theological method in Book Four focuses on the *homo vivens*, the living human being who is the glory of God and who is saved through Christ's work. For Irenaeus, as we have stressed, Christ's interpretation of scripture is not an academic exercise. One needs to understand what in scripture ought to be read literally and what ought to be read metaphorically, because knowing this

3. This schematic comes from Mary Ann Donovan's discussion of Phillipe Bacq's magisterial study of Book Four. See Mary Ann Donovan, *One Right Reading?: A Guide to Irenaeus* (Collegeville, Minn.: Liturgical Press, 1997), 285–86. Donovan notes her indebtedness to Bacq, *De l'ancienne à la nouvelle alliance*.

helps a person accept the salvation that the Father offers in Christ.[4]

Although the manifestation of God in Christ is the central message in Irenaeus's work, it would be fair to say that Irenaeus's most distinctive contribution is the understanding of Christ within the economy of God's salvific plan.[5] This theme is not peculiar to Irenaeus—Paul famously describes the *oikonomia* in the letter to the Ephesians—but Irenaeus offers a full account of that *oikonomia* in terms of human progress toward salvation.[6] As I have noted already, the *oikonomia* also plays an epideictic role, educating the faithful about the history of God's love for humanity. Irenaeus's opponents "argue against the entire economy of God."[7] In order for Irenaeus to prove those opponents wrong, he must persuade his audience that Jesus Christ is the fulfillment of the Hebrew prophets and the Son of the same God who created the universe.

There is a rhetorical as well as a Pauline precedent for *oikonomia*. For the rhetor, *oikonomia* is the arrangement of the speech after he has decided what points he will discuss.[8] Of course, the word *oikono-*

4. I should note that although I agree with Bacq about the three major divisions of Book Four, I differ with him on divisions within each of those major divisions. Like him, I am interested in the internal coherence of the text and how its argument proceeds. See *De l'ancienne à la nouvelle alliance*, 14–15. Of course, I agree with Bacq that Book Four has a "remarkable architecture" that shows Christian truth, and no details get lost in that architecture (*De l'ancienne à la nouvelle alliance selon S. Irénée*, 281).

5. On Irenaeus's use of *oikonomia* generally, see A. d'Ales, "Le mot «oikonomia» dans la langue théologique de saint Irénée," *Revue des Etudes grecques* 32 (1919): 1–9. See also José Pedro Tosaus Abadía, *Cristo y el universo: estudio lingüístico y temático de Ef 1:10b, en Efesios y en la obra de Ireneo de Lión*, Plenitudo Temporis (Salamanca: Universidad Pontificia de Salamanca, 1995), 226–27. The whole book is a helpful exploration of Irenaeus's use of Eph 1:10.

6. Eph 1:10. See Richter, *Oikonomia*, 94. For the use of *oikonomia* in Philo and the *Martyrdom of Polycarp* see *Oikonomia*, 24. See also Fantino, *La théologie d'Irénée*, 108–16.

7. "et doctrinam quidem Christi praetermittentes, et a semetipsis autem falsa divinantes, adversus universam Dei dispositionem argumentantur" (4.1.1).

8. As George Kennedy notes in discussing Hermagoras, "The structure of Hermagoras' book was a modification of the system which was common since Aristotle, the parts of rhetoric. The discussion of invention was the most important section of the work and came first; arrangement and style were grouped together under the second heading *oikonomia*, which was subdivided into judgment, division, order, and style (Quintilian 3.3.9); memory and delivery perhaps followed." Kennedy, *The Art of Persuasion in Greece*, 304.

mia itself means the management of a household.[9] In this sense the economy of God can be understood as God's rule over and care for creation.[10] The history of salvation is God's ordered *oikonomia*, the management of God's household. Christ, as the Word of God, is the speech through which God recapitulates all of creation. To say "all of creation" is to say all of the history of creation, especially as the Word tells the history of the people of Israel.

In Book Four, Irenaeus offers an *epideixis* of praise of this economy. Irenaeus's rhetoric persuades his audience to see the economy of God as it is recounted in scripture. More specifically, he hopes to persuade them that the economy denotes the covenant between God and human beings.[11] If Irenaeus can offer a persuasive account of how the Law and the prophets look forward to Christ and how Christ confirms the teaching of the Law and the prophets, he has refuted his opponents' claims that Christ is in no way connected with the teaching of the Old Covenant.[12] I should note that Irenaeus continues to track the argument of the faith, which I traced in my discussion of Book One. The faith began with God, then moved to the work of the Spirit through the prophets, and ended with Christ's work of recapitulation: *probatio, refutatio, recapitulatio*. Book Three marks the beginning of Irenaeus's positive teaching of Christian revelation, where he identifies Christ as the word of the Father, as the manifestation of God in flesh. Book Four, then, shows the Spirit of God who spoke through the prophets. Irenaeus must turn his attention to the connection between the witness of the Old Covenant and the words and actions of Christ. Indeed for Irenaeus, Christ can only be fully understood in light of the Old Covenant and the Old Covenant receives its proper interpretation through Christ.

9. "Hermagoras iudicium partitionem ordinem quaque sunt elocutionis subici oeconomiae, quae Graece appelata ex cura reru, domesticarum et hic per abusionem posita nomine Lationo caret." Quintilian, *The Orator's Education* 3.3.9.

10. Richter points to a catechetical sense of *oikonomia* in the work of Quintilian, *Oikonomia*, 15. Fantino, *La théologie d'Irénée*, 117–18.

11. See Fantino, *La théologie d'Irénée*, 236. For a study of Irenaeus and covenant see Susan Graham, "'Zealous for the Covenant': Irenaeus and the Covenants of Israel" (PhD diss., University of Notre Dame, 2001).

12. As Nielsen points out, Irenaeus's opponents' use of *oikonomia* indicates the ordering of salvation within the Pleroma. He points to Irenaeus's discussion in 1.6.1, 1.7.1, and 1.9.2. Nielsen, *Adam and Christ*, 66.

Probatio, 4.1–19: God

Jesus Christ is both the interpreter and the interpretation of scripture. Irenaeus and his opponents agree on this point. They further agree that Christ is the center of the economy of salvation. Thus the debate between Irenaeus and his opponents centers on *how* Christ interprets and is interpreted by the scripture; how, in other words, he is the center of the economy of salvation. Book Four continues the epideictic of praise found in Book Three. In Book Four Irenaeus both praises Christ and refutes his opponents' teaching. Because Christ is the fulfillment of the Law and the prophets, Irenaeus is particularly interested in how Christ himself interprets scripture in the New Covenant because Irenaeus sees himself as continuing the line of teachers begun by Christ.

In order to understand God's manifestation in the history of salvation, the reader of scripture should look to Christ's own words. After all, they set the terms for a proper discussion of God's identity. To set the terms here, Irenaeus quotes Jesus telling the disciples to confess no Father "except the one in heaven" (Mt 23:9) who, alone, is God and Father. Thus, Christ himself understood his own Father and the creator of the world to be one and the same. If one is confused about what is spoken metaphorically about God and what is spoken literally, Jesus' own words can clear up that confusion. And if Irenaeus's opponents are correct in their interpretation, then Jesus Christ is wrong. Both Irenaeus and his opponents agree that Christ's words are essential to unlocking the scriptures. Irenaeus uses Christ's own words to identify the God and Father of Christ.

The words Christ speaks must be understood literally. "Openly and without parables, the Son teaches that he is truly God."[13] His opponents cannot "say that these things are said ironically because they are convinced these words are said in truth."[14] Indeed, "the one who spoke was himself Truth."[15] This Johannine theme is key to Irenaeus's

---

13. "Non enim a Patre accipiunt cognoscere Filium, nec a Filio discunt Patrem, manifeste et sine parabolis eum Deum qui est vere docente" (4.2.5).

14. "Sed nec per ironiam quidem haec dicta esse poterunt dicere, cum convincantur ab ipsis dictis quoniam in veritate dicta sunt" (4.2.6).

15. "Etenim veritas erat ipse qui loquebatur" (4.2.6).

argument in the first section of Book Four. Because Jesus Christ is the truth, his clear words in the scriptures must be true, even if few of his words are easy to understand. If Christ's words are true, they must be the starting point for any interpretation of scripture. This is part of what it means for Christ to be the key to scriptural interpretation. Only once a reader has understood Christ's clear words can he move on to the more difficult sayings of Christ, the parables. In this, his *probatio* of Book Four, Irenaeus aims to instruct his reader. Like Christ, Irenaeus aims to use clear words so that the reader can understand Christ in light of the prophecies of the Old Covenant.

In setting up the terms for debate, Irenaeus is not afraid to address difficult scriptural passages that could easily be misread and, as a result, cause misunderstandings about the identity of God. For example, Irenaeus's opponents point to places in the scripture that seem to suggest that the God of the Old Covenant is only temporary.[16] Such people forget Paul's words in 1 Corinthians: "The figure of this world will pass away." Irenaeus sees a similar misunderstanding in their interpretation of Jerusalem.[17] What his opponents do not understand is that Jerusalem was like a grain of wheat. It is necessary, Irenaeus explains, for Jerusalem to have an end with the New Covenant. His opponents misunderstand why Jerusalem perished because they do not understand the scriptures according to the faith. The faith clearly explains the history of salvation in light of the Old and the New Covenant.

Ultimately what we have here is a problem of reading. Yes, all sorts of issues that later become known as "doctrinal" are at stake between Irenaeus and his opponents. On the most fundamental level, though, Irenaeus believes that he reads the scriptures according to their true hypothesis, which is the hypothesis of the faith. His opponents, so he believes, follow a different hypothesis, one that is opposed to the faith of the Apostles. Nowhere is this more clear, in Irenaeus's mind, than in the way his opponents provide overly complex readings of the clear words

---

16. "Si quidem caelum thronus Dei est et terra suppedaneum eius [see Is 66:1], dictum est autem praeterire caelum et terra [see Lk 21:33], hisque praetereuntibus oportere enim hunc Deum qui sit Omnia" (4.3.1).

17. "si esset magnis regis civitas [see Mt 5:35], non derelinqueretur" (4.4.2).

of Christ. And in doing so, they misidentify God. Christ identifies God as his Father and identifies himself as the key to the Father's revelation. As the Word, he makes the Father known because "all things are manifested through the Word."[18] Because the Son only teaches the true Father, "we do not receive another Father except him who is revealed by the Son," and this Father is "the creator of heaven and earth."[19] Christ revealed the Father when he was living on earth and will judge all people when he returns in glory. But Irenaeus argues that Christ's manifestation is continual. As the faith proclaims, the Spirit was at work in the prophets. Because he is setting up the terms for debate, he is showing the close connection between Jesus and the Father. This is important in Book Four because Irenaeus argues that Christ's revelation of the Father occurs in the Old Covenant as well as the New.

The status of the Old Covenant is part of Irenaeus's polemic with his opponents, but more importantly it points to the nature of Christ. Whether or not Christ fulfills the Law and the prophets is precisely the point at issue between him and his opponents. Therefore, Irenaeus has to show those places in scripture, especially those places where Christ himself speaks, in which Christ fulfills the covenant. For Irenaeus, Abraham, although he did not know Christ, "desired to see the day" of Christ's coming so that "he might embrace Christ." The witness of Abraham in the Old Covenant finds completion in the New. Through his faith, Abraham showed "that all who from the beginning have knowledge of God and prophesy the coming of Christ" will "accept revelation from the Son himself."[20] Jesus "established the faith of Abraham in us."[21] Abraham shows the link between the Old Covenant and the New, and all Christians who follow the Apostles' interpretation of scripture share Abraham's faith.

18. "Agnitio enim Patris est Filii manifestatio: omnia enim per Verbum manifestantur" (4.6.3).
19. "alterum non recipiamus Patrem nisi eum qui a Filio revelatur" (4.6.3). "Hic autem est Fabricator caeli et terrae" (4.6.4).
20. "Non enim tantum propter Abraham haec dixit, sed ut ostenderet quoniam omnes qui ab initio cognitum habuerunt Deum et adventum Christi prophetaverunt revelationem acceperunt ab ipso Filio" (4.7.2).
21. "Hoc autem fecit Jesus, a lapidum religione extrahens nos, et a dura et infructuosa cognatione transferens nos, et similem Abrahae fidem in nobis constituens" (4.7.2).

We now come to perhaps the biggest interpretative sticking point for Irenaeus: the status of the Law of the Old Covenant. This is also the challenge point for his *refutatio*. If the Old Covenant is no longer valid, then whatever interpretative traditions spring up are equally valid. There is no older tradition to check them, and if there are no older traditions to use as a precedent, then the identity of God (which is still Irenaeus's focus here) is an open question. If the nature of prophecy is up for grabs, so is the identity of God. His opponents think this is the case. "The tradition of their elders," Irenaeus writes, "which they pretend observes the law, was contrary to the law that was given trough Moses. This is why, Isaiah said, 'The tradesmen mix wine with water, which shows that their elders mixed a watered tradition with the austere precept of God.'"[22] Yet Christ's plain words prohibit such action. He says, as Irenaeus points out, "Why do you trade the precepts of God for your own tradition?" Irenaeus goes so far as to call his opponents Pharisees because they would rather "vindicate their traditions" than be "subject to the laws of God instituted by the coming of Christ."[23] Irenaeus argues that love is the highest precept of the Law because knowledge, faith, and prophecy are all empty without it (see 1 Cor 13). Without knowledge of the traditions of the Old Covenant, one cannot interpret Christ's love correctly.

This love, of course, is the whole point. In the *Adversus Haereses*, Irenaeus wants to counter his opponents' philosophical speculations with a discussion of God's love for humanity. In order to do that, he wants to show how the economy of salvation is present in the beginning of the scriptures. In other words, the manifestation of God's love began in and through the prophecies of the Old Covenant. "In the beginning," Irenaeus reminds his readers, "although God was not in need of human beings, he formed Adam so that he could have in him

22. "Seniorum enim ipsorum traditio, quam ex lege observare fingebant, contraria erat legi quae data est per Moysen. Propter hoc et Esaias ait: Caupones tui miscunt vinum aquae, ostendens quod austero Dei praecepto miscerent seniores aquatam traditionem" (4.12.1).

23. "Quare vos transgredimini praeceptum Dei propter traditionem uestram? ... Quas traditiones volentes vindicare, legi Dei instituenti eos ad adventum Christi non subjecti esse voluerunt" (4.12.1).

someone on whom to bestow his benefits."[24] "As much as God is in
need of nothing, so human beings are in need of communion with
God."[25] And the way human beings come into communion with God
is through observing the commandments. Irenaeus explains that for
the Jews, "the law is both discipline and prophecy of the future. God,
who admonishes them, demanded nothing more from them than what
he gave through natural precepts." That is to say, for Irenaeus, the Law
points beyond itself. It is a necessary part of the economy of salvation,
but it does not grant salvation itself. As he notes, "If someone does
not observe the Decalogue, he does not obtain salvation."[26] Thanks to
the Law, the Israelites learn to love God with their whole heart.[27] The
Law is not a sign of God's weakness; it is meant to help the Israelites'
weakness. "God always safeguards liberty and human free choice and
his exhortation to them so that those who are not obedient are judged
justly, since they do not obey, and those who obey and believe in him
are crowned with incorruptibility."[28]

This incorruptibility comes when human beings accept God's offer
of friendship. It does not come from human works such as circumcision
and sacrifice. What God requires instead, Irenaeus notes, quoting Deuteronomy 10:12, is fear of the Lord, walking in his ways, and loving and
serving the Lord with one's whole heart and soul.[29] Doing such things
leads to friendship with God. This friendship, however, "presents nothing to God, for God is not in need of the love of men. Man is in need of
the glory of God, which he is able to receive in no way unless through

24. "Igitur initio, non quasi indigens Deus hominis, plasmavit Adam, sed ut haberet
in quem collocaret sua beneficia" (4.14.1). On this paragraph, see Gilles Pelland, "Le décalogue dans la théologie d'Irénée de Lyon (Aduersus Haereses iv, 14, 1s)," in *Décalogue
au miroir des pères*, ed. R. Gounelle and J.-M. Prieur (Strasbourg: Université Marc Bloch,
2008): 93–106.
25. "In quantum enim Deus nullius indigens, in tantum homo indiget Dei com-
munione" (4.14.1).
26. "Itaque lex et disciplina erat illis et prophetia futurorum. Nam Deus primo
quidem per naturalia praecepta quae ab initio infixa dedit hominibus admonens eos,
hoc est per Decalogum—quae si quis non fecerit, non habet salutem" (4.15.1).
27. "sed toto corde discerent diligere eum" (4.15.2).
28. "et id quod erat semper liberum et suae potestatis in homine semper servasse
Deum et suam exhortationem: ut iuste qui non obaudiunt ei judicentur, quoniam non
obaudiunt, et qui obaudiunt et crediderunt ei coronentur incorruptibilitate" (4.15.2).
29. 4.16.4.

obedience to him."[30] Thus Irenaeus's *refutatio* in this first section of Book Four shows that the God of the Old Covenant and the God of the New Covenant are one and the same because this same God offers his friendship in both covenants. Prophecy is only prophetic if it is fulfilled. In turn, the fulfillment can only be understood in light of the prophecy.

This offer of love is, in fact, central to God's identity. The prophecies found in the Old Covenant are part of the economy of salvation that must be continuous with the realities found in the New Covenant. The same God, Irenaeus stresses, receives worship in both covenants as part of the same economy. Here we would expect Irenaeus to begin to engage in a deliberative discourse that shows his readers what interpretative choices are before them and what the consequences of those choices are. Thus far we have seen Irenaeus argue that Christ's words show that he acknowledges only one Father. Christ's own words must be taken literally. He did not metaphorically mean that his Father was somehow different from the creator of the universe. This acknowledgment led, in turn, to Irenaeus's discussion that the Law was a vital part of the economy of salvation. The types of sacrifice in the Old Covenant look forward to Christ's sacrifice.

It is particularly fitting that Irenaeus ends his *probatio* with a discussion of worship because someone cannot respond to God's offer of salvation unless he worships God properly. When his opponents' exegesis disregards earlier members of the church, it also disregards sacrifices made to God, and it refuses to see that these sacrifices are types of the Eucharistic sacrifice of the church. The Eucharist is the "offering of the Church, which the Lord teaches to be offered in the whole world."[31] It is the "Church alone" that "offers this pure offering to the Creator, offering to him with the action of grace from his creatures."[32] It is accepted by God, unlike the sacrifices of the Old Covenant, because it is offered "in pure thought and faith without hypocri-

---

30. "nec enim indigebat Deus dilectione hominis. Deerat autem homini gloria Dei [see Rom 3:23], quam nullo modo potera percipere, nisi per eam obsequentiam quae est erga eum" (4.16.4).

31. "Igitur Ecclesiae oblatio, quam Dominus docuit offerri in universo mundo" (4.18.1).

32. "Et hanc oblationem Ecclesia sola puram offert Fabricatori, offerens ei cum gratiarum actione ex creatura eius" (4.18.4).

sy, in firm hope, in fervent love."[33] This sacrifice, Irenaeus explains, is "the bread ... is the body of the Lord and the cup of his blood."[34] The bread is *literally* the body of the Lord. The distinction between literal and metaphorical language, which is necessary for understanding the scriptures, takes on an added importance in a discussion of the appropriate way to worship God. A proper understanding of the Eucharist is the result of a proper understanding of Christ. In Irenaeus's view, the Eucharist and the faith mutually reinforce each other. The union of flesh and Spirit, of creation and God, is the very point of the economy of salvation. Just as beholding the vision of God enables human beings to partake in the life of God, participating in the Eucharist leads to incorruptibility: "our bodies participating in the Eucharist are no longer corruptible but have the hope of resurrection in eternity."[35]

Images of God giving life are found in the New Covenant as well as the Old. These images are often connected with eschatological passages, which is perfectly appropriate in this final section of Irenaeus's *probatio*. For example, Irenaeus explains Matthew 25 by writing, "Although he was not in need of these things, nevertheless he wishes that they come about by us for us, lest we be unfruitful, he gave his Word to the people, as a precept for making offerings."[36] Human beings make offerings to God "so that they may learn to serve God just as he wishes, to offer gifts at the altar frequently and without intermission."[37] Irenaeus then refers to the Book of Revelation: "There is an altar in heaven where our prayers and offerings are directed."[38] Worshipping

33. "in sententia pura et fide sine hypocrisi, in spe firma, in dilectione ferventi, primitias earum quae sunt eius creaturarum offerentes" (4.18.4).

34. "Quomodo autem constabit eis eum panem in quo gratiae actae sint corpus esse Domini sui, et calicem sanguinem eius" (4.18.4). On this section, see G. Levesque, "Consonance chrétienne et dissonance gnostique dans Irénée Adversus Haereses IV 18,4 à 19,3," *Studia Patristica* 16, no. 2 (1985), 193–96.

35. οὕτως καὶ τὰ σώματα ἡμῶν μεταλαμβάνοντα τῆς εὐχαριστίας μηκέτι εἶναι φθαρτά, τὴν ἐλπίδα τῆς εἰς αἰῶνα ἀναστάσεως ἔχοντα (4.18.5).

36. "Sicut igitur non his indigens, vult tamen a nobis propter nos fieri, ne simus infructuosi, ita id ipsum Verbum dedit populo praeceptum faciendarum oblationum" (4.18.6).

37. "quamvis non indigeret eis, uti discerent Deo servire, sicut et ideo nos quoque offerre vult munus ad altare frequenter sine intermissione" (4.18.6).

38. "Est ergo altare in caelis, illuc enim preces nostrae et oblationes diriguntur" (4.18.6).

God in the heavenly Jerusalem is the ultimate fulfillment of the prophecies of the Old Covenant.

It is especially interesting here that Irenaeus uses worship to undergird the Apostolic exegesis of scripture.[39] Moses worships the same God that the Christians of Irenaeus's day do. This worship links the two covenants and links the interpretation of both. In his opponents' view, "things that are supercelestial and spiritual and invisible and ineffable to us are types of another heaven and another Pleroma and the image of another God the Father which wandered from the truth."[40] This view, Irenaeus tells us, is "foolish and stupid."[41] Here Irenaeus uses deliberative language that appeals to his audience's *pathos*. Instead of building their typology on things of the earth and the things of the Old Covenant, his opponents build their typology on invisible and ineffable things with no connection to the Old Covenant. As a result, Irenaeus believes they never "fix their soul on the one true God."[42] An improper worship of God goes hand-in-hand with an improper understanding of God. And both of these, as we have seen, relate to a misunderstanding of the nature of prophecy in the scriptures, especially a misunderstanding of Christ's clear words interpreting the Old Covenant.

Excursus, 4.20: Theological Method, *Homo Vivens*

With 4.20, we come to another section where Irenaeus steps back and offers us a "method" to his argument. We saw in Books Two and Three that this section came at the end of the *refutatio*. In Book One, it began and ended the *refutatio*. And here in Book Four, Irenaeus begins the *refutatio* with his methodology chapter. As we would expect, Irenaeus's discussion here turns on the rule of prophecy in interpreting

---

39. We saw in chapter 1 how Irenaeus's various opponents used worship to undergird their interpretation of scripture; see, e.g., *AH* 1.13 and 1.21.

40. "Quae autem supercaelestia et spiritalia sunt et, quantum ad nos spectat, invisibilia et inenarrabilia, typos rursum alterorum caelestium dicere et alterius Pleromatis et Deum alterius Patris imaginem esse, et errantium est a veritate" (4.19.1).

41. "et omnimodo stultorum et hebetum" (4.19.1).

42. "et numquam fingere animum suum in uno et vero Deo" (4.19.1).

scripture. Although prophecy is grounded in the past, Irenaeus is clear that it continues. Indeed, as we will see presently, the one who reads the scriptures correctly—Irenaeus calls him the *homo vivens*—understands himself to be a living continuation of the words of the prophets in the economy of salvation.

In Book One, we focused on the faith, which is the basis for Irenaeus's interpretation of scripture. In Book Two, we saw Irenaeus argue that his opponents inserted an alien methodology, based on Greek literature and philosophy, into their interpretation of scripture. Their methodology was its own rule, but not a rule that was based on the scriptures or handed down by the Apostles. In Book Three, we saw how Irenaeus used *ekphrasis* to paint a picture that would help his audience understand how Christ is the foundation of the faith and how Christ is both the key to unlock the scriptures and the treasure to be found therein. And now in Book Four, we see Irenaeus argue that Christ is present in the Old Covenant as well as the New. Indeed, it is precisely as the Word of God that Christ spoke through the Law and the prophets.[43] That same Word continues to speak to the Christian community in Irenaeus's day, and the community can understand the Word thanks to the faith and to the celebration of the Eucharist that grounds the community's thought.

Irenaeus's focus on theological methodology in 4.20 has shifted ever so slightly from what he discussed in previous discussions of method. The previous discussions focused on how one ought to read the scriptures so that the proper image emerges (or as we saw in Book Two, does not emerge). But in Book Four, Irenaeus presents an image of the one who interprets the scriptures correctly. The methodology chapter (4.20) has received extensive attention by scholars in the twentieth century, in large part because in it we find Irenaeus's celebrated dictum *"homo vivens, gloria Dei,"* the living human being is the glory of God.[44] The question, of course, is: what does this mean? The whole chapter is important for my discussion of Irenaeus because it brings

43. See John Behr, *The Way to Nicaea* (Crestwood, N.Y.: St. Vladimir's Seminary Press, 2001), 1:49–70. I shall return to Behr's argument in the conclusion.

44. See Barbara Aland, "Fides und Subiectio: zur Anthropologie des Irenäus," in *Kerygma und Logos: Beiträge zu den geistesgeschichtlichen Beziehungen zwischen Antike*

together his praise for God's love and his stress on proper interpretation. Once this proper interpretation is in place, one can see the glorious vision of the economy of God's salvation as it is recounted in the
scriptures. Once one partakes of this vision, one is truly a living human being and reflects the glory of God, and the only proper response
to beholding this vision is praising God.

This chapter is also important because it stresses the limits of human knowledge about God. Human beings do not know God according to his magnitude, Irenaeus writes, but according to his love. That
love leads "those who are obedient" to him "through his Word" to
God. Ultimately, God's *oikonomia*, which is recounted in the scriptures, educates human beings. The end of this education is recognizing
the love of God. When the human being is "embraced by the Spirit
of God," he "may accede to the glory of the Father."[45] This embrace
occurs, then, throughout the economy of salvation. In order to interpret the scriptures correctly, one must recognize that all of scripture
recounts the embrace of the Spirit.

Once a person understands this, he can see the vision that the
entire economy of the scripture provides. At one level, Christ can
be seen in the consecrated Eucharistic bread and wine. But Irenaeus's understanding of vision is more expansive than this; it is not
straightforwardly pictorial. Irenaeus argues that the prophets—from
Abraham forward—saw God "through the Spirit." The vision of God

---

und Christentum, ed. Adolf Ritter (Göttingen: Vandenhoeck and Ruprecht, 1979), 9–28;
Mary Ann Donovan, "Irenaeus: At the Heart of Life, Glory," in *Spiritualities of the Heart:
Approaches to Personal Wholeness in the Christian Tradition*, ed. Annice Callahan (Mahwah, N.J.: Paulist Press, 1990), 11–22; Antonio Orbé, "Gloria Dei Vivens Homo (Analisis
de Ireneo, Adv Haer IV,20,1–7)," *Gregorianum* 73, no. 2 (1992): 205–26; Thierry Scherrer,
La glorie de Dieu dans l'oeuvre de saint Irénée (Rome: Editrice Pontifica Universita Gregoriana, 1997).

45. "faciens nos servire sibi in sanctitate et justitia omnes dies nostros, uti complex-
us homo Spiritum Dei in gloriam cedat Patris" (4.20.4). Donovan writes, "Both in the
prophetic seeing and in the adoptive, it is the one Word of God who shows the Father
to the one who accepts the guidance of the Spirit. We begin to see that what unites the
two testaments is the similar actions of the one same God who consistently works in
the same way for our salvation. If we submit to the guidance of the Spirit, the Word
shows us the Father. It is this which has always been the role of the Word: to show us the
Father." Mary Ann Donovan, "Alive to the Glory of God: A Key Insight in St Irenaeus,"
Theological Studies 49, no. 2 (1988): 283–97, at 285.

is something like the vision of light. To see light is to recognize that it illumines what we see. In this way "those who see God participate in life."⁴⁶ Such people recognize what the prophets recognized, namely that they are part of God's economy of salvation—an economy that was announced by the prophets, recapitulated by Christ, handed down by the Apostles, and lived in the church. Even though not everyone recognizes it, all who are alive participate in salvation. "Since it is not possible to live without life, the reality of life becomes participation in God."⁴⁷

Here we come to the heart of Irenaeus's rhetoric and the heart of his argument. As a rhetor, when Irenaeus properly interprets the scriptures, he helps his readers participate in the life of God by beholding the manifestation of God. Another way of saying this, of course, is that Irenaeus's interpretation shows that Jesus Christ, the manifestation of God in the flesh, can only be understood in light of the prophecies of the Old Covenant, because he himself gives those prophecies their definitive interpretation. Because the structure of Irenaeus's argument mirrors the structure of the faith, and because the structure of the faith *is* Irenaeus's argument, by placing Jesus in his proper context of the prophets, Irenaeus places the reader in his proper context of the economy of salvation. In the economy of salvation, "he who is ungraspable and incomprehensible and invisible presents himself to be seen and comprehended and grasped by the faithful."⁴⁸ Yet Irenaeus's rhetoric depends on God's love, which ultimately allows human beings to participate in God. Human beings are "made immortal through the vision and they reach out to God."⁴⁹ God makes human beings immortal through his manifestation in Christ. It is Irenaeus's task to persuade his readers to see this manifestation. In order to do this, he must show that a proper understanding of God's love includes God's work in the Law and the prophets.

46. Ζωῆς οὖν μετέξοθσιν οἱ ὁρῶντες Θεόν (4.20.5).
47. Ἐπεὶ ζῆσαι ἄνευ ζωῆς οὐχ οἷον τε ἦν ἡ δὲ ὑπαρξις τῆς ζωῆς ἐκ τῆς τοῦ θεοῦ περιγίνεται μετοχῆς μετοχὴ δὲ θεοῦ ἐστι (4.20.5).
48. Καὶ διὰ τοῦτο ὁ ἀχώρητος καὶ ἀκατάληπτος καὶ ἀόρατος ὁρώμενον ἑαυτὸν καὶ καταλαμβανόμενον καὶ χωρούμενον τοῖς πιστοῖς παρέσχεν (4.20.5).
49. "Homines igitur videbunt Deum ut vivant, per visionem immortales facti et pertingentes usque in Deum" (4.20.6).

Understanding the scriptures with the light of Christ allows the reader to see what the prophets saw. The issue is what this seeing entails, for "according to his magnitude and his untellable glory, no one will see God and live" (Ex 33:20). Yet, "according to his love," God "concedes this to those who love him, that is to see God, which the prophets prophesied."[50] Irenaeus argues that the community of believers is bound by a common vision, from the prophets to Irenaeus's own day.

To say that the faithful share a common vision is not to say that all faithful people see the same thing. Again, this would be too simplistic an understanding of vision. Through his *epideixis*, Irenaeus interprets the visions of the Old Covenant through the person of Christ. The work of the Son has enabled manifestations of God to occur and these manifestations continue. Not everyone sees the manifestation of God in the same way. Some "saw the prophetic Spirit and his works poured out in all kinds of gifts." Others saw "the coming of the Lord and that dispensation which is from the beginning, through which he accomplishes the will of the Father." Still others saw "the paternal glories adapted for the times."[51] God has been manifested in these ways, Irenaeus tells us.[52]

Here we get to the rub of Irenaeus's argument. The core debate between Irenaeus and his opponents—as I have stressed throughout—is how God reveals himself in Christ. My focus in this chapter has been on God's revelation in history, more specifically in Jesus Christ, and how the revelation of Jesus Christ can only be understood in light of the prophecies of the Old Covenant. Indeed, Irenaeus argues that "from the beginning the Son is the interpreter of the Father." The Word

50. "Sed secundum magnitudinem quidem eius et inenarrabilem gloriam nemo videbit Deum et vivet, incapabilis enim Pater, secundum autem dilectionem et humanitatem et quod omnia possit. etiam hoc concedit his qui se diligunt, id est videre Deum, quod et prophetabant prophetae" (4.20.5).

51. "Quidam enim eorum videbant Spiritum propheticum et operationes eius in omnia genera charismatum effusa; alii vero adventum Domini et eam quae est ab initio administrationem, per quam perfecit voluntatem Patris quae est in caelis et quae est in terris; alii vero et glorias paternas temporibus aptas, et ipsi qui videbant et qui tunc audiebant et hominibus qui deinceps audituri erant" (4.20.6).

52. 4.20.6.

is "the dispenser of paternal grace" and on account of this, he "shows God to men and exhibits men to God."[53] Thus human beings can only see the vision of God because of the Word, who "shows God visibly to men through many economies."[54] This line is the immediate context for Irenaeus's dictum that the living human being is the glory of God. Indeed, the next part of that line is "the life of man is the vision of God." He goes on to define vision more fully: "If the vision of God that is throughout creation presents life to all living who are on the earth, how much more does the manifestation of the Father that is through the Word present life to those who see God."[55] The manifestation of God occurs through the economy of God's creation.[56]

Now we are in a position to understand what Irenaeus means here and why it is so important to his argument. Who is the *homo vivens*? The one to whom God has manifested the Word. And this human being can only see God because he has understood that the scriptures recount the economy of God's salvation. Indeed, such an understanding *is* seeing God, which is simply another way to talk about human salvation. The story found in the economy of salvation is the story of preparing for the Lord's arrival. It is ultimately the story of understanding oneself in light of the economy of salvation. Irenaeus hopes to persuade his audience that God's economy—proclaimed in the Law and the prophets, lived in and through Christ, and taught by the Apostles—makes them fully alive.

The prophecy of the Old Covenant not only tells of the coming of the Lord, but through its telling it prepares human beings for his arrival. The vision that God offers—and that Irenaeus attempts to describe—is the result of God's love for humanity. It is not enough that

53. "Enarrator ergo ab ignitio Filius Patris .... Et propterea Verbum dispensator paternae gratiae factus est ad utilitatem hominum, propter quos fecit tantas dispositiones, hominibus quidem ostendens Deum, Deo autem exhibens hominem" (4.20.7).

54. "hominibus per multas dispositionis ostendens Deum" (4.20.7).

55. "Si enim quae est per conditionem ostensio Dei vitam praestat omnibus in terra viventibus, multo magis ea quae est per Verbum manifestatio Patris vitam praestat his qui vident Deum" (4.20.7).

56. Fantino explains that the idea of the economy is of an organizing action that gives and organizes realities according to a specific purpose. Fantino, *La théologie de saint Irénée*, 93. We certainly see that in this section.

the Son and the Father "are spoken prophetically" but that God "may be seen by all sanctified members." The prophets taught "by vision and way of life and actions which they performed according to what that Spirit suggested."[57] The prophets did not see the face of God, but they saw the "economies and mysteries" through which human beings began to see God.[58] Yet just as one has to be in light to recognize the light, one needs to be within the economy of God in order to recognize it. Those who follow Christ are in the best position to understand themselves in the economy of salvation, for "the Word himself is the interpreter of the Father." But even this has its limits because the Father is "rich and multiple. He is not seen in one figure nor in one character by those who see him but according to the causes or efficacy of his economy."[59] As we have seen, Irenaeus's use of the rhetorical tradition can never fully capture the vision experience the Father offers through the Word. Irenaeus recognizes the limits of his own interpretative model.

Refutatio, 4.21–35: Scripture/Economy

Thus 4.20 argues that the *homo vivens*, who is the glory of God, is the one who beholds the vision of the economy of salvation that the scriptures offer. As we just saw, Irenaeus argues that in order to understand this economy, one must understand that Christ names the God of the Old Covenant as his own Father and that the Word is present in the Old Covenant. With this, Irenaeus has set the terms for the discussion of the relationship between the Old Covenant and the New. He has also described the reader who understands this relationship. Once he has established his parameters in 4.1–20, Irenaeus comes to the heart of his *refutatio* in the *Adversus Haereses*. In 4.21–35, Irenaeus's task is to show how scripture, when properly interpreted, sustains the vision of

57. "Non enim solum sermone prophetabant prophetae, sed et visione et conversatione et actibus quos faciebant secundum id quod suggerebat Spiritus" (4.20.8).
58. "Non igitur manifeste ipsam faciem Dei videbant prophetae, sed dispositiones et mysteria per quae inciperet homo videre Deum" (4.20.10).
59. "Et ipse autem interpretator Patris Verbum, utpote dives et multus exsistens, non in una figura neque in uno charactere videbatur videntibus eum, sed secundum dispensationum eius causas sive efficaciam" (4.20.11).

God that the economy of salvation offers. In 4.20, Irenaeus argued *how* the prophets could see Christ in love because they understood themselves within the economy of salvation. In 4.21–35, Irenaeus shows how the prophets *do see* Christ in love. Irenaeus begins his discussion in 4.21 by addressing Abraham, whom he sees as the beginning of the line of prophets. Abraham is also, of course, a primary figure in the economy of salvation. Thus, it makes sense for Irenaeus to start a new section of his argument with Abraham.

Irenaeus first reminds his readers that "Christ did not only come for those who believed in him in the time of Tiberius Caesar."[60] Just as Irenaeus has a more expansive understanding of vision than we might have, he also has a more expansive understanding of time. Christ came for all ages and he redeemed those faithful Israelites who longed to see him. He also opens the covenant to the pagans. Because of Paul's writings, the pagans can understand that they too are included in the economy of God's salvation, even though learning this was, for them, "foreign instruction and new teaching."[61] Paul could not rely on the pagans knowing the Old Covenant as the Jews knew it.[62]

Abraham is both the beginning of the covenant and in a way both a Jew and a pagan. Abraham is the "father of all who follow the Word of God and who sustain pilgrimage in this world."[63] This includes both the circumcised and the uncircumcised. Irenaeus cannot discuss Abraham without offering an *epideixis* of praise to him. He wants his discussion of Abraham to delight his audience because the teaching and example of Abraham is directly connected to the life of the church. "The prophets and the patriarchs disseminate the word about Christ" and the word "is reaped by the Church."[64] The point here is clear: Irenaeus refutes his opponents by showing that the writings in the Old Covenant do not refer to some alien god, but to the God who

60. "Non enim propter eos solos qui a temporibus Tiberii Caesaris crediderunt eu venit Chirstus" (4.22.2).

61. "Hic vero peregrina quaedam eruditio et nova doctrina" (4.24.2).

62. Here Irenaeus is returning to themes we have seen already in 3.12.

63. "pater omnium qui sequuntur Verbum Dei et peregrinationem in hoc saeculo sustinent" (4.25.3).

64. "seminaverunt enim sermonem de Christo patriarchae et prophetae, demessa est autem Ecclesia" (4.25.3).

prophesied the coming of Christ, the God who planted what will be reaped.

The Word is reaped by the church when the church sustains the vision of the economy of salvation, and central to this vision is Christ's presence through the economy that the scriptures recount. If Irenaeus cannot show Christ's presence in the scriptures, he cannot praise Christ properly, which is the goal of this epideictic moment of his speech. Irenaeus realizes, of course, that Christ's presence is not always self-evident. That Irenaeus has to argue for a proper understanding of God's economy and of the role of prophecy in that economy means that the economy and prophecy have to be interpreted in the proper way. Irenaeus believes, of course, that if a person directs his energies in the right way, he will see the word about Christ throughout the Old Covenant. Yet Irenaeus also recognizes that "Christ is the 'hidden treasure in the field,' which in the Scriptures means the world."[65] This treasure, although hidden, is "revealed to all and explained by the cross of Christ." And once it is explained, God's economies become visible and "announce that the man who loves God in this way progresses so that he may see God and hear his word." To read the scriptures is to be "a perfect disciple."[66] Indeed, we might even say that such a person is the *homo vivens*, who is the glory of God. But one cannot be a perfect disciple on one's own. The believer needs the help of the church, which guards the faith, to read the scriptures properly.

Christ's cross reveals that Christ is hidden in the prophecies of the Old Covenant.[67] The cross shows the wisdom of God. This revelation, though, can only be understood within Christ's community,

---

65. For a thorough study on the interpretation of this passage, see David W. Jorgensen, *Treasure Hidden in a Field: Early Christian Reception of the Gospel of Matthew* (Berlin: de Gruyter, 2016).

66. "A Christianis vero cum legitur, thesaurus et absconsus in agro, cruce vero Christi revelatus [est] et explanatus, et ditans sensus hominum, et ostendens sapientium Dei, et eas quae sunt erga hominem dispositiones eius manifestans, et Christi regnum praeformans, et hareditatem sanctae Hierusalem praeevangelizans, et praenuntians quoniam in tantum homo diligens Deum proficiet, ut etiam videat Deum et audiat sermonem eius, et ex auditu loquelae eius in tantum glorificatibur, uti reliqui non possint intendere in faciem gloriae eius" (4.26.1).

67. For a discussion of the role that the cross plays in Irenaeus's work, see Daniel Wanke, *Das Kreuz Christi bei Irenaeus von Lyon* (Berlin: Walter de Gruyter, 2000).

the church. Yes, thanks to the cross, the *homo vivens* can see God and hear his Word, but he needs the teachers of the church to preserve the prophecy of the Old Covenant and help its members recognize Christ in that covenant.

Irenaeus began Book Three with a long discussion of the church and its teachers, in order to set the terms of the debate he was having with his opponents. In Book Four we find another discussion of teachers, but here it comes not in the *probatio* of Irenaeus's argument, but in the *refutatio*. This is significant. For Irenaeus, the work of interpretation falls to the elders of the community. Because he has already set the terms of his debate with his opponents, he can now refute those opponents. However, a central aspect of this refutation is that his interpretation is *his* only insofar as he is a member of the community that interprets this way. Irenaeus connects himself to a line of teachers whose interpretation stands in continuity with the Apostles. Thus Irenaeus's interpretation itself has a history just as the Word historically appears in the Old Covenant. By stressing this history, Irenaeus is offering a refutation of his opponents.

In fact, in 4.26–32, Irenaeus quotes a certain unnamed presbyter and offers that elder's interpretation of the relationship between the Old Covenant and the New.[68] This elder (who could be Polycarp) sustains the vision of the economy of salvation. In order to do this, he must tackle the strongest argument that Irenaeus's opponents make: namely, the sinful behavior found in the Old Covenant. Indeed, the immoral actions described in the Hebrew scriptures might lead one to

---

68. The role of the presbyter has been debated extensively in secondary literature on Irenaeus. See Loofs, *Theophilus von Antiochen Adversus Marcionem*; F. R. Montgomery Hitchcock, "Loofs' Theory of Theophilus Von Antioch as a Source of Irenaeus," *JTS* 38 (1937): 254–66, and "Loofs' Asiatic Source (I.Q.A.) and the Pseduo-Justin De Resurrectione," *Zeitschrift für die neutestamentliche Wissenschaft* 36, no. 1 (1937): 35–60. For a thorough account see Benoit, *Saint Irénée*, 21–22, and Bacq, *De l'ancienne à la nouvelle alliance*, 333–61. Charles Hill argues that Polycarp is the presbyter; see Hill, *From the Lost Teaching of Polycarp*. See also Jeffrey G. Sobosan, "Role of the Presbyter: An Investigation into the Adversus Haereses of Saint Irenaeus," *Scottish Journal of Theology* 27, no. 2 (1974): 129–46. I have already argued that 4.20 represents Irenaeus's "theological methodology" for Book Four; however, 4.26–32 is also a good candidate. Whereas 4.20 focuses on the *homo vivens* who sees himself in the economy of salvation, 4.26–32 focuses on the teacher who helps his students to see this.

believe that neither the Father nor the Son was present in the Old Covenant. Irenaeus addresses this issue by describing the sinful actions of David and Solomon. The scriptures include the sins of David and Solomon not to valorize their actions, but to show that in the economy of salvation Christ comes to forgive all sins. In this refutation, Irenaeus is showing why the Old Covenant is important. Indeed, Irenaeus is simply following Paul's precedent. In 1 Corinthians 10:1–12, Paul discusses Israel's sins as a warning to the community in Corinth. Thus, the sins recounted in the Old Covenant do not show an alien god; they show the economy of salvation.

The elder's teaching helps human beings recognize themselves in the vision offered in the scriptures. By recognizing themselves in the vision of the economy of salvation, they share in salvation. This story, though, must include the history of sin and the need for judgment. David, Irenaeus notes, writes in the Psalms that "The face of the Lord is over all who do evil, so that he might lose their memory from the earth."[69] Irenaeus tells us that the elder's interpretation of scripture exposes the "truly insensible ones who, because of those things that befell those who did not obey God, tried to introduce another Father."[70] Irenaeus's opponents reject the true God because they reject the very possibility of God's judgment, and in rejecting God's judgment, they reject that they themselves are judged. By carefully attending to the economy of God's salvation as it is recounted in scripture, the reader of scripture will come to recognize that God is a just judge. But such careful attention can only occur with the aid of the teacher in the community of faith, the church.

As we have seen again and again, Irenaeus focuses on the proper way to interpret scripture and to do this he must tackle specific scriptural passages. It is fitting, then, that his discussion of just judgment should turn on a scripture passage that deals with vision. When Irenaeus's opponents object to the idea that the god of the Old Covenant judges justly, they point to the hardening of Pharaoh's heart. Irenae-

---

69. "Vultus autem Domini super facientes mala, ut perdat de terra memoriam ipsorum" (4.28.1); see Ps 33:17.

70. "valde insensatos ostendebat presbyter eos qui, ex his quae acciderunt his qui olim Deo non obtemperabant, temptant alterum Patrem introducere" (4.28.1).

us draws on the presbyter's interpretation and turns to the words of Christ, the interpreter *par excellence*, to understand God's motives. Christ himself quotes Isaiah, who says the people's ears are blocked and their eyes are blind.[71] "One and the same God brings blindness to those who do not believe ... just as the sun ... presents fuller and greater illumination of the mind to those who believe and follow him than to those who are not able to contemplate the light because of some infirmity of the eyes."[72] And from Christ (quoting Isaiah), Irenaeus turns to Paul for support. In the second letter to the Thessalonians, speaking about the Antichrist, Paul writes, "God sent the work of error to them, so that they might believe mendaciously so that all who do not believe the truth will be judged, but they will not commit iniquity" (2 Thes 2:11–12). With these passages in mind Irenaeus can respond to his opponents, "If God knows those who will not believe, since he has foreknowledge of all things, he hands them over to infidelity and turns their face from him, leaving them in the shadows which they choose for themselves, what wonder is it if the Pharaoh will never believe with those who are with them when God hands them over to their own infidelity?"[73] Here we have an example of Irenaeus's general pattern of interpretation. He has taken a difficult text, used the clear words of Christ to form the basis of an interpretation of that text, and then shifted to a text from Paul that can explain the difficult text in light of Christ's own words. The text itself is the *probatio*, Christ's words, which themselves interpret the Old Covenant, are the *refutatio*, and Paul's words are the *recapitulatio* because they focus specifically on judgment. By drawing on the elder, Irenaeus implies that this method is not his invention.

71. See Mt 13:10–17. Christ's point here, Irenaeus implies, is that knowing the history of the people of Israel allows one to interpret his words correctly. His point is *not* that one needs secret knowledge to understand Christ's words.

72. "Unus enim et idem Dominus his quidem qui non credunt sed nullificant eum infert caecitatem, quemadmodum sol qui est creatura eius his qui propter aliquam infirmitatem oculorum non possunt contemplari lumen eius" (4.29.1).

73. "Si igitur et nunc quotquot scit non credituros Deus, cum sit omnium praecognitor, tradidit eos infidelitati eorum et avertit faciem ab hujusmodi, relinquens eos in tenebris quas ipsi sibi elegerunt, quid mirum si et tunc nunquam crediturum Pharaonem cum his qui cum eo erant tradidit eos suae infidelitati?" (4.29.2).

That is to say, Irenaeus recalls the elder's teaching because the elder has understood the role of the prophecy of the Old Covenant in the economy of salvation. Irenaeus refers to the elder for this focus on judgment to show how the story of the Pharaoh and the Egyptians continues to have relevance for Christians. The Egyptians ruled the ancient Israelites, and the Romans rule Irenaeus's contemporaries. Irenaeus interprets Christ's words about caring for the poor by saying:

By the remaining things of good works we are justified, just as we redeem our things from foreign hands. I say not as if the world is alien to God, but since we have accepted things given by others, just as the Jews accepted from the Egyptians who did not know God. Through these things we have set up in ourselves the tabernacle of God, since God inhabits those things that are made well.[74]

When Irenaeus says "we redeem our things from foreign hands," he may well be suggesting that just as the Israelites took spoils from the Egyptians, Christians can take useful things from the Romans. In this way, he again shows how his own community is connected with the communities found in the Old Covenant, and although he does not say it here, perhaps Irenaeus is offering a subtle defense of his own borrowing of tropes and methods from the rhetorical tradition.

The elder and Irenaeus can connect their church community with this history of the Israelites because they understand the events of the Old Covenant as types for the New Covenant. "The whole exodus from Egypt that happened to the people of God was a type and image of the exodus of the Church from the gentiles."[75] Then the true leader of the exodus, according to Irenaeus, was not Moses, but the Word himself. Christ is the key to typological exegesis because his interpretation of the Old Covenant shows that he was present in it. Christ un-

74. "Cum facis misericordiam, non sciat sinistra tua quid faciat dextera tua, et reliqua quaecumque benefacientes justificamur, velut de alienis nostra redimentes: de alienis autem ita dico, non quasi mundus alienus sit a Deo, sed quoniam hujusmodi dationes ab aliis accipientes habemus, similiter velut illi ab Aegyptiis qui non sciebant Deum, et per haec ipsa erigimus in nobismetipsis tabernaculum Dei: cum bene enim facientibus habitat Deus" (4.30.3). For an extended discussion of this passage, see Graeme W. Clarke, "Irenaeus Adv Haer 4 30 I," *Harvard Theological Review* 59, no. 1 (1966): 95–97.

75. "Universa enim quae ex Aegypto profectio fiebat populi a Deo typus et imago fuit profectionis Ecclesiae quae erat futura ex gentibus" (4.30.4).

locks the scriptures by showing which passages to understand literally
and which passages to understand metaphorically. This distinction, of
course, is carried on by the interpretation of the Apostles.

Earlier we saw how Irenaeus sees Christ's cross as the key to revealing the "treasure hidden in the field." For Irenaeus, remember,
Christ is the interpreter of scripture *par excellence*. And so to say that
the cross is the key to interpretation is to say that Christ's death and
resurrection showed that Christ's divinity safeguarded his interpretation. In Irenaeus's view, of course, he carries on the Apostolic tradition
of interpretation, which comes from Christ himself. The Apostolic
tradition of interpreting prophecy relies on typology. This typological
relationship is especially important when trying to interpret the actions of the patriarchs, which often appear to be sinful. The task of the
interpreter of scripture is not to judge the figures in the Old Covenant.
Judgment is reserved for God alone. Instead, the task of the interpreter
of scripture is "to seek the type, for nothing which is hateful that is
placed in the Scriptures is without signification."[76] Indeed, once the
relationship between the two covenants is established, one can see how
everything in the Old Covenant, interpreted in light of the death and
resurrection of Christ, is important.

Irenaeus began his discussion of the presbyter in 4.26 with the
presbyter's interpretation of Paul. He ends his discussion by returning
to Paul in 4.32. As we have seen, Paul is the site of one of the main
interpretative disagreements between Irenaeus and his opponents.
According to Irenaeus, Paul shows "there is no other God than the
one who formed us. Those who would say our world was made either
through angels or through another power or by another god do not
have stable thought."[77] Irenaeus shows how the biblical text bears this
out by linking Genesis 1, John 1, and the letter to the Ephesians. Anyone who "reads the Scriptures diligently among those who are elders

76. "De quibus autem Scripturae non increpant, sed simpliciter sunt posita, nos
non debere fieri accusatores, non enim sumus diligentiores Deo, neque super magistrum possumus esse, sed typum quaerere: nihil enim otiosum est eorum quaecumque
inaccusabilia posita sunt in Scripturis" (4.31.1).

77. "Nec enim esse alterum Deum praeter eum qui fecit et plasmavit nos, nec fir-
mitatem habere sermonem eorum qui dicunt aut per angelos, aut per aliam quamlibet
virtutem, au tab alio Deo factum esse hun mundum qui est secundum nos" (4.32.1).

in the Church" will understand that these passages are indeed linked. These elders have the teaching of the Apostles. And the Apostles, Irenaeus explains, "teach that there are two covenants for the two people," but there is "one and the same God, who ordered both for the use of men."[78] The New Covenant does not "obviate what was given in the first covenant, but it shapes those to whom it was given for their benefit in the service of God."[79] God offers the New Covenant "since man is not yet able to see the things that are of God through the appropriate vision."[80] As we have seen, when Irenaeus discusses vision, he does not mean a straightforward pictorial representation. Instead, he means a way of understanding the entire economy of salvation and one's place in it.

In 4.33, Irenaeus shows that the spiritual man Paul discusses in 1 Corinthians 2:15 is, in fact, the true interpreter of scripture, not a distinct class of human being.[81] Irenaeus also lists various teachers in this chapter, and he shows where they go wrong. The chapter could serve as a précis of the *Adversus Haereses* as a whole. In 4.34, Irenaeus turns his attention to Marcion. For Marcion, Christ's coming obviated the Law and the prophets. For Irenaeus Christ's coming fulfilled the Law and the prophets. "He brought every novelty in bringing himself."[82] Christ's coming "fulfilled all things. He accomplished the New Covenant that had been predicted in the Church all the way to the consummation of the law."[83] Irenaeus even quotes Paul's letter to the Romans to show that Paul believed justification by faith was predicted

78. "Apostoli enim omnes duo quidem Testamenta in duobus populis fuisse docuerunt, unum autem et eundem esse Deum, qui disposuerit utraque ad utilitatem hominum" (4.32.2).

79. "quoniam non otiose neque frustra aut ut obvenit datum est prius Testamentum, sed illos quidem quibus dabatur in servitutem Dei concurvans ad utilitatem eorum" (4.32.2).

80. "Quoniam nondum poterat homo per proprium visum videre quae sunt Dei" (4.32.2).

81. For an extended discussion of this chapter, see Scott D. Moringiello, "The Pneumatikos as Scriptural Interpreter: Irenaeus on 1 Cor. 2:15," *Studia Patristica* 65, no. 1 (2013): 105–18.

82. "cognoscite quoniam omnem novitatem attulit semetipsum afferens, qui fuerat annuntiatus" (4.34.1).

83. "Omnia enim ipse adimplevit veniens et adhuc implet in Ecclesia usque ad consummationem a lege praedictum novum Testamentum" (4.34.2); see Mt 5:17–18.

by the prophets.[84] As Irenaeus makes clear, there can only be such accord between the New Covenant and the Old because both came from one and the same God.

Marcion is the most important Christian teacher to deny that the two covenants come from one and the same God. Marcion is important rhetorically for Irenaeus because Marcion's error is clear to see. In a sense, refuting Marcion is a ground-clearing exercise to show how Christians ought to understand prophecy. When Irenaeus turns in 4.35 to the "disciples of Valentinus and the rest of the falsely-named Gnostics," the situation is slightly different. These teachers deny that the prophets could have known anything about Christ, because Christ was not part of the economy of salvation. Irenaeus's opponents hid their teachings even though they "have various thoughts about the same Scriptures."[85] Because Christ would return soon, there was an urgent need to understand scripture correctly so that human beings could be saved. Without the guidance that the faith offers, followers of the Apostolic teaching will not recognize that the prophecies of the scriptures are occurring before their eyes. This faith enables believers to recognize the manifestation of God in the Son in the last times. It enables the believers to see the vision of the economy offered in the scriptures.

Each follower of the Son is called to perform the task that Irenaeus has taken up. Irenaeus helps his audience read scripture correctly so they can understand how God works for their salvation. He appeals to their *ethos* and aims to delight them. If someone disregards some part of scripture, he is in danger of rejecting his own salvation. Instead, Irenaeus and those who adhere to Apostolic teaching "follow the teaching of the one and only true Lord and have his words as the rule of truth."[86] Christ's words are the rule of truth because he is the

---

84. Rom 3:21.

85. "Adversus eos rursum qui sunt a Valentino et reliquos falsi nominis Gnosticos, qui aliquando quidem a Summitate quaedam eorum quae sunt in Scripturis posita dicta" (4.35.1). It is interesting to note here that Irenaeus uses the word "gnostics." Usually, Irenaeus is careful to distinguish the various schools he attempts to refute. Here, though, he distinguishes the Valentinians from the Gnostics.

86. "Nos autem unum et solum verum Dominum doctorem sequentes et regulam veritatis habentes eius sermones" (4.35.4).

recapitulation of the rule. The rule of truth, which is grounded in the Father, Son, and Holy Spirit, provides the ultimate refutation of heresy because it provides a recapitulation of the story of scripture. This salvation is the vision of God that the *homo vivens* sees.

Recapitulatio, 4.36–41: Christ/Recapitulation

We now come to the final section of Book Four (4.36–41), which comprises the *recapitulatio*. These chapters, as we have come to expect, focus specifically on questions of salvation. More specifically, though, Irenaeus stresses in these chapters that the God who promises salvation through Jesus Christ is the same God who began the economy of salvation in the Old Covenant. It is important to note that Irenaeus addresses Jesus' parables here, at the end of Book Four. It is only after one has gotten the clear words of Christ straight and understood those words in the context of the economy of salvation that the parables can be put in their proper context, when what ought to be understood metaphorically is more clear. Irenaeus, then, interprets these parables in light of the entire economy of salvation. And this economy of salvation, as Irenaeus has made clear throughout his work and makes clear again in 4.36, is the economy of the one God. (Indeed, we can see 4.36 as the beginning of a new section precisely because Irenaeus starts with a discussion of the one God.) One such parable Irenaeus discusses is the parable of the wedding feast.[87] In this parable, Irenaeus explains, Christ shows "one King and Lord, the Father of all."[88] By bringing together parables from Matthew with prophecy from Jeremiah, Irenaeus argues that the God "who called us through the apostles" also called the prophets.[89] So again we see in this chapter how Irenaeus sets the terms for the discussion by linking the Gospels with the prophets. Jesus' parables cannot be understood without this connection.

87. Mt 22:1–14.
88. "Manifeste enim et per haec uerba sua ostendit Dominus Omnia, et quoniam unus rex et Dominus omnium Pater" (4.36.5).
89. "qui igitur nos per Apostolos undique vocavit Deus" (4.36.5). Irenaeus draws on Jer 7:25–28 and 42:15.

As we have seen again and again, the structure of Irenaeus's argument *is* his argument, and so it is important to note that he shifts his discussion here to prophecy. When one understands the role of prophecy correctly, the point is not to acquire some new knowledge for interpreting the scriptures. Instead, the point is to see how the prophecy of the Old Covenant leads to its completion in Christ. Part of this completion is the role that free will plays in the lives of figures in the Old Covenant. To understand any parable correctly—and to understand salvation correctly—human beings must be free.[90] Whether or not they follow the teaching that has been offered to them determines whether or nor God will save them. Those who rejected the good "rightly fall into the just judgment of God."[91] There are not good people or evil people by nature. Instead, "all are of the same nature, they are able to possess and do the good and they are able to hold back and not do it."[92] Some "are praised and receive just testimony of the choice and of perseverance." Others "accuse and receive appropriate damnation for throwing away what is just and good."[93]

The prophets are part of the long economy of human progression toward God. This progression has a sacramental context, and in turn this context helps make sense of prophecy. As Irenaeus continues his discussion of the human progression toward God, he points to the importance of the Eucharistic meal. God was able to give humans im-

90. Many scholars have discussed the role of free will in Irenaeus's thought, and this section is the *locus classicus* for that discussion. See M. F. Berrouard, "Servitude de la loi et liberté de l'évangile selon saint Irénée," *Lumière et vie* 61, no. 1 (1963): 41–60; Roger Berthouzoz, *Liberté et grâce suivant la théologie d'Irénée de Lyon: Le débat avec la gnose aux origines de la théologie chrétienne* (Paris: Cerf, 1980); Pierre Évieux, "Théologie de l'accoutumance chez saint Irénée," *Recherches de science religieuse* 55, no. 1 (1967): 5–54; Christina Manohar, "The Salvific Work of God Is a Pedagogic Process: Insights from St Irenaeus," *UBS Journal* 1, no. 1 (2003): 57–65; E. P. Meijering, "Irenaeus' Relation to Philosophy in the Light of His Concept of Free Will," in *Romanitas et Christianitas*, ed. W. Den Boer (Amsterdam: North-Holland, 1973), 221–32.

91. "Abjicientes igitur bonum et quasi respuentes, merito omnes in justum judicium incident Dei" (4.37.1).

92. "Sed quoniam omnes eiusdem sunt naturae, et potentes retinere et operari bonum, et potentes rursum amittere id et non facere" (4.37.2).

93. "alii quidem laudantur et dignum percipiunt testimonium electionis bonae et perseverantiae, alii vero accusantur et dignum percipiunt damnum eo quod justum et bonum reprobaverint" (4.37.2).

mortality from the beginning, Irenaeus tells us, "but man was unable to receive it."[94] Irenaeus says specifically that this is why "our Lord, in these last times, recapitulating all things to himself, came to us."[95] The Eucharistic bread and wine nourishes believers as they progress toward life with God. We should note here that for Irenaeus, the Eucharist literally is the bread of immortality. The bread of the Eucharist transforms the one who receives it, making him accustomed to living in the kingdom of God to come. Irenaeus's remarks on the church and the Eucharist, and more specifically on the church as constituted by the Eucharist, rhetorically recapitulate the themes that have concerned us in this chapter: the work of Christ, the connection between the Old and New Covenants, and the nature of God. They also point forward to Irenaeus's discussion of salvation.

Those who accept the bread of immortality remain obedient to God. Irenaeus knows that human beings are not always obedient to God. If they were, there would not be the examples in the Old Covenant that Irenaeus thinks are important for the vision of the economy. But human disobedience is not the end of the story. Irenaeus writes, "According to his love and power, he conquered the substance of his created nature, then after it was conquered, the mortal was absorbed by the immortal and the corruptible by the incorruptible and man came about according to the image and likeness of God, having accepted the knowledge of good and evil."[96] These words are a preview of Book Five, where Irenaeus will begin with a discussion of 1 Corinthians 15 and end the book by interpreting 1 Corinthians 15 in light of Genesis 1:26–28.

Throughout this final section of Book Four, Irenaeus links proph-

94. ὁ δὲ ἄνθρωπος ἀδύνατος λαβεῖν αὐτό (4.38.1). Robert F. Brown, "'On the Necessary Imperfection of Creation': Irenaeus' Adversus Haereses Iv, 38," *Scottish Journal of Theology* 28, no. 1 (1975): 7–25.

95. ὁ Κύριος ἡμῶν ἐπ᾽ ἐσχάτων τῶν καιρῶν ἀνακεφαλαιωσάμενος εἰς ἑαυτὸν τὰ πάντα ἦλθε πρὸς ἡμᾶς (4.38.1).

96. "Secundum autem dilectionem et virtutem vincet factae natura substantiam. Oportuerat autem primo naturam apparere, post deinde vinci, et absorbi mortale ab immortalitate et corruptibile ab incorruptibilitate [see 2 Cor 5:4, 1 Cor 15:53], et fieri hominem secundum imaginem et similtudinem Dei, agnotione accepta boni et mali [see Gn 3:5]" (4.38.4).

ecy to judgment. Indeed, you cannot have one without the other because both are part of God's economy of salvation. This offer of incorruptible bodies is only open to those who believe in Christ, and "God,
foreknowing all things, prepared appropriate homes" for those who
were obedient and those who were disobedient.[97] The choice, Irenaeus
stresses, belongs with his audience. At the end of Book Four, he has
shifted to a deliberative rhetoric where he employs *pathos*. Those who
turned away from the light did so out of their own free will. To flee
the eternal light of God is to miss the vision of the economy that God
offers in Christ. By focusing at the end of Book Four on what awaits
those who praise Christ and those who do not, Irenaeus prepares his
audience for the deliberative discourse that marks Book Five. In that
book, as we will see, Irenaeus offers two competing visions: of Christ
and of the Devil.

In the last two chapters of Book Four, Irenaeus stresses again that
one and the same God is found in the Old Covenant and the New.
To say this in terms that are familiar to us now, the prophets of the
Old Covenant prophesy the New Covenant. The structure of the scriptures is the structure of the faith, which is the structure of the *Adversus Haereses*. Jesus is the Son of the same God of judgment found in
the Old Covenant. This judgment is part of the economy of salvation.
"One and the same Lord demonstrated that the whole human race is
separated in judgment."[98] Jesus' words in Matthew 25 show there is
only one God. In this way, judgment is both a refutation of his opponents' teaching and a reminder of what awaits those who do not follow
the faith when reading the scriptures. God castigated the wicked in
the time of the Law and the prophets, and Jesus Christ, Son of the
same God, will return in judgment to do the same. The Lord, Irenaeus
reminds his readers, "had mercy on the man who disobeyed his commandment."[99] The Lord "recapitulated this enemy in himself. He was
man 'born of a woman' [Gal 4:4] and stepped on his head."[100] Once

---

97. "Deus autem omnia praesciens utrisque aptas praeparavit habitationes" (4.39.4).

98. "Sed quoniam unus et idem Dominus separari demonstravit in judicio omne
genus humanum" (4.40.2).

99. παραδεξάμενον τὴν παρακοὴν ἄνθρωπον ἐλέησε (4.40.3).

100. ὁ Κύριος εἰς ἑαυτὸν ἀνακεφαιώσατο «γενόμενος ἐκ γυναικὸς» ἄνθρωπος καὶ
πατήσαω αὐτοῦ τὴν κεφαλὴν.

again, we see Irenaeus argue that Christ is the beginning, the center, the end, and the fulfillment of the economy of salvation.

From this evocation of the Lord recapitulating Satan, Irenaeus ends Book Four with a discussion of judgment. God's judgment responds to human choice, not to human nature. There are two ways to understand sonship, Irenaeus explains. One is according to nature and the other according to obedience. "According to nature, which is according to creation, we are all sons of God because we are all made by him." Conversely, "according to obedience and teaching we are not all sons of God but only those who believe in him and do his will. Those who do not believe and do not do his will are sons and angels of the Devil."[101] Those who "do not obey" God "cease to be his sons." Thus, "they are not able to receive his inheritance."[102]

Irenaeus tells his readers that after Book Four, it is necessary for him "to add to this composition in the following book the teaching of Paul, and to examine his thought, and to explain the Apostle."[103] He will "dispose of the rest of the words of the Lord about the Father, which he taught not by parables but plainly, along with the explanation of the epistles of the blessed Apostle."[104] With the completion of Book Five, "we have trained ourselves and you in five books in the refutation of all the heretics."[105] Here we clearly see Irenaeus refer to the structure of his own argument. He recognizes that there are five books, and he is clear that he is moving from the clearer words of Jesus to the more difficult words of Paul.

101. "Secundum igitur naturam, quae est secundum conditionem, ut ita dicam, omnes Dei filii sumus, propter quod ab eo facti sumus. Secundum autem dictoaudientem et doctrinam, non omnes filii Dei sunt, sed qui credunt ei [see Jn 1:12] et faciunt uoluntatem eis [see Mt 12:50]. Qui autem non credunt et non faciunt eius uolentatem filii et angeli sunt diaboli, secundum id quod opera diaboli faciunt [see Jn 8:41, 44]" (4.41.3).

102. "apud Deum qui non obaudiunt ei abdicate ab eo desierunt filii eius esse. Unde nec hereditatem eius percipere possunt" (4.41.3).

103. "Necessarium est autem conscriptioni huic in sequenti post Domini semones subiungere Pauli quoque doctrinam, et examinare sententiam eius et Apostolorum exponere" (4.41.4).

104. "Reliquos igitur sermones Domini, quos quidem non per parabolas sed simpliciter ipsis dictionibus docuit de Patre, et expositionem epistolarum beati Apostoli in altero libro disponentes" (4.41.4).

105. "Nos ipsos et te ad contradictionem omnium haereticorum in quinque exercentes libris" (4.41.4).

We must remember that Irenaeus's goal in the *Adversus Haereses* is both to persuade his readers of the proper interpretation of scripture and to persuade those who have been misled by his opponents' interpretation of scripture. In this way, Irenaeus's deliberative rhetoric is essential. He reminds his audience of the examples in the Old Covenant when sinners "converted and did penance" and then "were able to be sons of God and to follow the inheritance of incorruptibility that was presented" by God.[106] Irenaeus wants to refute his opponents' errors so that they can be "converted to the truth and saved."[107] To borrow from the language of Ephesians with which we began, Irenaeus hopes to make known to his audience the mystery of God's will that he set forth in Christ as a plan for the fullness of time. As he ends Book Four, he signals that he will turn his attention to Paul in Book Five. Like the words in the letter to the Ephesians, Irenaeus will recapitulate his argument in Book Five. Like Irenaeus, we will do the same.

---

106. "cum autem conuerterentur et paenitentiam agerent et quiescerent a militia, filii poterant esse Dei et hereditatem consequi incorruptelae quae ab eo praestatur" (4.41.3).

107. "ad ueritatem conuerti et salvari" (4.41.4).

5 ✣ JUDGMENT

> This I declare, brothers: flesh and blood cannot inherit the king-
> dom of God, nor does corruption inherit incorruption.
>
> 1 CORINTHIANS 15:50

The living human being is the glory of God, and the vision of God is
the life of man. Thus in order to be the glory of God, human beings
must see the vision of God. I have argued throughout this book that
Irenaeus thinks one can apprehend the vision of God by recognizing the economy of salvation that scripture recounts. One has to look
to the past, to the history of the Law and the prophets, and realize that
one is part of that past. The church, as a community of believers and
interpreters of scripture, finds its roots in the Old Covenant. But the
church also looks forward. If Book Four focused on how the prophecies of the Old Covenant foretold the New Covenant, Book Five focuses on how the words of the New Covenant prophesy the eschaton.
And nowhere in the life of the church is the prophecy of the eschaton
more important than in the deaths of the martyrs.

The key scriptural passage here is 1 Corinthians 15:50, cited above.[1]
It would not be an exaggeration to say that this passage is *the* central
scriptural text under dispute between Irenaeus and his opponents.
This Pauline passage addresses both the nature of human beings and

---

1. Needless to say, Irenaeus's use of Paul has received a great deal of attention. In
some ways, every study of Irenaeus is a study of Irenaeus's interpretation of Paul. For two
specific studies, see Andrew J. Bandstra, "Paul and an Ancient Interpreter: A Comparison of the Teaching of Redemption in Paul and Irenaeus," *Calvin Theological Journal* 5,
no. 1 (1970): 58–61, and Benjamin C. Blackwell, "Paul and Irenaeus," in *Paul and the Second Century* (New York: T and T Clark, 2011).

the nature of salvation. For Irenaeus, the passage needs to be understood in light of Christ's works, teaching, and passion, as well as in the context of Paul's other writings. In his interpretation of 1 Corinthians 15:50, Irenaeus continues to be concerned about the role that the faith plays in any interpretation, but with this verse especially we see how the faith may *govern* the use of metaphorical language, without *determining* the specific metaphor. In one way, Irenaeus does interpret this verse metaphorically because he believes that Paul did not literally mean that human flesh plays no role in the kingdom of God. Instead, Irenaeus uses the faith to determine that in this case, Paul uses "flesh" metaphorically to mean "sin." The task of this chapter will be to spell out how Irenaeus uses the faith to distinguish what ought to be read literally from what ought to be read metaphorically in the words of Paul in his letters, of Christ in the Gospels, and of John in the Book of Revelation. In this way, the faith helps the reader of scripture see what awaits him in the eschaton. For Irenaeus, as we will see repeatedly, any discussion of the eschaton is also a discussion of judgment. Irenaeus's exegesis helps his readers judge which interpretations—which rule— they want to follow to understand the scriptures.

We can divide Irenaeus's discussion in Book Five into three major parts.[2] These parts mirror the three major moments of the faith. In 5.1–14, he focuses on an exegesis of Paul that proves the resurrection of the flesh. These chapters demonstrate the power of God the Father. In 5.15–24, he shows how the unity of God the creator and God the Father of Jesus Christ is shown in the life of Christ. In these chapters Irenaeus shows the unity of the God of the Old and New Covenants by explaining how Christ interprets the words of the prophets in his life and teaching. In 5.25–36, he shows how the unity of God the creator and God the Father of Jesus Christ is portrayed through an exegesis of the scriptures concerning the end times.[3] These latter chapters, then,

2. Here I follow the editors of the SC edition. I should note, though, that in his analysis of the book, Overbeck divides Book Five in the following way: (a) 1–14, (b) 15–20, (c) 21–30, and (d) 31–35 (Overbeck, *Menschwerdung*). See also Antonio Orbé, *Teología de San Ireneo, Comentario al libro 5 del Adversus Haereses*, Biblioteca De Autores Cristianos (Madrid: Editorial Católica, 1985).

3. I have learned much from Rolf Noormann, *Irenäus als Paulusinterpret: zur Rezeption und Wirkung der paulinischen und deuteropaulinischen Briefe im Werk des Irenäus*

focus on Christ's work of recapitulation. In summary, 5.1–14 serve as the *probatio* of the case Irenaeus is trying to make, 5.15–24 serve as the *refutatio* that backs up that case, and 5.25–36 serve as the *recapitulatio* of the book and the peroration of the *Adversus Haereses* as a whole. In 5.1–14, Irenaeus's discourse is largely forensic and relies on *logos* as he prosecutes a false understanding of Paul. In 5.15–24, Irenaeus's discourse shifts to the epideictic because he is praising the economy of salvation. Here he relies on *ethos*, while in 5.25–36, Irenaeus's discourse is deliberative, as he relies on *pathos* there. He wants to present as clearly as he can the choice that faces a reader of scripture so that the reader will choose to accept the salvation that God offers in Christ. As we will see, the saved human being is the *homo vivens*, who partakes in the vision of God. As with each of the previous four books, we find in Book Five a section that we can describe as an example of Irenaeus's theological method. In 5.21–24, Irenaeus offers an interpretation of Christ's temptation by the Devil. These chapters serve as the fifth theological excursus of the *Adversus Haereses*. Irenaeus understands this temptation as an argument about scriptural interpretation. In these chapters, Irenaeus recapitulates his arguments found throughout the *Adversus Haereses*, and he casts himself in the role of Christ, with his opponents in the role of Satan. Throughout Book Five, Irenaeus focuses his attention on the future judgment that awaits all people.

In the previous chapter, I discussed how Book Four uses Christ's interpretation to set the rule for interpreting the past, specifically the relationship between the Old Covenant and the New. In this chapter we shall observe how Irenaeus uses the interpretation of Paul and Christ to set the rule for interpreting the future, specifically the relationship between the text of the scriptures, in both the Old and the New Covenants, and the eschaton. Just as his opponents misunderstand the role of the Old Covenant, they misunderstand the eschaton and Christ's salvific work. We could even say that his opponents misunderstand this relationship precisely because they lack the proper rule to interpret the Old Covenant in terms of the New. As a result,

---

Von Lyon (Tubingen: Paul Siebeck, 1994); Mutschler, *Irenäus als johanneischer Theologe*; and Bingham, *Irenaeus' Use of Matthew's Gospel*. But my basic argument has been that Irenaeus's genius is the way in which he blends these voices in his own theological work.

they cannot interpret the relationship between the New Covenant and the eschaton.

It is fitting, of course, that Irenaeus sums up his own discourse with an interpretation of the end times. I began the previous chapter with a brief discussion of Ephesians 1:8–10 and the role that Christ plays in summing up God's *oikonomia*. The specific word for "summing up" there is *anakephalaiosis*, which has a rhetorical valence. According to Quintilian, the *anakephalaiosis* or *recapitulatio* is the final moment in a forensic speech. He specifically says that in this part of the speech, the rhetor should put the issues in front of the eyes of the audience.[4] Irenaeus does exactly this.[5] Following Aristotle, Irenaeus must dispose his audience favorably to himself, he must praise and deprecate, he must excite the emotions of the audience, and he must recapitulate the issues.[6] The emotional appeal is particularly important in the recapitulation. As Quintilian notes, "proofs may lead judges to *think* our cause is the better one, but it is our emotional appeals that make them also *want* it to be so; and what they want they also believe."[7] Here we begin to see a distinction between the primarily epideictic discourse found in Books Three and Four and the deliberative discourse found in Book Five. The goal of epideictic discourse is to praise or blame, but the goal of deliberative discourse is a decision by the audience.[8] By employing emotional appeals, the orator leads

4. Quintilian, *The Orator's Education* 6.1.1. Aristotle specifically uses the word sight in his discussion of the *recapitulatio*. Aristotle, *Rhetoric* 1362a.

5. Of course, we have seen recapitulations throughout the *Adversus Haereses*, and this too fits with Quintilian's proscription (*The Orator's Education* 6.1.8). Aristotle lists four parts that the epilogue should have. Aristotle, *Rhetoric* 1419b.

6. Kennedy, *The Art of Persuasion in Greece*, 122.

7. "Probationes enim efficiant sane ut causam nostram meliorem esse iudices putent, adfectus praestand ut etiam veliat; sed id quod volunt credunt quoque" (Quintilian, *The Orator's Education* 6.2.5). Dionysius of Helicarnassus says this specifically in *Critical Essays, Volume I: Ancient Orators. Lysias. Isocrates. Isaeus. Demosthenes. Thucydides*, trans. Stephen Usher (Cambridge, Mass.: Harvard University Press, 1974), Demosthenes 13. See Michael de Brauw, "The Parts of the Speech," in *A Companion to Greek Rhetoric* (ed. Worthington), 197. Kennedy notes, "Emotional appeal in oratory is most clearly developed in the peroration. After the judges' sympathy has been secured by exhibition of the good character of the speaker, the facts are narrated for their instruction and the proof advanced for their conviction" (*The Art of Persuasion in Greece*, 93).

8. For a good introduction to deliberative discourse, which is also called symbol-

his audience toward that decision. *Pathos* has as much of a role to play in Irenaeus's argument as *ethos* and *logos*.

The different types of discourse also relate to different temporalities. Forensic rhetoric looks to the past and epideictic to the present. According to Aristotle, deliberative rhetoric looks to the future "for the speaker, whether he exhorts or dissuades, always advises about things to come."[9] As we will see, Irenaeus focuses on the things to come in Book Five. More precisely, he focuses on two people who will come at the end of time: the Antichrist and Christ. At that point the dead will rise, participate fully in God's kingdom, and be alive through the Spirit. Irenaeus urges his audience to follow the Apostolic teaching, which comes from Christ, instead of his opponents' teaching, which comes from the Devil.

Besides the precedent in the Greco-Roman rhetorical tradition, Irenaeus also has precedent from the *corpus paulinum* for the uses of *anakephalaiosis*. We find the word or its related verbal form twice in the New Testament, once in explicit reference to Christ and once in reference to Christ's commandments and the Law. In the letter to the Romans, Paul writes, "The commandments 'You shall not commit adultery, you shall not murder, you shall not steal, you shall not covet' and whatever other commandment there may be are summed up [*anakephalaioûtai*] in this: 'You shall love your neighbor as yourself.'"[10] Jesus Christ who, as the Word of God, had been present when Moses received the commandments, recapitulates these commandments when he summarizes them as "love your neighbor as yourself."[11] The quotation from Paul's letter to the Romans points to Christ's ethical teaching, but the other use of *anakephalaiosis* points to Christ's role in the economy of salvation. In Book Five, Irenaeus concerns himself with more than Christ's teaching. Irenaeus wants to

---

eutic discourse, see Stephen Usher, "Sumbouleutic Oratory," in *A Companion to Greek Rhetoric* (ed. Worthington), 220–35.

9. μὲν συμβουλέυοντι ὁ μέλλων (περὶ γὰρ τῶν ἐσόμενων συμβουλεύει ἢ προτρέπων ἢ ἀποτρέπων) (Aristotle, *Rhetoric* 1358b).

10. τὸ γὰρ οὐ μοιχεύσεις, οὐ φονεύσεις, οὐ κλέψεις, οὐκ ἐπιθυμήσεις, καὶ εἴ τις ἑτέρα ἐντολή, ἐν τῶι λόγωι τούτωι ανακεφαλαιοῦται ἐν τῶι αγαπήσεις τὸν πλησίον σου ὡς σεαυτόν (Rom 13:9).

11. See Mt 5:43, 19:19, 23:39; Mk 12:31; Lk 10:27.

rouse his audience to recognize the eschatological vision that the Apostolic tradition provides. This vision centers on the *homo vivens*, the living human being who is the glory of God. This *homo vivens*, as we saw in the previous chapter, can participate in God's glory because he understands himself in light of the economy of salvation. The life of Christ and the work of the Holy Spirit effect the salvation of the whole human person, flesh as well as soul, and this salvation enables human beings to participate fully in the life of God.

Before human beings can come to the vision of God that is offered at the eschaton, they must attend to the appearances that Irenaeus discusses throughout Book Five. Here, Irenaeus focuses his attention not on his opponents' teaching, nor on the Law and prophecy of the Old Covenant as he did in Book Four, but on Jesus' teaching, especially in the parables, and in the Apostolic letters, especially the *corpus paulinum*. This is particularly appropriate for the *recapitulatio*, where Irenaeus discusses Christ, who himself is the *anakephalaiosis* of God's *oikonomia*. The purpose of Book Five is the same as that of the other four books. Irenaeus will "try to present proofs from the rest of the words of our Lord's teaching and from the Letters of the Apostles." He wants to "strengthen the minds of the neophytes, that they may guard the faith secure." And so, by reading this, the reader "will contradict [his opponents] legitimately" and "reject their thoughts just like dung by means of heavenly faith, following the only firm and true teacher, the Word of God Jesus Christ our Lord."[12] The Word of God teaches what needs to be known for salvation. Irenaeus, in his interpretation of Christ's words and deeds, continues the work of Christ. Irenaeus's interpretation and his use of persuasion must be done with love, for Christ "through his great love made us as we are, so that he may perfect us to be what he is."[13] In order to persuade his audience of the truth of his interpretation, Irenaeus must focus their gaze on the future judgment that awaits them all.

12. "sic enim et legitime eis contradices et de praeparato accipies adversus eos contradictiones, illorum quidem sententias per caelestem fidem velut stercora abjiciens, solum autem firmum et verum magistrum sequens, Verbum Dei, Jesum Christum Dominum nostrum" (5.P.1).

13. "qui propter immensam suam dilectionem factus est quod sumus nos, uti nos perficeret esse quod est ipse" (5.P.1).

Probatio, 5.1–14: God

The faith, as Irenaeus presents it in Book One, begins with a discussion of God. Irenaeus also begins Book Five with a discussion of God, but here with a focus appropriate to his goal of understanding God's future judgment. In 5.1–14, Irenaeus focuses his attention on Paul's argument about the resurrection of the flesh. Is God powerful enough to raise powerless human flesh as a part of human salvation? According to Irenaeus, to understand Paul's words one must remember that Jesus is the teacher of scripture *par excellence.* And to to be reminded that Jesus is the proper teacher of scripture, one must recognize that Christ comes to the church in the breaking of the bread. Irenaeus's meditation on the Eucharist in 5.1–7 sets the context for any proper interpretation of the scriptures. That is to say, in order to understand what Paul says about the resurrection of the flesh, one must first understand how Christ's flesh is present in the Eucharist. Like the faith, the Eucharist puts the interpretation of scripture in its proper context. For Irenaeus, the Eucharist sets the terms of debate for any discussion of scripture.

The crux of Irenaeus's argument is simple: he offers the same interpretation of the scriptures as Jesus himself offers.[14] And this is the same interpretation that Christ has handed down to the Apostles. We have seen already that Irenaeus begins with what is more clear and then moves to what is less clear. To begin with Christ as teacher is to begin with how Christ himself interprets the scriptures, how he interprets the Law and the prophets. When Christ interprets the scriptures, he begins with the most clear statement of when the text of scripture ought to be taken literally and when it ought to be taken metaphorically. We can also understand Irenaeus's focus on the Son as an interpreter in light of the rhetor as an interpreter of texts. Like the rhetor's audience, Christ's followers perceive his voice and are moved by what he says. Christ's teaching goes beyond rhetorical categories, though. For example, unlike a political assembly contemplating a course of action, the followers of Christ "are made new" by "him who has the gift of incorruptibility."[15] Like Hellenistic rhetors, Christ directs his

---

14. I shall return to this in my treatment of 5.21–24.

15. "a perfecto et eo qui est ante omnem conditionem augmentum accipientes qui

listeners toward a certain course of action. Unlike Hellenistic rhetors, Christ makes his followers new and endows them with incorruptibility. In this incorruptibility, human beings "are formed according to his likeness, so that we, who do not yet exist, are predestined according to the foreknowledge of the Father."[16] Irenaeus wants his audience to know that even the future is within God's economy of salvation. Like a good rhetor, Christ offers his teaching *persuasively*. Even though he is the Word of God, Jesus Christ himself needs to use persuasion to convince his audience, because his audience is made up of human beings who were made free to choose between good and evil. In this recapitulation, Irenaeus hopes to rouse the audience to choose the teaching of the Apostles regarding scripture and the person of Christ. He believes that the teaching of the Apostles will enable the reader of scripture to understand not only the history of God's promise of salvation but the future salvation and judgment itself.

For Irenaeus, the arrival of Christ is not some distant future event. Christ is with the church in and through the Eucharist. Because Jesus is present in the Eucharist, it offers its own interpretative lens to understand scripture. It does so because it is *literally* the body and blood of Christ. "When the mixed chalice and broken bread call down the word of God and becomes the Eucharist and the body of Christ, the substance of our flesh is strengthened and affirmed."[17] And if this is the case, as Irenaeus clearly believes it is, he asks, "why do they say the flesh is incapable of the gifts of God, which is eternal life, which is the nourishment of the body and blood of the Lord and his members?"[18] The Eucharist nourishes every part of the human being. The nourish-

---

nunc nuper facti sumus, a solo optimo et bono et ab eo qui habet donationem incorruptibilitatis" (5.1.1). The question of incorruptibility in Irenaeus is ably addressed in de Andia, who notes that the access to glory is gradual, but the entire economy moves toward human salvation (*Homo Vivens*, 139).

16. "in eam quae est ad eum similitudinem facti, praedestinati quidem ut essemus qui nondum eramus secundum praescientiam Patris" (5.1.1).

17. Ὁπότε οὖν καὶ τὸ κεκραμένον ποτήριον καὶ ὁ γεγονὼς ἄρτος ἐπιδέχεταιτὸν λόγον τοῦ Θεοῦ καὶ γίνεται εὐχαριστία καὶ σῶμα Χριστοῦ, ἐκ τούτων τε αὔξει καὶ συνέστηκεν ἡ τῆς σαρκὸς ἡμῶν ὑπόστασις (5.2.3).

18. πῶς δεκτικὴν μὴ εἶναι τὴν σάρκα λέγουσι τῆς δωρεᾶς τοῦ Θεοῦ, ἥτις ἐστὶ ζωὴ αἰώνιος, τὴν ἀπὸ τοῦ σώματος καὶ αἵματος τοῦ Κυρίου τρεφομένην καὶ μέλος αὐτοῦ ὑπάρχουσαν (5.2.3).

ment one receives in the Eucharist empowers the bodies of believers to rise again. "The Word of God gives resurrection … for the glory of God the Father, who encircles immortality to the moral and gives incorruptibility to the corruptible."[19] We might go so far as to say here that Irenaeus thinks God raises the dead to confound his opponents! The Eucharist and the network of scriptural texts governed by the faith reinforce each other. Without either the Eucharist or the faith, there can be no proper interpretation of scripture. It is essential that Irenaeus establish this at the beginning of Book Five, because the difference between how he and his opponents understand the Eucharist play into their respective interpretations of Paul.

Both Irenaeus and his opponents agree that the flesh is weak. For his opponents, this weakness is proof that the flesh is incapable of incorruptibility. For Irenaeus, who believes he is following Paul here, the weakness is a site for the manifestation of the power of God. The workings of the human body reveal the glory of God. As he draws contrasts between his and his opponents' exegesis, Irenaeus offers his audience a choice between an interpretative technique that views the body as a hindrance to salvation and one that views the body as a manifestation of God's power. Irenaeus's point is clear: by denying the Father's power to make weak things strong, his opponents weaken the Father himself. In their quest to protect God's strength, they wind up undermining it, and if they undermine God's strength, they also undermine his ability to save them.

Irenaeus believes that Paul's writings show the power of God. There is no better display of God's power, according to Irenaeus, than God's concern for—and indeed nourishment of—frail human bodies. Irenaeus creates a narrative out of a range of scriptural passages from both the Old and New Covenants that show God caring for the just.[20] Even though Irenaeus admits that such a concern for human bodies

19. τοῦ Λόγου τοῦ Θεοῦ τὴν ἔγερσιν αὐτοῖς χαριζομένου εἰς δόξαν Θεοῦ. καὶ Πατρός, ὃς ὄντως τῷ θνητῷ τὴν ἀθανασίαν περιποιεῖ καὶ τῷ φθαρτῷ τὴν ἀφθαρσίαν προσχαρίζεται (5.2.3).

20. These include verses from Psalms, Genesis, Wisdom, Hebrews, 2 Kings, and 2 Corinthians. Irenaeus does not offer direct quotations here, but rather allusions to texts in the Old and New Covenants.

seems impossible, he reminds his readers that things that are impossible for man are possible for God.[21] Just as in Book One, where Irenaeus began his exposition of Ptolemy's teaching to show how he ended up limiting the power of God, Irenaeus returns to this key theme in Book Five. When Paul is interpreted properly, his letters show that God is so powerful that he can raise frail human bodies from the dead and make them worthy of the kingdom of heaven. In this way, God does not only care for those bodies now, but he will also care for them at the resurrection of the dead.

Irenaeus discusses the nature of human beings in his *recapitulatio* in Book Five because the entire *Adversus Haereses* lays out and refutes his opponents' teaching on human salvation. A human being "is made according to the image of God" "through the hands of the Father, that is through the Son and Spirit."[22] The human being is made perfect when the soul assumes the Spirit of the Father.[23] For Irenaeus the soul or spirit is not the whole of the human being. "For if someone takes away the substance of the flesh, that is of the formation and understands it only as naked spirit, then this is not a spiritual man but the spirit of man or the spirit of God."[24]

Of course, what Paul means by "spiritual man" is exactly what is at issue between Irenaeus and his opponents. After all, the argument about the faith is an argument over the proper interpretation of the scriptural text. He argues that the proper interpretation of Paul's use of the term "spiritual man" in 1 Corinthians 2:15 and 3:1 includes the body. For example, Irenaeus argues that when Paul describes the body as a temple (1 Cor 3:16–17), "most clearly he was saying that the body

---

21. 5.5.2 (see Lk 18:27).

22. "Per manus enim Patris, hoc est per Filium et Spiritum, fit homo secundum similitudinem Dei, sed non pars hominis" (5.6.1). D. Jeffrey Bingham, "Himself within Himself: The Father and His Hands in Early Christianity." *Southwestern Journal of Theology* 47, no. 2 (2005): 137–51. See also Jean Mambrino, "'Les deux main de Dieu' dans l'oeuvre de s. Irénée," *Nouvelle revue théologique* 79 (1957): 355–70.

23. "perfectus autem homo commixtio et adunitio est animae assumentis Spiritum Patris et admixtae ei carni quae est plasmata secundum imaginem Dei" (5.6.1).

24. "Si enim substantiam tollat aliquis carnis, id est plasmatic, et nude ipsum solum spiritum intellegat, iam non spiritalis homo est quod est tale, sed spiritus hominis aut Spiritus Dei" (5.6.1).

is a temple in which the Spirit dwells."[25] Paul also says that human beings are members of the body of Christ. Only when the faith governs the reading of scripture can one see that the term "spiritual man" is not to be read literally as some type of ghost, but instead to be read metaphorically as a man in whose body the Spirit dwells. Ultimately, though, this discussion has less to do with the constitution of human beings and more to do with the power of God.

The faith helps the reader of scripture to see that Paul's use of the term "spiritual man" is metaphorical, not literal. The faith also helps the reader of scripture to see that Christ's death and resurrection in the flesh is literal, and not metaphorical. Eschatological bodies remain carnal, but they are infused with the Spirit "so that they may always have permanent life through the Spirit."[26] At that time, "our face will see the face of God and will rejoice with indescribable joy, just as when he sees his own joy."[27] Irenaeus's interpretation—learned from the Apostles—helps his readers to see the vision that the scriptures provide and prepares them for the time when they will see God face to face.

Human beings encounter God while they are alive in this life as their human bodies. To say this is to interpret Paul in a particular way. Paul's writings can confound the most careful readers because the distinction between literal and metaphorical language is so difficult to parse. Understanding the full extent of God's power is always a challenge, and nowhere is this distinction more important than in Paul's use of the word "flesh." The "perfect man," composed of body and soul, participates in the Spirit of God. "We receive some part from his Spirit for the purpose of perfection and preparation for incorruptibility. Little by little we become accustomed to receive and bear God."[28] Ire-

25. "Manifeste corpus templum dicens in quo habitat Spiritus" (5.6.2).
26. "uti per Spiritum semper permanentem habeant vitam" (5.7.2). For an analysis of Ireaneus's understanding of participation in the Spirit, see Julie Canlis, "Being Made Human: The Significance of Creation for Irenaeus' Doctrine of Participation," *Scottish Journal of Theology* 58, no. 4 (2005): 434–54.
27. "Facies enim nostra videbit faciem Dei, et gaudebit gaudio inenarrabili, videlicet cum suum videat gaudium" (5.7.2).
28. "Nunc autem partem aliquam a Spiritu eius sumimus ad perfectionem et praeparationem incorruptelae, paulatim assuescentes capere et portare Deum" (5.8.1).

naeus has to justify this position through an appeal to scripture, and
he recognizes that a reading of some scriptural passages would not
permit this. For example, when confronted with the passage, "But you
are not in the flesh; on the contrary, you are in the spirit, if only the
Spirit of God dwells in you. Whoever does not have the Spirit of Christ
does not belong to him" (Rom 8:9), Irenaeus comments, "This comes
about not according to the rejection of the flesh but according to the
communion of the Spirit."[29] In a further contrast with his opponents,
Irenaeus writes, "incorporeal spirits are not spiritual men, but our substance, that is, the union of flesh and soul, assuming the Spirit of God,
completes man as spiritual."[30] Not only does Paul stress that human
beings are bodies but he also stresses that their bodies need to become
accustomed to God. This long accommodation is itself the economy of
salvation whose end is the salvation of human flesh and blood.

Irenaeus counters his opponents' exegesis of 1 Corinthians 15:50 by
placing the verse in the context of what Paul writes in the rest of the
epistle as well as in other letters and the rest of scripture. He discusses
this verse in Book Five because his argument has built to a discussion
of human salvation in light of the weakness of the human flesh. We
have seen many times how Irenaeus interprets the scriptures to argue
that human beings are made up of body, soul, and spirit. But because
he bases this interpretation in part on Paul, Irenaeus must account for
the fact that Paul recognizes the weakness of human flesh. According
to Irenaeus, Paul "says without the heavenly Spirit we have lived in the
old age of the flesh, not obeying God, thus we now accept the Spirit
[and] 'we will walk in the newness of life,' obeying God."[31] In Irenaeus's words, "if it is necessary to tell the truth the flesh does not inherit

29. "Si ergo pignus hoc habitans in nobis jam spiritales efficit et absorbetur mortale
ab immortalitate Vos enim, ait, non estis in carne sed in Spiritu, siquidem Spiritus Dei
habitat in vobis, hoc autem non secundum jacturam carnis sed secundum communionem Spiritus fit" (5.8.2).

30. "quoniam Spiritus Dei habitat in ipsis: incorporales enim spiritus non erunt
homines spiritales, sed substantia nostra, hoc est animae et carnis adunatio, assumens
Spiritum Dei spiritalem hominem perficit" (5.8.2).

31. "Sicut igitur, ait, sine Spiritu caelesti conversati sumus aliquando in vetustate
carnis, non obaudientes Deo, sic nunc accipientes Spiritum in novitate vitae ambulemus,
obaudientes Deo [see Rom 6:4]" (5.9.3).

but is inherited."[32] The flesh "is not able to possess the kingdom of God as an inheritance, but it is able to be possessed in the kingdom as an inheritance by the Spirit."[33] God is the one who can raise the flesh of the dead. God does this because human beings—flesh and blood, body and soul—are part of God's economy of creation and salvation that Christ, who himself was the Word made flesh, recapitulates.

Commenting on 1 Corinthians 15:50, Irenaeus clarifies his view of what the perfect human being is. "The perfect man consists in flesh, soul, and spirit. One of these saves and forms, this is the Spirit, the other is saved and formed, that is the flesh, and the third, which is between the two, that is the soul, which following the spirit is lifted up by it."[34] A proper interpretation of scripture shows that the Spirit of God offers life. It is the Spirit of God who lives, and human beings live by participating in the Spirit.[35] To be alive is to possess the Spirit of God, and those who possess the Spirit of God inherit the kingdom of God. Those who wander from the faith of the Apostles will not inherit the kingdom.

As I have noted, in Book Five Irenaeus looks to the future as well as to the past. He can do this because he believes the scriptures that he interprets recount the economy of salvation. By attending to the economy of salvation, Irenaeus stresses that humans become transformed into spiritual men and women because they can progress in faith. In order to be a human being, one must possess both body and soul, and to be a complete human being, one must also participate in the Spirit of God. In the same way, the "man who does not assume the engrafting of the Spirit through faith will remain as he was, flesh and blood, not able to possess the kingdom of God as an inheritance."[36] Therefore,

32. Εἰ γὰρ δεῖ τἀληθὲς εἰπεῖν, οὐ κληρονομεῖ ἀλλὰ κληρονομεῖται ἡ σάρξ (5.9.4).

33. ἡ σὰρξ καθ᾽ ἑαυτὴν βασιλείαν Θεοῦ κληρονομῆσαι οὐ δύναται, κληρονομηθῆναι δὲ εἰς τὴν βασιλείαν τοῦ Θεοῦ δύναται (5.9.4).

34. "perfectus homo constat, carne, anima et spiritu, et altero quidem salvante et figurante, qui est Spiritus, altero quod salvatur et formatur, quod est caro, altero quod inter haec est duo, quod est anima: quae aliquando quidem subsequens Spiritum, elevatur ab eo" (5.9.1).

35. 5.9.4.

36. "sic et homo non assumens per fidem Spiritus insertionem perseverat hoc esse quod erat ante, caro et sanguis, regnum Dei hereditate possidere non potens" (5.10.2).

when Paul writes, "Flesh and blood are not able to possess the kingdom of God" (1 Cor 15:50) and "Those who are in the flesh are not able to please God" (Rom 8:8), he does not advocate escaping the body as a means of salvation.[37] God's creation is not a hindrance to salvation. Instead, the hindrance is the perverted desires of human beings who have been seduced by temptation. God's work of persuasion through Christ corrects those carnal desires. In the same way, Irenaeus's work of persuasion seeks to correct those Christians who have been seduced by his opponents' teaching. This seduction consists in misconstruing the distinction between literal and metaphorical language.

Irenaeus spends so much time discussing the future because by doing so, he can highlight the importance of understanding the scriptures correctly. And understanding the scriptures correctly means understanding God's identity and God's power. Being able to distinguish between which passages to understand metaphorically and which passages to understand literally is important because human salvation is at stake. For example, when Paul proclaims in his first letter to the Corinthians that through Christ human beings are cleansed, Irenaeus makes clear, "We have cleansed not the substance of our body nor the image of the formation, but the earlier life of vanity." That is, human beings progress from an earlier life of vanity to a new life in the Spirit. "Therefore," Irenaeus continues, "we are given life in these same members, working those things which are of the Spirit."[38]

Human beings have the ability to choose which interpretation of Paul they want to follow: one that stresses the power of God to raise human flesh or one that limits God's power because it says human flesh cannot be saved. If they do not wander they will progress from having the breath of life, which all have by virtue of living, to partic-

37. As Olson writes, "Paul was really using the phrase 'flesh and blood' to refer to the wicked who will not inherit the kingdom because of their evil works of the flesh" (*Irenaeus, the Valentinian Gnostics, and the Kingdom of God*, 14). See also Godehard Joppich, *Salus Carnis: Eine Untersuchung in der Theologie des hl. Irenäus Von Lyon* (Münsterschwarzach: Vier-Türme-Verlag, 1965), 27–38.

38. "Abluti autem sumus non substantiam corporis neque imaginem plasmatis, sed pristinam vanitatis conversationem. In quibus igitur periebamus membris, operantes ea quae sunt corruptelae, in iisdem ipsis vivificamur, operantes ea quae sunt Spiritus" (5.11.2).

ipating in the Spirit of God. The breath of life "completes the psychic man" and the Spirit of God "completes the spiritual man."[39] Irenaeus then comments, "the breath is given commonly to all the people on earth. The Spirit tramples in its own way those with earthly desires."[40] The progression between the breath of life and the Spirit of God is the Pauline progression between Adam and Christ. Thanks to Christ one can assume the "life-giving Spirit" and "find life." Christ offers a cure for the corruptible flesh of human beings.[41] Christ is the key to salvation, but this salvation can only be accepted if one accepts the interpretation of scripture that Christ, through the Apostles, has offered.

Whenever Irenaeus brings an eschatological lens to his interpretation, he draws contrasts between his exegesis and that of his opponents. Nowhere is the eschatological focus of the Gospels more clear than in episodes regarding how the dead are raised. If Paul only meant that bodies metaphorically rise, then the literal resurrections found in the Gospels would not make sense. Christ, of course, is not the only person in the New Testament to rise from the dead. Irenaeus points to the dead daughter of the high priest, the son of the widow, and Lazarus, and he asks his opponents, "in what bodies did they rise?" "Clearly," Irenaeus answers, "in the same ones in which they died, for it was not in the same ones then it was not the same people who rose."[42] "Therefore," he continues, "just as those who were cured were

---

39. Ἕτερόν ἐστι πνοὴ ζωῆς ἡ καὶ ψυχικὸν ἀπεργαζομένη τὸν ἄνθρωπον, καὶ ἕτερον Πνεῦμα ζωοποιοῦν τὸ καὶ πνευματικὸν αὐτὸν ἀποτελοῦν (5.12.2). Here Irenaeus is building on themes found in 1 Cor 14:45–49.

40. Καὶ διὰ τοῦτο Ἡσαΐας φησίν· «Οὕτω λέγει Κύριος ὁ ποιήσας τὸν οὐρανὸν καὶ στερεώσας αὐτόν, ὁ πήξας τὴν γῆν καὶ τὰ ἐν αὐτῇ, καὶ διδοὺς πνοὴν τῷ λαῷ τῷ ἐπ' αὐτῆς καὶ Πνεῦμα τοῖς πατοῦσιν αὐτήν», τὴν μὲν πνοὴν κοινῶς παντὶ τῷ ἐπὶ τῆς γῆς λαῷ φήσας δεδόσθαι, τὸ δὲ Πνεῦμα ἰδίως τοῖς καταπατοῦσι τὰς γεώδεις ἐπιθυμίας (5.12.2).

41. "Oportuerat enim primo plasmari hominem et plasmatum accipere animam, deinde sic communionem Spiritus recipere. Quapropter et primus Adam factus est a Domino in animam viventem, secundus Adam in Spiritum vivificantem. Sicut igitur qui in animam viventem factus est devertens in peius perdidit vitam, sic rurus idem ipse in melius recurrens et assumens vivificantem spiritum, inveniet vitam" (5.12.2).

42. "Dicant enim nobis hi qui contraria dicunt, hoc est qui contradicunt suae saluti, summi sacerdotis mortua filia, et viduae filius qui circa portam mortuus efferebatur, et Lazarus qui in monumento quartam habebat diem, in quibus resurrexerint corporibus? In iisdem ipsis scilicet in quibus et mortui fuerant: si enim non in iisdem ipsis, videlicet nec iidem ipsi qui mortui erant resurrexerunt" (5.13.1).

in the same bodies in which they rose, the members and their bodies receive the cure and the life which was given by the Lord."[43]

Throughout Book Five Irenaeus draws stark contrasts, as a rhetor would when presenting deliberative oratory. Irenaeus distinguishes between these two modes of scriptural interpretation so that his audience will have a basis for comparison. And, in doing this, he makes ethical, emotional, and logical appeals. Ultimately, his opponents do not *see*. They are "vain and sorry" because "they do not wish to see what is clear and manifest, but flee from the light of truth."[44] In this case, "the light of truth" concerns the proper interpretation of scripture. Irenaeus's opponents cannot see the visions that scripture offers because "they do not search out the thought of the Apostle nor the power of his words."[45] Instead, "they hold on nakedly to the words alone." When they do this, "they turn away from the whole economy of God."[46] The implicit contrast here is with the Apostolic teaching that accounts for God's economy. Any one scriptural passage must be read in light of the faith and with the context of the rest of scripture handed down by the Apostles. Exegetical mistakes are theological mistakes and vice versa. Indeed, for Irenaeus, exegesis (with the faith in mind) *is* theology.[47] If the Apostle contradicts himself he should not be trusted as a teacher. According to Irenaeus's opponents, Paul contradicts himself; according to the Apostolic faith, he does not. To put it another way, if Paul does contradict himself, his writings are not worthy of discussion.

Paul's letters provide the interpretative context to understand what he meant to be taken literally and what he meant to be taken metaphorically. This context helps the reader to see the vision of the

---

43. "Sicut igitur qui curati sunt in his quae ante passa fuerant membra curati sunt et mortui in iisdem surrexerunt corporibus, membris et corporibus ipsorum percipientibus curationem et eam vitam quae dabatur a Domino [see 1 Cor 15:53–55]" (5.13.1).

44. Μάταιοι οὖν ὄντως καὶ ἄθλιοι, οἱ τὰ οὕτως ἔκδηλα καὶ φανερὰ μὴ θέλοντες συνορᾶν ἀλλὰ φεύγοντες τὸ φῶς τῆς ἀληθείας (5.13.2).

45. οὔτε τοῦ Ἀποστόλου κατεῖδον οὔτε τὴν δύναμιν τῶν λεγομένων προερευνήσαντες (5.13.2).

46. ψιλῶς δὲ αὐτῷ μόνον τὰς λέξεις κρατοῦντες περὶ αὐτὰς ἀποθνήσκουσι, τὴν πᾶσαν οἰκονομίαν τὸ ὅσον ἐφ᾽ ἑαυτοῖς ἀνατρέποντες τοῦ Θεοῦ (5.13.2).

47. It is worth remembering that Irenaeus never uses the word "theology." The distinction between exegesis and theology that burdens Christian thinkers today was unknown to him.

eschaton that Paul provides. Irenaeus's interpretation helps readers to see Paul's teaching about the coming judgment. The body of which Paul speaks "is the flesh, which when it falls, is lowered to the earth." Thanks to the work of God, the body will be transformed: "the immortal encircles the mortal and the incorruptible the corruptible."[48] The economy of salvation ends with the bodies of the just becoming incorruptible, and Irenaeus stresses that these bodies will glorify God. "The mortal will be absorbed by life when the flesh will remain not dead but living and incorruptible, singing hymns to God, who perfected us in this. So that we may be perfected, he said well to the Corinthians 'Glorify God in your body' [1 Cor 6:20]. God is the maker of incorruptibility."[49] The transformation begun in the heart (2 Cor 3:3), thanks to belief in Christ, culminates in the incorruptible resurrected body. "Therefore," Irenaeus writes, "if now fleshly hearts became capable of the Spirit, what wonder if in the resurrection they are capable of that life which is given by the Spirit."[50] Paul's vision of the future is in deep continuity with the present. The same Spirit that changes hearts in this life revivifies bodies in the life to come. According to Irenaeus, "the apostle has not pronounced against the very substance of flesh and blood, that it cannot inherit the kingdom of God, the same apostle has everywhere adopted the term 'flesh and blood' with regard to the Lord Jesus Christ."[51] According to Irenaeus, the goal of the economy of salvation, the eschaton, is none other than Christ himself. The Word can come into communion with human beings and save human beings because he has flesh and blood. And because he is God he can offer incorruptibility to those who believe in him.

48. Φανερὸν ὅτι τὸ σῶμα, ὅπερ ἐστὶν ἡ σάρξ, ἥτις καὶ ταπεινοῦται πίπτουσα εἰς τὴν γῆν. Μετασχηματισμὸς δὲ αὐτῆς... τῷ θνητῷ τὴν ἀθανασίαν καὶ τῷ φθαρτῷ περιποιήσασθαι τὴν ἀφθαρσίαν (5.13.3).

49. Καταπίνεται γὰρ τὸ θνητὸν ὑπὸ τῆς ζωῆς, ὅτι μηκέτι σάρξ νεκρὰ ἀλλὰ ζῶσα καὶ ἄφθαρτος ἀναμένει, ὑμνοῦσα τὸν εἰς αὐτὸ τοῦτο κατεργασάμενον ἡμᾶς Θεόν. Ut ergo in hoc perficimur, bene Corinthiis ait: Glorificate Deum in corpore vestro. Deus autem incorruptibilitatis est effector (5.13.3).

50. "Si ergo nunc corda carnalia capacia Spiritus fiunt, quid mirum si in resurrectione eam quae a Spiritu datur capiunt vitam?" (5.13.4).

51. "Quoniam autem non adversus ipsam substantiam carnis et sanguinis dixit Apostolus non possidere eam regnum Dei, ubique idem Apostolus in Domino nostro Jesu Christo usus est carnis et sanguinis nomine" (5.14.1).

Irenaeus began Book Five by discussing God through an examination of the Eucharist. The Eucharist acts as a conduit for God's power because in consuming the Eucharist, one is consuming Christ himself, the Word made flesh. This consumption prepares the body for incorruptibility. Jesus Christ, as a human being, shares the same flesh with the human race. Because he is the Word made flesh, his flesh gives life to all who believe in him. "If someone says that that flesh of the Lord is different from our flesh, since it did not sin nor 'was any deceit found in his soul' [1 Pt 2:22], he says rightly that we are sinners."[52] Christ, because he is the Word of God, does not have the carnal desires of the flesh that all other human beings do. But because he is the Word of God, "the Lord has reconciled man to God the Father through his communion, reconciling us to himself through the body of his flesh and redeeming us by his blood."[53] Through Christ, there is true reconciliation with God. "What was once in enmity is reconciled. If the Lord carried flesh from another substance, that which had been made an enemy through transgression would not be reconciled to God."[54] Christ's flesh is human flesh. God's power—the power of the God of the Old Covenant and the New—saves human flesh. This flesh is strengthened by Christ's flesh in the Eucharist and saved by Christ's flesh through his death and resurrection. Christ's coming is not simply some event that occurs in the future at the eschaton or in the past at the incarnation. Christ comes at each Eucharistic meal and in so doing strengthens the flesh of all who partake in him.

Christ himself offers salvation. Irenaeus encourages his readers to remember what Christ has done so that each reader will choose Christ's recapitulation as it is understood in the Apostolic faith. Irenaeus concludes this first major section of Book Five by telling his reader that by using these examples from scripture, "You will easily overturn, as we

52. "Si quis igitur secundum hoc alteram dicit Domini carnem a nostra carne, quoniam illa quidem non peccavit neque inventus est dolus in anima eius, nos autem peccatores, recte dicit" (5.14.3).

53. "reconciliavit Dominus hominem Deo Patri, reconcilians nos sibi per corpus carnis suae et sanguine suo redimens nos" (5.14.3).

54. "Reconciliatur enim illud quod fuit aliquando in inimicitia. Si autem ex altera substantia carnem attulit Dominus, jam non illud reconciliatum est Deo quod per transgressionem factum fuerat inimicum" (5.14.3).

have demonstrated, all the thoughts that were invented by the here-tics."[55] (We can tell this ends a section because Irenaeus uses the phrase "we have demonstrated.") The main goal, however, is not overturning heresies so much as it is reading the scriptures correctly so that one can be saved. Irenaeus leaves this choice to his reader.

Refutatio, 5.15–24: Scripture/Economy

As we have discussed, the proper interpretation of Paul was the main dispute at issue between Irenaeus and his opponents in Book Five. Irenaeus argued that his opponents misunderstood Paul's use of key terms such as "flesh" and "resurrection" and "spiritual man." There were times when these words ought be understood metaphorically and times when they ought to understood literally, but the only way to tell the difference was to read Paul in light of the faith. Irenaeus's dis-cussion of Paul was his proof, his *probatio*. Irenaeus needed to discuss Paul first in Book Five because that discussion sets the terms for the debate he is having with his opponents. While 5.1–14 dealt with the proper exegesis of Paul, Paul himself was discussing the power of God to raise human beings in the flesh.

If the first fourteen chapters of Book Five deal with the power of God, 5.15–24 deal with the *oikonomia* of God's salvation in the life of Jesus Christ. Once again, the structure of Irenaeus's argument mir-rors the structure of the faith. Thus after discussing God, Irenaeus must turn to a discussion of the Spirit speaking through the prophets. Here, Irenaeus lays out how Christ interprets the prophets in his own words. We have already noted how the letter to the Ephesians states that all things are recapitulated in Christ. For Irenaeus, understand-ing the way Christ interprets the scriptures is part of understanding *both* the *oikonomia* of God's creation and salvation, *and* the recapit-ulation Christ performs. Irenaeus's particular focus in these chapters is on Christ's own interpretation of the scriptures. In these chapters, Irenaeus shifts from a discussion of Paul's letters to a discussion of the

---

55. "utens etiam his ostensionibus quae sunt ex Scripturis, facile evertes, quemad-modum demonstravimus, omnes eas quae postea affictae sunt haereticorum sententias" (5.14.4).

Gospels. Following the structure for which we have argued through-out, Irenaeus uses 1.15–24 as a *refutatio* of his opponents' arguments. He began with the difficult work of parsing Paul's words. In order to show how Paul follows the faith, Irenaeus turns to the words of Jesus. Jesus' words show that he is the son of the God of the Old Covenant. His words also show that this God saves human beings in the flesh. Irenaeus uses Christ's own words to clear up any confusions that might remain about Paul's writings.

Even Christ's words need the proper context, though, so Irenaeus begins this section by placing Christ in the context of the whole economy of salvation. In order to understand Christ's words about future judgment, one must understand his words about past prophecy. It should come as no surprise that Irenaeus relies on a visual metaphor when discussing the economy. This economy begins with the Book of Genesis. For Irenaeus, Christ, as the Word of God, has been present throughout creation. Irenaeus begins by interpreting the story of Jesus healing the man born blind (Jn 9:3) in light of the story of God's creation of Adam (Gn 2:3). Because of sin, Adam lost his way. Because of Christ's work, human beings can now see God clearly thanks to the interpretation of the economy that Christ offers. Because it is clear that human bodies come from this earth, it is clear that they will return to this earth. Christ also recapitulates in himself the creation and salvation of human beings. The Lord "formed us from the beginning all the way to the end and adapted us to life and is present with his formation and perfects it according to the image and likeness of God."[56] He can perfect human beings according to God's image and likeness because he became a human being himself.

The things of God are made visible because in Christ, God becomes part of his creation. "This is shown to be true," Irenaeus writes. "The Word of God was made man [*homo*], assimilating himself to man [*homo*] and man [*homo*] to himself."[57] The Word does this "so that through that likeness to the Son, man [*homo*] becomes precious

---

56. "ab initio usque ad finem format nos et coaptat in vitam et adest plasmati suo et perficit illud secundum imaginem et similitudinem Dei" (5.16.1).

57. "Tunc autem hoc verum ostensum est, quando homo Verbum Dei factum est, semetipsum homini et hominem sibimetipsi assimilans" (5.16.2).

to the Father."⁵⁸ Through the incarnation, however, the Word "established the likeness, firmly making man [*homo*] for the invisible Father through the visible Son."⁵⁹ Not only does Christ manifest the
Father by giving sight to the blind, but he also manifests the Father
through his own suffering. Because of his obedience to the point of
death on a cross (Phil 2:8), he cleansed the disobedience of human
beings through his own obedience. If Christ had come from another
Father, and if he did not truly suffer, he could not have been obedient
in this way. Christ's obedience places him in the economy of salvation and this position allows human beings to come into a relationship with God. Indeed, this relationship—in its various forms—is the
whole point of the manifestation of the Word. Christ shows that God
is "the Creator, who according to his love, is Father, according to his
power, Lord, according to his wisdom, our Maker and Former. When
we transgress his commandments, we make ourselves an enemy to
him." All is not lost, though, because "at the critical time, the Lord
established us in friendship through his incarnation, becoming the
'mediator of God and man' [1 Tm 2:5]."⁶⁰ When he forgave sins, Christ
showed who he truly was. Because he forgave sins and cured the sick,
Irenaeus says, "it is manifest that he himself was the Word of God
made son of man."⁶¹ The order of the entire universe is directed for
the purpose of the judgment and salvation of human beings. Through
his own interpretation of scripture, Irenaeus hopes to make that manifestation clear to his audience.

In Book Five, remember, Irenaeus focuses on the future judgment
and on what human beings need to do in order to live in accordance
with God's love. The Word offers salvation through those aspects of
the economy that led human beings away from salvation. Christ saves
both humanity and the creation that bears it. Through Christ's reca-

58. "ut per eam quae est ad Filium similitudinem pretiosus homo fiat Patri" (5.16.2).
59. "ipse hoc fiens quod erat imago eius, et similitudinem firmans restituit, consim-
ilem faciens hominem invisibili Patri per visibile Verbum" (5.16.2).
60. Ἔστι δὲ οὗτος ὁ Δημιουργός, ὁ κατὰ μὲν τὴν ἀγάπην Πατήρ, κατὰ δὲ τὴν
δύναμιν Κύριος, κατὰ δὲ τὴν σοφίαν Ποιητὴς καὶ Πλάστης ἡμῶν, οὗ καὶ τὴν ἐντολὴν
παραβάντες ἐχθροποιήθημεν πρὸς αὐτόν. Καὶ καιρῷ εἰς φιλίαν ἀποκατέστησεν ἡμᾶς ὁ
Κύριος διὰ τῆς ἰδίας σαρκώσεως, «μεσίτης Θεοῦ τε καὶ ἀνθρώπων» γενόμενος (5.17.1).
61. "Manifestum est quoniam ipse erat Verbum Dei Filius hominis factus" (5.17.3).

pitulation the earth is joined to God. As befitting a minor recapitulation, Irenaeus sets up a contrast between Eve's disobedience and
Mary's obedience.[62] The themes of persuasion and seduction are most
important in Irenaeus's discussion of Eve and Mary. Like all human beings they can be swayed by rhetoric. Yet not all human beings are persuaded to such consequence. "As one was seduced by the angelic word
so that she might flee God by wandering from his Word, so too the other, having been evangelized through the angelic word, might bear God,
being obedient to his word. And just as the one was seduced so that she
did not obey God, so too the other was persuaded to obey God."[63]

Irenaeus is concerned that Christians will be seduced to read the
scriptures according to his opponents' teaching instead of the Apostolic
faith. Only the faith is the sure protection against diabolic seduction. It
is also the backdrop of proper persuasion. Only the church, following
the tradition of the Apostles, guards the faith, which helps people to
see properly. "One and the same way of salvation is shown in the whole
world."[64] It is no accident that Irenaeus discusses light. Unlike the darkness of his opponents' teaching, which leads human beings away from
God, the light of God illuminates the wisdom of God through which
human beings are saved.[65] Irenaeus mocks his opponents as sophists
because they do not recognize any measure of truth beyond themselves. These sophists think they "find something above the truth."[66]
For Irenaeus the truth of God is found within the economy of salvation, not outside it. His opponents attempt to circumvent the economy
and end up circumventing the salvation that comes along with it.

Salvation comes through seeing the vision that the scriptures pro-

---

62. For a thorough discussion of Mary in Irenaeus's thought, see M. C. Steenberg,
"The Role of Mary as Co-Recapitulator in St Irenaeus of Lyons," *VC* 58, no. 2 (2004):
117–37.

63. "quemadmodum enim illa per angelicum sermonem seducta est ut effugeret
Deum praevaricata verbum eius, ita et haec per angelicum sermonem evangelizata est
ut portaret Deum obaudiens eius verbo; et sicut illa seducta est ut non obaudiret Deo,
sic haec suasa est obaudire Deo" (5.19.1).

64. "apud quam una et eadem salutis via in universo mundo ostenditur. Huic enim
creditum est lumen Dei" (5.20.1).

65. 5.20.1.

66. "Tales sunt enim omnes haeretici, et qui se plus aliquid praeter veritatem invenire putant" (5.20.1).

vide, and the teaching of the church is essential for one to see that vision. And so once again, Irenaeus stresses the centrality of the church. Unlike the stable Apostolic tradition, those who follow his opponents' teaching do "not always have the same thoughts about the same things."[67] Because of this, they can never find the truth. The scriptures, which contain the preaching of the Law, the prophets, Christ, and the Apostles, must be interpreted in the proper way. Irenaeus goes so far as to conceive of the church as the Garden of Eden, and so he picks up the discussion that he began earlier. "The Church has been planted as a paradise in this world."[68] In this way it is firmly within the economy of salvation. "Therefore 'you may eat the fruits of every tree of paradise,' the Spirit of God said, that is, eat the lordly Scriptures from everything."[69] The scriptural passage Irenaeus quotes is suggestive. God cast Adam and Eve from the Garden precisely because they ate the fruit that was forbidden to them. Had they eaten only the fruits allowed to them, they would have remained. Irenaeus's implication is clear: those who follow the scriptures that are forbidden, the scriptures that are not part of the Edenic church, cast themselves out of the church and away from the faith that it guards. Irenaeus, in this deliberative moment of his work, presents his audience with the same choice. He urges them to choose the Apostolic faith lest they eat or touch "the whole heretical dissent" thanks to their "puffed up sense" (see 1 Cor 8:1).[70] Like the serpent, his opponents "confess themselves to have the knowledge of good and evil and they throw their impious sense over the God who made them."[71] Here again we see Irenaeus not only distinguishing between two traditions of exegesis, but comparing these different exegeses to Christ and the Devil. This comparison only intensifies as he continues in Book Five.

67. "de iisdem non semper easdem sententias habentes" (5.20.2).

68. "Plantata est enim Ecclesia paradisus in hoc mundo" (5.20.2).

69. "Ab omni ergo ligno paradisi escas manducabitis, ait Spiritus Dei, hoc est ab omni Scriptura dominica manducate" (5.20.2).

70. "a superelato autem sensu ne manducaveritis neque tetigeritis universam haereticam dissensionem" (5.20.2). Again we see Irenaeus alluding to 1 Corinthians as a way to distinguish his interpretation from that of his opponents.

71. "Ipsi enim confitentur semetipsos agnitionem habere boni et mali, et super Deum qui fecit eos jaculantur sensus suos impios" (5.20.2).

Excursus: Theological Method, Christ's Own
Interpretation of Scripture

We now come to the final theological excursus in the *Adversus Haereses*. In Book One, Irenaeus laid out the faith. In Book Two, he showed how his opponents' exegesis relied on an unstable rule based on the vagaries of Greek philosophy. In Book Three, Irenaeus showed how he based his exegesis on Christ himself, as Christ is presented in the Gospels. In Book Four, with Christ as the basis, Irenaeus turned to the economy of salvation and the living human being who, thanks to Christ's work, can see the entire economy of God as it is recounted in scripture. In Book Five, Irenaeus recapitulates his discussion by showing how his interpretation is in line with the interpretation made by Christ himself. Whereas the focus in Book Four was the past, Irenaeus focuses on the future in this excursus. Notice how Irenaeus builds his argument to its strongest point. After all, what could be stronger evidence for Irenaeus's argument than aligning himself with Christ's own interpretation? He has exposed his opponents' fictions (Book Two), set the context for God's manifestation in Christ (Book Three), shown how that manifestation relies on a proper understanding of past prophecy (Book Four), and now argues that Christ's interpretation helps his readers understand God's future judgment, the recapitulation of God's economy of salvation and the recapitulation of Irenaeus's own speech.

I have argued that the *Adversus Haereses* centers on the proper interpretation of scripture and, relatedly, the proper interpretation of Christ. A host of other issues flow from these two: the identity of God, the nature of creation and human beings, the role of the church, and the question of human salvation. Irenaeus has prosecuted his opponents' beliefs, praised the interpretation of the scriptures that has been handed down from the Apostles, and made clear the decision that his audience has to make. Perhaps the most important chapters of the entire *Adversus Haereses* are 5.21–24. These chapters most clearly set up Christ as the interpreter of scripture *par excellence*, and it is fitting that they are found in the *refutatio* of Book Five. In these chapters,

Irenaeus interprets the Devil's temptation of Christ in the Gospels.[72] Irenaeus sees his own situation reflected in this Gospel passage. The Devil tempts Christ three times. First, he tells Christ to turn stones to bread. Then, the Devil tells Christ to throw himself off the parapet of the Temple so that angels will save him. Finally, the Devil offers Christ power over all the kingdoms of the world if Christ would worship him. The Devil tempts Christ by quoting the scriptures to him; Christ responds by quoting scripture back. For Irenaeus, then, this episode is so fundamental because it shows the kind of disagreement about scripture that engages Irenaeus and his opponents. And of course, it is through Christ's words that Irenaeus believes he has refuted his opponents.[73]

Irenaeus begins this section by noting that Christ recapitulates all things. He brings together Genesis 3, where the serpent tempts Eve, with Galatians 4, where Paul talks about Christ being born of a woman. In this way, Irenaeus himself recounts the economy of salvation. "The enemy was not conquered justly unless the man who conquered him was born of a woman."[74] Satan "dominated man through a woman, establishing himself against man from the beginning."[75] Christ "did not destroy [Satan] from another place, except from the words of the Law, and he used the judgment of the Father for the destruction and the unmasking of the apostate angel."[76] Thus, the first step in Irenaeus's argument is showing how Christ fits into the economy of salvation.

Irenaeus is clearly offering an *epideixis* of praise in this chapter. His praise of Christ here focuses on how Christ argues with the Devil about the proper interpretation of scripture. Understanding Christ's

---

72. See Mt 4:1–11. Irenaeus draws on Matthew rather than the parallel accounts at Mk 1:12–13 or Lk 4:1–13.

73. For an extended discussion of this episode, see Rémi Gounelle, "L'ultime combat de Dieu: le face à face infernal du Christ et du diable," *Foi et vie* 110, no. 2 (2011): 36–47.

74. "Neque enim juste victus fuisset inimicus, nisi ex muliere homo esset qui vicit eum" (5.21.2).

75. "Per mulierem enim homini dominatus est, ab initio semetipsum contrarium statuens homini" (5.21.2).

76. "Et propter hoc non aliunde eum destruxit, nisi ex dictionibus legis, et Patris praecepto adjutore usus ad destructionem et traductionem apostatae angeli" (5.21.2).

argument with the Devil in terms of scriptural exegesis both casts Christ as an interpreter of scripture and forms two rival genealogies of interpretation: the divine and the diabolical.[77] Irenaeus's scriptural interpretation extends beyond exegesis of the narrative of the text. He attends to Gospel parallels and to etymologies. Irenaeus begins his discussion of Christ's temptation by noting that Christ fasted for forty days, just as Moses and Elijah did. By mentioning Moses and Elijah, Irenaeus reminds his reader that Christ stands in the line of the Jewish Law and prophets. Christ, as the center of the economy of salvation, stands between prophecy and judgment and encompasses them both. When the Devil first tempted Christ by using the words of scripture and said, "If you are the Son of God, say the word and these stones become bread," Christ quotes a passage from the Old Covenant, in the Book of Deuteronomy, which goes on to say that human beings do not live on bread alone but from every word that comes from the mouth of the Lord.[78] Understanding the scriptures gives life; misunderstanding the scriptures brings death. Irenaeus's whole task is to help his audience participate in the life that Christ offers, and they can only do that if they understand the scriptures with the faith. As Irenaeus notes, Christ countered the Devil's "first assault through the word of the Father."[79]

In the second temptation, Satan raised the stakes. When the Devil led Jesus to the precipice and tempted him to jump so that the angels would catch him, Irenaeus says that the Devil "hid his mendacity through Scripture, which all heretics do."[80] Irenaeus notes, "the puffed up sense, which was in the serpent, was dissolved through humility, which was in man."[81] With these words, Irenaeus recalls 1 Corinthi-

---

77. Wingren notes two characteristics of Irenaeus's theology. "First, the whole of his theology is marked by his contrast between God and the Devil, and the ceaselessly raging conflict between the two powers, a conflict which is fought out in the midst of our humanity; and second, this humanity, independently of the conflict we have mentioned, is continually in the process of change, developing and altering its form, but never remaining in the same fixed pattern." Wingren, *Man and the Incarnation*, 104.

78. "Si filius Dei es, dic ut lapides isti panes fiant" (5.21.2).

79. "et per paternam dictionem primum eius impetum euacauit" (5.21.2).

80. "mendacium abscondens per Scripturam, quod faciunt omnes haeretici" (5.21.2).

81. "Dominus itaque legitime confutavit eum, dicens: Item scriptum est: Non temptabis Dominum Deum tuum, per eam vocem quae est in lege ostendens id quidem

ans 8:1. There Paul says that knowledge (*gnosis*) puffs up, but love (*agapē*) builds up. Satan's response to Christ was the same as his temptation of Eve in the guise of a serpent. In both cases, Satan was puffed up rather than being built up by the love of God. Satan could not really know the scriptures because he had rejected God's love. As we have seen, love is the foundation for God's relationship with humanity and thus for the economy of salvation. Satan's pride, based as it is on an ersatz knowledge, has puffed him out of that economy. Anyone who follows Satan's interpretation risks doing the same.

Satan's third temptation deals with a misunderstanding of salvation. Satan shows Christ the kingdoms of the world and promises them to him only if Christ will worship him. Clearly Satan thinks Christ desires an earthly kingdom of the present. But of course that is not Christ's desire. Instead, Christ's words point to the future judgment. As Irenaeus writes, Christ "exposed" Satan "through his name and showed who he was. For the word 'Satan' signifies 'apostate' in Hebrew."[82]

Chapter 21 offers a précis of Book Five. Remember that the structure of Irenaeus's argument is Irenaeus's argument. Christ's three temptations map onto the three sections of Book Five. We can understand the first temptation as a clear allusion to the Eucharist. Human beings do not live on bread alone, but they live on the Word that transforms bread into the body of Christ. As we saw, Irenaeus spent the first part of Book Five discussing the Eucharist and how Paul's words, properly understood, show that God makes corruptible bodies incorruptible. The second temptation deals with the proper interpretation of the Old Covenant. Christ does not refute the Law of the Old Covenant, but uses the Law to refute the Devil. We have seen in the second section of Book Five how Irenaeus places Christ in the economy of salvation and places Christ's interpretation of the scriptures at the heart of his discussion. The Devil's final temptation deals with the kingdom of God,

quod est secundum hominem, quoniam non debet homo temptare Deum, quantum autem ad illum, quoniam in eo homine qui videbatur non temptaret Dominum Deum suum. Elatio itaque sensus quae fuit in serpente dissoluta est per eam quae fuit in homine humilitas" (5.21.2).

82. "Per hoc nomen et [se] ostendens qui erat Satana enim verbum hebraice apostatam significant" (5.21.2).

and Irenaeus spends the third section of Book Five writing of the kingdom of God, which raised corporeal bodies will enjoy. Those bodies will properly—and continually—praise God in that coming kingdom. All of this can be understood only because of Christ's interpretation of scripture.

Irenaeus does not say this explicitly, but we can see how he projects his own battles with his opponents onto this confrontation between Christ and the Devil. By doing this, Irenaeus has Christ recapitulate his own battle. One way in which Christ saves human beings as a human being is by offering them the proper interpretation of the scriptures. Irenaeus, as a disciple of Christ, seeks to do the same.

Irenaeus understands the future by looking at the past, so in order to draw the proper vision of the coming kingdom of God, Irenaeus looks back to how the Devil convinced Adam and Eve to disobey God.[83] Irenaeus makes this comparison for good rhetorical reasons. Through his words, he links his opponents with their ideological father, Satan. In doing so, he discredits them. When Adam and Eve disobeyed God, they gave themselves over to death. But Christ, in "recapitulating in himself the whole human race from the beginning to the end, has recapitulated even his death."[84] Nothing is beyond Christ's recapitulation of God's economy of salvation.

In drawing a contrast between Christ and the Devil—and therefore between the exegesis of the Apostles and of his opponents—another characteristic of Irenaeus's exegetical method comes to the fore: his use of scripture to interpret other parts of scripture. Irenaeus, interpreting the Lucan account of Jesus' temptation, writes, "Just as he deceived in the beginning, he will deceive in the end, saying 'All these things are handed over to me and to whom I wish to give them.'"[85] Irenaeus reminds the reader that the Devil "did not determine the kingdoms of this age," God did. Then, quoting Proverbs, he writes, "the heart of the king is in the hand of God" (Prv 8:15–16). He then

---

83. 5.23.1.

84. "Recapitulans enim uniuersum hominem in se ab initio usque ad finem, recapitulates est et mortem eius" (5.23.2).

85. "Sicut ergo in principio mentitus est, ita et in fine mentiebatur dicens: Haec omnia mihi tradita sunt, et cui volo do ea" (5.24.1).

quotes from Paul's letter to the Romans. "It does not carry the sword with a reason, for it is the minister of God to inflict vengeance on the one who does evil."[86] Irenaeus then draws the comparison between the Devil and his opponents' interpretation when he writes that Paul "said these things not about invisible rulers, as they dared to explain, but about those things which were powers according to men."[87] From Proverbs to Paul, Irenaeus then turns to Christ: "And the Lord confirmed this, not doing what he was persuaded [to do] by the Devil."[88] Not only does Irenaeus show how scriptural passages need to be read in light of each other, more importantly he shows how Christ himself recapitulates and confirms other scriptural teaching. Irenaeus can interpret scripture this way because Christ did so, and on this crucial point about the rulers of the world, Irenaeus uses the scriptures to show that thanks to the death and resurrection of Christ, the Devil does not have power over this world or the world to come. Following the Apostolic faith makes the scriptures clear on this point.

Recapitulatio, 5.25–36: Salvation/Christ

As he concludes the *Adversus Haereses* in 5.25–36, Irenaeus looks to the future when he offers his final *recapitulatio*. He began Book Five by discussing the proper interpretation of Paul, which was the proper interpretation of God's power to save. He then moved to discussing Christ's own interpretation of the scriptures, which, he noted, was the interpretation offered by the God who becomes part of the economy of salvation. In these two sections, Irenaeus shifted from forensic oratory to epideictic oratory, from accusing his opponents of misinterpreting Paul to praising Christ's proper interpretation. In this final section,

86. "Non enim ipse determinavit hujus saeculi regna, sed Deus: Regis enim cor in manu Dei ... non enim sine causa gladium portat: Dei enim minister est, vindex in iram ei qui male operatur" (5.24.1). See Rom 13:4.

87. "Quoniam haec autem non de angelicis potestatibus nec de invisibilibus principibus dixit, quomodo quidam audent exponere, sed de his quae sunt secundum homines potestates" (5.24.1).

88. "Hoc autem et Dominus confirmavit, non faciens quidem quod a Diabolo suadebatur, tributorum autem exactoribus jubens pro se et pro Petro dari tributum, quoniam ministri Dei sunt, in hoc ipsum deservientes" (5.24.1).

Irenaeus recapitulates his arguments. Although, as I have argued, the overall tone of the *Adversus Haereses* is forensic discourse, in this last section Irenaeus offers deliberative discourse by presenting his audience with a choice: they can choose either the interpretation of Satan or the interpretation of Christ.

In order to make clear the decision that his audience faces, Irenaeus must present the competing visions that the diabolical and Apostolic exegesis each offer. His rhetoric turns deliberative as he aims to move his audience. A large part of that task is showing the Devil himself, and how the Devil will appear at the end of time. Irenaeus has just shown how Christ defeated the Devil. Now he begins the final section of the *Adversus Haereses* by explaining how the scriptures discuss the final confrontation between Christ and the Devil. Irenaeus begins 5.25 by discussing the "apostate and mercenary" Antichrist, who "wishes to be adored as God."[89] This is the same one who sat on top of the Temple tempting Christ.[90] Irenaeus points out that both the Book of Daniel and the Gospels discuss the Antichrist.[91] In order to show the future, Irenaeus must interpret the visions of the past, especially the Book of Daniel. "For if the prophecies of Daniel are about the end, the Lord confirms them by saying, 'when you will see the abomination of desolation which is told by the prophet Daniel.'"[92] Christ's words recorded in the Gospels are necessary to understanding Daniel's prophecy correctly. The visions recorded in the texts of scripture call for interpretation. Irenaeus links Daniel's prophecy to the angel Gabriel's annunciation to Mary. "The angel Gabriel interprets the vision of Daniel. He is the archangel of the Creator and he is the one who evangelized to Mary the manifest coming and incarnation of Christ."[93] Because of Christ "one and the same God is shown most

---

89. "apostata et latro quasi Deus vult adorari" (5.25.1).

90. 5.25.2.

91. 5.25.3–5.

92. "Si enim quae a Daniele prophetata sunt de fine Dominus comprobavit, Cum videritis, dicens, abominationem desolationis quae dicta est per Danielem prophetam" (5.25.5).

93. "Danieli autem angelus Gabriel exsolutionem visionum fecit, hic autem est archangelus Demiurgi et hic idem Mariae evangelizavit manifestum adventum et incarnationem Christi" (5.25.5).

clearly who sent the prophets, and promised the Son and called us into his own knowledge."[94] All visions in the scriptures are linked. Without the proper interpretation, it is easy to mistake the Antichrist for Christ. Indeed, that is precisely what has happened to those swayed by Irenaeus's opponents' teaching.

Without the proper interpretation of the scriptures, Satan himself would go unrecognized. "Justin said well that before the coming of the Lord, Satan did not dare blaspheme God. Indeed, he did not know his own damnation because it laid in parables and allegories."[95] Satan did not know he was damned because he did not know how to interpret what was literal and what was metaphorical in Christ's own words. Satan, in other words, was a poor interpreter of scripture. But after Christ's life, death, and resurrection, Satan "knew manifestly from the Lord's words and the apostles' that the eternal fire was prepared for him."[96] This is important to underline. After Christ came, Satan was able to see something he could not previously see, namely his own damnation. Thanks to Irenaeus's interpretation, his audience can see what awaits them. He wants them to understand their place in the economy of salvation.

Just as an orator makes clear the decision that lies before his audience clear, Christ's advent makes God's judgment clear. "The word came 'for the ruin and resurrection of many' [Lk 2:34].... Therefore if the coming of the Lord came over all similarly, it is just to separate the believing from the unbelieving because the believers do his will ... and the disobedient do not accede to his teaching."[97] Although there are

94. "unus et idem Deus manifestissime ostenditur qui prophetas misit et Filium praemisit et nos vocavit in agnitionem suam" (5.25.5).

95. "Nam ipse per semetipsum nude non audet blasphemare suum Dominum, quemadmodum et initio per serpentem seduxit hominem, quasi latens Deum. Καὶ καλῶς ὁ Ἰουστῖνος εἶπεν ὅτι πρὸ μὲν τῆς τοῦ Κυρίου παρουσίας οὐδέποτε ἐτόλμησεν ὁ Σατανᾶς βλασφημῆσαι τὸν Θεόν, ἅτε μηδέπω εἰδὼς τὴν ἑαυτοῦ κατάκρισιν, διὰ τὸ ἐν παραβολαῖς καὶ ἀλληγορίαις κεῖσθαι" (5.27.1). On the relationship between Irenaeus and Justin, see Michael Slusser, "How Much Did Irenaeus Learn from Justin?," *Studia Patristica* 40 (2006): 515–20.

96. μετὰ δὲ τὴν παρουσίαν τοῦ Κυρίου ἐκ τῶν λόγων αὐτοῦ καὶ τῶν ἀποστόλων μαθὼν ἀναφανδὸν ὅτι πῦρ αἰώνιον αὐτῷ ἡτοίμασται (5.27.1).

97. "Verbum venit in ruinam et in resurrectionem multorum: in ruinam quidem non credentium ei .... Si ergo adventus Filii super omnes quidem similiter advenit,

epideictic elements in Irenaeus's discussion of Christ here, he intends this praise of Christ to lead his audience to decide to follow Christ and gain communion with God. The choice is clear: "to those who guard their love for God, he will give his communion. Communion with God is life and light and the fruit of good things from him."[98] Of course, the words "light" and "life" here should recall Irenaeus's discussion of the *homo vivens* and his many allusions to vision. On the other hand, "he separates himself from those who renounce their feeling of God. Separation from God is death and separation from light is darkness and separation from God is sending away all good things from him."[99] In the light of God human beings will come to the heavenly vision of salvation. Although Irenaeus's rhetoric itself cannot offer that vision, it can warn its audience of the dangers of being separated from the Apostolic faith. The good orator persuades; Satan seduces. Just as Christ recapitulates the economy of God's salvation, Satan comes "in his own opinion to recapitulate the unbelief to himself ... so that many, having been seduced by him, might worship him as Christ."[100] Irenaeus wants his audience to read the scriptures the way Christ himself read the scriptures. Irenaeus's praise of Christ extends to a praise of those martyred because of their faith in him. The martyrs saw the vision of the economy of scripture that Christ's interpretation recapitulates. Irenaeus's audience would have honored the martyrs they knew personally.

---

iudicialis est autem et discretor credentium et non credentium—quoniam ex sua sententia credentes faciunt eius voluntatem et ex sua sententia indicto audientes non accedunt ad eius doctrinam" (5.27.1).

98. "Et quicumque erga eum custodiunt dilectionem, suam his praestat communionem. Communio autem Dei, vita et lumen et fruitio eorum quae sunt apud eum bonorum" (5.27.2).

99. Ὅσα ἀφίστανται κατὰ τὴν γνώμην αὐτῶν τοῦ Θεοῦ, τούτοις τὸν ἀπ' αὐτοῦ χωρισμὸν ἐπάγει· χωρισμὸς δὲ Θεοῦ θάνατος, καὶ χωρισμὸς φωτὸς σκότος, καὶ χωρισμὸς Θεοῦ ἀποβολὴ πάντων τῶν παρ' αὐτοῦ ἀγαθῶν (5.27.2).

100. τοῦ μὲν γὰρ ἐρχομένου ἰδίᾳ γνώμῃ τὴν ἀπιστίαν ἀνακεφαλαιουμένου πρὸς ἑαυτὸν καὶ αὐτεξουσίου πράξαντος ὅσα καὶ πράξει καὶ εἰς τὸν ναὸν τοῦ Θεοῦ καθίσαντος, ἵνα ὡς Χριστὸν αὐτὸν προσκυνήσουσιν οἱ πλανώμενοι ὑπ' αὐτοῦ (5.28.2). In 5.28.2–3, Irenaeus shows the deeply millenarian aspects of his theology. For more on this see Charles E. Hill, *Regnum Caelorum: Patterns of Millennial Thought in Early Christianity*, 2nd ed. (Grand Rapids, Mich.: Eerdmans, 2001).

If Satan's interpretation cannot penetrate the faith that the church guards, that does not mean that the church is a place that guarantees physical safety. The acts of the martyrs teach as much. In the person of the martyr, we find both characteristics of the church: the interpretation of scripture and the embodiment of the eschatological community. Irenaeus praises the martyr and presents the martyr as worthy of emulation because the Spirit of God rests on him or her. The Spirit prompts the tribulation that announces the eschaton. Like the prophets, the martyrs prepare Christians who have followed the faith to endure tribulation. Irenaeus explicitly connects martyrdom and the economy of salvation back to the Eucharist by quoting Ignatius of Antioch. "I am the wheat of God and because of the teeth of the beasts I am spoken of truly in order that I may be found to be pure bread."[101] Although Irenaeus does not mentions Ignatius by name, he clearly puts himself in the same line of teaching as Ignatius. Ignatius, like Polycarp, is a teacher of scripture whose martyrdom offers proof of his teaching.

Ignatius, Polycarp, and Irenaeus are all members of the church that share Jesus' interpretation of the scriptures. Just as the church extends from the present to the past, it also extends from the present to the future. Irenaeus writes that "all things came about for the salvation of man" and later he notes "this is why in the end the Church is gathered together." At that time the wheat will be separated from the chaff so that "insofar as it is useful, it presents blades to add to the wheat and its chaff is put in the fire for burning."[102] The church, in Irenaeus's account, is the group of people who, because of their faith, have obeyed the will of God. The church is gathered together because Christ warns, "there will be a tribulation" (Mt 24:21). This tribulation, according to Irenaeus, "is the end of the conflict of the just, in which the victors are crowned with immortality."[103] There can only be victors—and persua-

101. ὡς εἶπέ τις τῶν ἡμετέρων διὰ τὴν πρὸς τὸν Θεὸν μαρτυρίαν κατακριθεὶς πρὸς θηρία, ὅτι «σῖτός εἰμι τοῦ Θεοῦ καὶ διὰ ὀδόντων θηρίων ἀλήθομαι, ἵνα καθαρὸς Θεοῦ ἄρτος εὑρεθῶ» (5.28.4). The text from Ignatius is his *Letter to the Romans* 4.1. See Holmes, *The Apostolic Fathers*, 171.
102. "πάντα τὰ τοιαῦτα ὑπὲρ τοῦ σῳζομένου ἀνθρώπου γέγονεν ... Καὶ διὰ τοῦτο, ἐν τῷ τέλει ἀθρόως ἐντεῦθεν τῆς ἐκκλησίας ἀναλαμβανομένης, quantum utilitatis praestat stipula ad tritici augumentum, et palea eius in ustionem ad operationem auri" (5.29.1).
103. Καὶ διὰ τοῦτο, ἐν τῷ τέλει ἀθρόως ἐντεῦθεν τῆς ἐκκλησίας ἀναλαμβανομένης,

sion and seduction can only occur—if human beings have free will in the first place. For Irenaeus, free will is essential to understanding the human relation with God because it not only allows one to mature toward immortality, but it also allows one to be persuaded. Were it not for free will, Irenaeus's rhetoric could not persuade his audience to follow the Apostolic faith. Without free will, the church cannot gather its members in the future because no one in the church can make any decisions.[104]

Free will, then, allows human beings to follow the recapitulation of Christ. Recapitulation, either by Christ or by Satan, brings the beginning to the end. Irenaeus's discussion of the end times is particularly vivid. This vividness also serves to make the decision before his audience clear and it serves the end of *pathos*. At the end of time, there will be a "recapitulation of all injustice and all pain" that will occur in the coming of the beast. Thanks to this recapitulation, "all apostate power" will come together and "be cast into the oven of fire."[105] Irenaeus makes sure his audience knows that the Antichrist recapitulates just as Christ does. The Antichrist "recapitulates in himself the whole cataclysm of evil which came about from the angelic apostasy."[106] Unlike those who follow Christ, those who follow the recapitulation of the Antichrist follow an apostate who will lead them into the oven of fire.

Irenaeus discusses the future coming of the Antichrist because he finds this in the Book of Revelation. He interprets parts of Revelation literally because he believes that the faith demands a literal interpretation of the text.[107] In contrast to Irenaeus's picture of per-

---

«ἔσται», φησίν, «θλῖψις, οἵα οὐκ ἐγένετο ἀπ' ἀρχῆς οὐδ' οὐ μὴ γένηται».Ἔσχατος γὰρ ἀγὼν οὗτος τῶν δικαίων, ὃν νικήσαντες στεφανοῦνται τὴν ἀφθαρσίαν (5.29.1).

104. It is interesting to note here that Irenaeus has a similar discussion of free will at a similar place in Book Four. This should come as no surprise, given the overall structure that I have been arguing for. At both points, Irenaeus uses deliberative rhetoric to urge his audience to use their free will to make the right choice about Christ's coming.

105. Καὶ διὰ τοῦτο εἰς τὸ θηρίον τὸ ἐρχόμενον ἀνακεφαλαίωσις γίνεται πάσης ἀδικίας καὶ παντὸς δόλου, ἵνα ἐν αὐτῷ συρρεύσασα καὶ συγκλυδωνισθεῖσα πᾶσα δύναμις ἀποστατικὴ εἰς τὴν κάμινον βληθῇ τοῦ πυρός (5.29.2).

106. ἀνακεφαλαιούμενον ἐν ἑαυτῷ τὴν πρὸ τοῦ κατακλυσμοῦ πᾶσαν τῆς κακίας ἐπίδειξιν ἐξ ἀγγελικῆς ἀποστασίας γεγενημένης (5.29.2).

107. Although scholars have not cast Irenaeus's eschatological discussion in rhetorical terms, his thoughts on eschatology have garnered much scholarly attention. See

suasion through rhetoric, his opponents' interpretation depends on static categories based on numerology. Such numerology is not governed by the faith and as a result it misunderstands the scriptures it is supposed to help interpret. Irenaeus has little patience for the numerology found in identifying the Antichrist with the number 666. Such numerology depends on the Greek alphabet, but "it is the Latins who now reign."[108] Christians need to be on guard against the Antichrist, but they should realize that "his name is silent, because it is not worthy to be foreknown by the Holy Spirit."[109] Irenaeus does believe that the Book of Revelation provides some insight about the future that awaits Christians. "When the Antichrist will have destroyed all the things in this world, he will have reigned for three years and six months and he will have sat on the temple in Jerusalem." At that point, "the Lord will come down from heaven on the clouds in the glory of the Father, sending those who were obedient to the Antichrist into a pool of fire."[110] Christ will lead the just to a place of rest, and he will reestablish the promise of Abraham's inheritance.

The comparisons Irenaeus draws between Christ and the Devil are a metonymy for the differences between two differing interpretations of the Book of Revelation. These comparisons are ultimately about the proper vision of the judgment that awaits all human beings. Those who do not believe that the just will rise from the dead in the flesh "have the sense of heretics in themselves" because they "despise

Dominique Bertrand, "L'eschatologie de Saint Irénée," *Théophilyon* 16, no. 1 (2011): 113–48; M. O'Rourke Boyle, "Irenaeus's Millenial Hope: A Polemical Weapon," *Recherches de théologie ancienne et medieval* 36, no. 1 (1969): 5–16; Jacques Fantino, "Ordre social et politique, temps et eschatologie: la lecture de l'Apocalypse par Irénée," *Studies in Religion/Sciences religieuses* 37, nos. 3–4 (2008): 481–96; Hill, *Regnum Caelorum*; William P. Loewe, "Irenaeus' Soteriology: Transposing the Question," in *Religion and Culture: Essays in Honor of Bernard Lonergan, S.J.*, ed. T. Fallon and P. Riley (Albany: State University of New York Press, 1987), 167–79; Antonio Orbé, "San Ireneo y el regimen del milenio," *Studia Missionalia* 32, no. 4 (1983): 345–72.

108. "Latini enim sunt qui nunc regnant" (5.30.3).

109. "nomen autem eius tacuit, quoniam dignum non est praeconaria sancto spiritu" (5.30.4).

110. "Cum autem devastaverit Antichristus hic omnia in hoc mundo, regnaverit annis tribus et mensibus sex et sederit in templo Hierosolymis, tunc veniet Dominus de caelis in nubibus in gloria Patris, illum quidem et obaudientes ei in stagnum ignis mittens" (5.30.4).

the formation of God and they do not accept the salvation of their flesh."[111] As a result they misunderstand Christ's death and resurrection. Irenaeus refutes his opponents' understanding by pointing to Christ's manifestation to his disciples after the resurrection. "He rose corporeally and was assumed after the resurrection, it is manifest for his disciples because the Lord did these things."[112] In fact, Christ's literal bodily resurrection is the key to understanding the Book of Revelation. What happened to the Lord will happen for all people at the end of time. The visions of God Irenaeus has described throughout the *Adversus Haereses*, the vision that the prophets and the martyrs glimpsed, can only be seen by embodied human beings. Only in the corporeal resurrection of the just is the promise to Abraham fulfilled.

The final chapters of the *Adversus Haereses* deal, appropriately enough, with the resurrection of the dead. Christ's death and resurrection cause the dead to rise. Through his resurrection, Christ *shows* his disciples what resurrected bodies will look like. It is not enough that Christ will effect the salvation of human beings; he also presents a vision of what that salvation will entail. Christ's resurrection, in other words, offers the definitive interpretation of texts from the Old Covenant about God's promise of life and resurrection. His resurrection is also the key with which to interpret the New Covenant. He stayed in the lower parts of the earth "until the third day" and then rose "in the flesh, so that He even showed the print of the nails to his disciples." He then ascended to the Father.[113] Christ ascended to the Father after he had gone out "into the shadow of death [Ps 23:4], where the souls of the dead are."[114] Christ's actions not only have repercussions for the disciples who saw him ascend to the Father, but also for all the dead.

111. "haereticos sensus in se habentes haeretici enim despicientes plasmationem Dei et non suscipientes salutem carnis suae" (5.31.2).

112. "post deinde corporaliter resurrexit et post resurrectionem assumptus est, manifestum est quia et discipulorum eius propter quos et haec operatus est Dominus" (5.31.2).

113. "Si ergo Dominus legem mortuorum servavit, ut fieret primogenitus a mortuis, et commoratus usque in tertiam diem in inferioribus terrae, post deinde surgens in carne, ut etiam fixuras clavorum ostenderet discipulis, sic ascendit ad Patrem" (5.31.2).

114. "Cum enim Dominus in medio umbrae mortis abierit, ubi animae mortuorum erant" (5.31.2).

After the dead rise, just as the Lord rose, and receive their bodies back "they come into the sight of God."[115] Just as Christ shows himself as resurrected to his disciples, resurrected human beings present themselves to be seen by God. Irenaeus makes clear the connection between Christ's actions and human hope. Irenaeus recapitulates his own discussion, reminding his readers that the God of the Old Covenant is the Father of Jesus Christ, and this God will judge them. If one does not understand the place of the prophets in the scriptures, one does not understand the Christ to whom they refer. Without understanding Christ, of course, one risks future damnation.

The journey toward salvation needs the nourishment of the Eucharist. Irenaeus began Book Five by showing how the Eucharist and the scriptures reinforce each other. Near the end of Book Five, Irenaeus returns to a discussion of the Eucharist to underline that the just will rise as bodies. The Eucharist in this account is always eschatological. Human beings need bread and wine because they are embodied. Christ offered the first Eucharist to signify that salvation was corporeal. And because salvation is corporeal, the renewed and redeemed earth will nourish the resurrected bodies. "A grain of wheat will guarantee thousands of ears and each ear ten thousand grains and each grain gives the world two pounds." All the animals too will eat this food.[116] "It is necessary that the renewed creation obey and all the animals be subjected to man and turn back to the first fruit given by God."[117] As we have seen before, Irenaeus looks to the future by interpreting biblical texts of the past. Here he understands the new creation with the help of Isaiah. In the new creation, lions will feed on straw. Irenaeus recognizes how unbelievable these images are. It is one thing to understand the importance of the Eucharist, but it is another thing to say that straw will satiate lions. Irenaeus is keen to stress that

115. "post recipientes corpora et perfecte resurgentes, hoc est corporaliter, quemadmodum et Dominus resurrexit, sic venient ad conspectum Dei" (5.31.2).
116. "Similiter et granum tritici decem millia spicarum generaturum, et unamquamque spicam habituram decem millia granorum, et unumquodque granum quinque bilibres similae dare mundae" (5.33.3).
117. "et oportet conditione revocata obaudire et subiecta esse omnia animalia homini et ad primam a Deo datam reverti escam" (5.33.4).

his interpretation accords with the elders "who saw John, the disciple of the Lord"[118] and with Papias, who said, "These things are believable for those who believe" (5.33.4).[119] Indeed, it is precisely because of the importance of the Eucharist that one can believe that bread and wine in the new creation will provide all the nourishment the just need. If Christ can be present in the Eucharist, the new creation can sustain beasts with straw alone.

This image of the new creation is also a Johannine theme, and near the very end of the *Adversus Haereses*, Irenaeus turns to John's vision of the New Jerusalem.[120] "After these things have passed away, John, the disciple of the Lord, said that the higher Jerusalem descended over the new earth, as a spouse adorned for her husband and this is the tabernacle of God in which God will dwell with men."[121] Like the rest of scripture, these images must be interpreted. The tabernacle was prefigured with Moses. Irenaeus uses typological exegesis to understand the relationship between the Old and New Covenants. And it is important to stress that Irenaeus employs typology and not allegory. Allegory, according to Irenaeus, does not accord with the faith, but typology does. Thus Irenaeus uses typology and his opponents use allegory.[122] Irenaeus is quick to point out that the image from the Book of Revelation is not something that can be explained away through allegory. "Nothing is able to be allegorized but all things are firm and true and have substance, made by God for the enjoyment of just men."[123] Irenaeus makes clear: "As it is truly God who raises man, so it is truly man who rises from the dead and not allegorically ... And thus he truly rises, he truly is predestined for incorruptibility and he is increased and thrives in the times of the kingdom, so that he may be capable of the glory of

118. "qui Johannem discipulum Domini viderunt" (5.33.3).
119. "Haec autem credibilia sunt credentibus" (5.33.4).
120. For a study of Irenaeus's use of John's Gospel, see P. Ferlay, "Irénée de Lyon exégète du quatrième évangile," *Nouvelle Revue Théologique* 106, no. 1 (1984): 222–34.
121. "His itaque praetereuntibus, super terram novam superiorem Hierusalem ait Domini discipulus Johannes descendere, quemadmodum sponsam ornatam viro suo, et hoc esse tabernaculum Dei in quo inhabitabit Deus cum hominibus" (5.35.2).
122. For Irenaeus's idiosyncratic definitions of these words, see Moringiello, "Allegory and Typology in Irenaeus of Lyon."
123. "Et nihil allegorizari potest, sed omnia firma et vera et substantiam habentia, ad fruitionem hominum justorum a Deo facta" (5.35.2).

the Father. And then after all things have been renewed, truly he will
live in the city of God."[124] Life in the city of God awaits those who
understand scripture correctly and see the visions it provides. In order
to see these visions, in order to distinguish what is metaphorical and
what is literal, the reader of scripture must follow Irenaeus in reading
the scriptures along with the faith. Only such a reading enables one to
see the typological rather than the allegorical interpretation do justice
to God's economy of salvation.

Irenaeus ends the *Adversus Haereses* by reminding his readers that
the salvation of human beings is at the center of God's economy of
salvation. Here he argues that in the scriptures and the economy of
salvation "the same God the Father is shown in all." This God "formed
man and promised the inheritance of land to the Fathers." God led this
inheritance "into the resurrection of the just and fulfilled the promises
of the kingdom in his Son."[125] Thanks to the work of the Son, human
beings can become *homines viventes*, because they "were capable of
the Word and ascended to him, going above the angels and becoming
according to the image and likeness of God."[126]

Of course, for Irenaeus, human beings are created in the image
and likeness of God *because of* and not in spite of their bodies. The
image and likeness of God, the prototype for the *homo vivens*, is Jesus
Christ, who was truly human in soul and body. In Book Five, Irenaeus
has recapitulated the major themes of the *Adversus Haereses* so that

124. "Quomodo enim vere Deus est qui resuscitat hominem, sic et vere resurget
homo a mortuis et non allegorice, quemadmodum per tanta ostendimus; et sicut vere
resurget, sic et vere praemeditabitur incorruptelam et augebitur et vigebit in regni temporibus, ut fiat capax gloriae Patris; deinde omnibus renovatis, vere in civitate habitabit
Dei" (5.35.2). On Irenaeus and the earthly kingdom of God, see J. F. Glasson, "The Temporary Messianic Kingdom and the Kingdom of God." *JTS* 41, no. 4 (1990): 517–25, and
Orbé, "San Ireneo y el regimen del milenio."

125. "Et in omnibus his et per omnia idem Deus Pater ostenditur, qui plasmavit
hominem et hereditatem terrae promisit patribus, qui eduxit illam in resurrectione justorum et promissiones adimplet in Filii sui regnum" (5.36.3). On the resurrection of the
flesh, see Anders-Christian Jacobsen, "The Philosophical Argument in the Teaching of
Irenaeus on the Resurrection of the Flesh," *Studia Patristica* 36 (2001): 256–62.

126. "ut progenies eius primogenitus Verbum descendat in facturam, hoc est in
plasma, et capiatur ab eo, et factura iterum capiat Verbum et ascendat ad eum, supergre-
diens angelos et fiens secundum imaginem et similitudinem Dei" (5.36.3). The best book
on image and likeness in Irenaeus is Fantino, *L'homme, image de Dieu*.

he can help his readers make the decision that is before them. They can choose to follow the exegesis of the Apostles, which teaches that the economy of salvation recounted in the Old and New Covenants is recapitulated in Christ, taught by the Apostles, embodied in the martyrs, and leads to the vision of God. Or they can choose to follow the exegesis of Irenaeus's opponents, which denies that economy and disparages both the Apostles and the martyrs. Irenaeus wrote in the shadow of the persecution his community suffered in 177. Little did he know as he wrote that another persecution was imminent, and his community would once again face a persecution that forced them to witness to their faith in the economy of God recapitulated by Christ.

CONCLUSION

I began my argument by criticizing approaches to the study of early Christianity that reduced its study to questions of sociology. But it is clear that members of the early Christian community were interested in defining who was a Christian and on what basis they could claim that identity or how the community could claim it for them. The issue, then, is not whether identity is important. The issue instead is: what is the site for arguments about identity? I fear that if we misplace the site of these arguments, we misunderstand their importance. Of course, in this book I have argued that, for Irenaeus, questions of identity play themselves out in terms of debates about the interpretation of texts. I have argued that the structure of Irenaeus's argument in the *Adversus Haereses* is based on the faith of the church. The faith of the church, moreover, provides the proper interpretative key for the scriptures—both of the Old Covenant and the New.

In this conclusion, I wish to make three points. First, I will recapitulate my own argument about Irenaeus's understanding of Christian identity. To perform this recapitulation, I want to move from the *Adversus Haereses* to Irenaeus's *Demonstration of the Apostolic Preaching*. Second, I will explore what my understanding of Irenaeus might offer the scholarly world of the study of religion and the study of late antiquity. Third, I will conclude with some reflections on how my understanding of Irenaeus might inform the world of Christian theology. Irenaeus would not have seen himself as either a student of "religion" or a figure of late antiquity or even as a theologian. He was the leader of a Christian community who wanted that community to understand the scriptures in a certain way.

If the faith structures the *Adversus Haereses*, how might that faith structure the life of the reader of the *Adversus Haereses*? In other words, how does the faith, on which Irenaeus's text is built, identify the reader of Irenaeus's text? How does the faith identify a Christian? The clearest answer to these important questions is found not in the *Adversus Haereses*, but in the other complete text of Irenaeus that we have, the *Demonstration of the Apostolic Preaching*.[1] I want to turn my attention to this text because we see there how Irenaeus believes that baptism makes a person a Christian. Part of being a Christian— perhaps the most important part of being a Christian—is understanding oneself within the economy of salvation that the scriptures recount and that Christ recapitulates. This economy of course includes the work of the Father, the Son, and the Holy Spirit. The faith, as we have seen, provides the guide for interpreting scripture and the economy that it recounts correctly.

Some scholars argue that Irenaeus originally meant to follow the first two books of the *Adversus Haereses* with what is now the *Demonstration*.[2] Other scholars have placed the *Demonstration* in the context of catechetical initiation. Of course, both arguments could be right. If the *Demonstration* was meant to "finish" the *Adversus Haereses* or whether it was meant to stand alone, Irenaeus is primarily concerned with forming Christians through the scriptures. To be Christian is to be part of a community that has been taught to interpret the scriptures in the way that the Apostles themselves did.

Before we turn to the text itself, let me say a bit about its structure. I stressed in my argument about the *Adversus Haereses* that Irenaeus follows the pattern of *probatio*, *refutatio*, and *recapitulatio* throughout his text. Irenaeus based this pattern both on the tradition of rhetoric that he learned and on the faith as he laid it out throughout the text. We should not expect an exact correspondence between the structure

---

1. The text of the *Demonstration* comes down to us in an Armenian translation. See Irenaeus, *Eis Epideixin Tou Apostolikou Kerugmatos = The Proof of the Apostolic Preaching: With Seven Fragments: Armenian Version* (Turnhout: Brepols, 1974). In the few places where I have quoted the *Demonstration* here, I have relied on Behr's translation because I could not improve on it. See Irenaeus, *On the Apostolic Preaching*. See also Irenaeus, *Irenaeus's Demonstration of the Apostolic Preaching: A Theological Commentary and Translation*, trans. Iain M. Robinson MacKenzie (Burlington, Vt.: Ashgate, 2002).

2. Behr, *Irenaeus of Lyons*, 76.

of the *Adversus Haereses* and the structure of the *Demonstration*. Nevertheless, we do find some similarities.

Here I draw on the work of James Wiegel, who has recently argued for a Trinitarian structure of the *Demonstration*.[3] Throughout my argument, I have suggested that Ireaneus bases the structure of the *Adversus Haereses* on the structure of the faith as he lays it out in 1.10.1. Wiegel argues that Irenaeus structures the *Demonstration* in the same way. Chapters 1–7 form a preface to the work, chapters 8–30 form the first part, chapters 31–42a the second part, 42b–97 the third part, and 98–100 the conclusion of the work. Although Weigel does not connect the *Demonstration* to the rhetorical tradition the way I have, I think his framework fits the one that I have argued for. Chapters 8–30 are the *probatio* that assert God's identity. As Weigel puts it, the concern in this section is "the rhetorical-narrative continuity between the scriptures and the apostolic kerygma."[4] The second section, chapters 31–42a, then, serves as a *refutatio* by showing how Christ is present in the economy of salvation. And the final section, chapters 42b to 98, serves as the *recapitulatio* and focuses on how the Holy Spirit reveals the salvific work of Christ.[5] Indeed, the faith is based on Christ's identity, his role in the economy of salvation, and his work as savior. That is who Christ is and that is the whole point of the scriptures, as Irenaeus understands them. All of this, according to Irenaeus, is there in the books of the Old Covenant. The only thing new that Christ brings, as Irenaeus puts it in the *Adversus Haereses*, is himself.[6]

I do not want to spend this conclusion arguing for my interpretation of the structure of the *Demonstration*. I do, however, want to examine the *Demonstration* in light of questions of Christian identity.

3. James B. Wiegel, "The Trinitarian Structure of Irenaeus' Demonstration of the Apostolic Preaching," *St. Vladimir's Theological Quarterly* 58, no. 2 (2014): 113–39. Wiegel argues against an interpretation that sees the *Demonstration* organized into two parts as argued by Everett Ferguson and Susan Graham. See Everett Ferguson, "Irenaeus' Proof of the Apostolic Preaching and Early Catechetical Instruction," *Studia Patristica* 18, no. 3 (1989): 119–35, and Susan L. Graham, "Irenaeus and the Covenants: 'Immortal Diamond,'" *Studia Patristica* 40 (2006): 393–98.

4. Wiegel, "The Trinitarian Structure," 128. As Wiegel notes, he too shares Behr's understanding of the structure of the *AH*.

5. Wiegel, "The Trinitarian Structure," 132.

6. See *AH* 4.33.1.

Most relevant for my purposes are the beginning and end of the text where Irenaeus discusses baptism and the faith. As we will see, the faith that is poured onto the believer at baptism is the same faith that structures the correct reading of scripture. Indeed, if one is baptized, then one has all that is necessary to interpret the scriptures correctly, provided that one follows the faith of the church as received at baptism. Irenaeus's concern, then, is much more than identifying some Christians as part of a group and identifying other Christians as part of another group. No doubt he is interested in such questions, but those questions point to a more fundamental issue. The faith allows people a "true comprehension of what is."

The faith is personal and communal. At the beginning of the *Demonstration*, Irenaeus writes to Marcianus and tells him: "to demonstrate by means of a summary, the preaching of the truth, so as to strengthen your faith." Thanks to what Irenaeus writes, Marcianus will "understand all the members of the body of truth, and through a summary receive the expositions of the things of God." With these expositions, Marcianus will be able to "bear [his] own salvation," confound those who hold false opinions, and deliver "our sound and irreproachable word" to all who desire to know. But the faith is not merely personal. Properly speaking, the faith belongs to the church, which guards it. Irenaeus tells Marcianus "we must keep the rule of faith unswervingly and perform the commandments of God, believing in God and fearing him for he is Father."[7] Irenaeus notes that truth brings about faith. "For faith," he writes, "is established upon things truly real, that we may believe what really is, as it is, and [believing] what really is, as it is, we may always keep our conviction of it firm. Since, then, the conserver of our salvation is faith, it is necessary to take great care of it, that we may have a true comprehension of what is."[8]

We should note here how high the stakes are for Irenaeus. The Christian is marked by the faith he receives at baptism. This faith gives the baptized a "true comprehension of what is." In this light, the *Adversus Haereses* takes on a new importance. If, as I argued, the structure of the *Adversus Haereses* is the argument of the *Adversus Haereses*,

7. See *AH* 4.20.1.
8. All references to the *Demonstration* are to paragraph numbers.

and if the faith is the basis of the structure, then the *Adversus Haereses* does far more than "defeat heretics." Indeed, that is an ancillary goal at best. Instead, the *Adversus Haereses* performs the faith. Through this performance of the faith, the reader of the *Adversus Haereses*, who has been baptized into that faith, can see the vision of the economy of salvation that the scriptures offer.

Let us return to the *Demonstration* and examine three paragraphs where Irenaeus links the faith to baptism. Irenaeus reminds Marcianus that what he writes comes down from "the elders, the disciples of the apostles."[9] He tells Marcianus that they have received "baptism for the remission of sins, in the name of God the Father, and in the name of Jesus Christ, the Son of God, [who was] incarnate, and died, and was raised, and in the Holy Spirit of God." This baptism, moreover, is "the seal of eternal life and rebirth unto God, that we may no longer be sons of mortal men, but of the eternal and everlasting God."[10] Obviously baptism here is the mark of a new identity where one's sins are forgiven through a relation with God the Father, the Son of God, and the Holy Spirit of God. This same God, of course, created the world. The faith states that there is "One God [the] Father, uncreated, invisible, Creator of all, above whom there is no other God, and after whom there is no other God. And as God is verbal, therefore He created things by the Word; and God is Spirit, so that He adorned all things by the Spirit."[11] Thanks to baptism, one can know "the Spirit demonstrates the Word, and because of this, the prophets announced the Son of God, while the Word articulates the Spirit, and therefore it is He Himself who interprets the prophets and brings man to the Father."[12] This is all another way of saying that thanks to baptism, a person can understand the scriptures. This understanding occurs because the faith received at baptism—the faith that proclaims the Father, Son, and Holy Spirit—is the same faith that undergirds the hypothesis of the scriptures themselves.

Such an understanding, moreover, brings a person closer to God.

---

9. See *AH* 4.32.
10. *Demonstration* 3.
11. *Demonstration* 5.
12. *Demonstration* 5.

For Irenaeus, being closer to God is not primarily intellectual, as if knowledge of the scriptures were cognitive. Instead, the faith, he writes, is the "foundation of [the] edifice and the support of [our] conduct." The faith is the basis for every aspect of a Christian's life and identity, not just what the Christian knows. And baptism, as I have noted, imparts the faith. Irenaeus's key point is that baptism brings with it the interpretation of the scriptures. It does this because a person is baptized into the faith, which has three headings. The first heading or article of the faith is "God, the Father, uncreated, uncontainable, invisible, one God, the creator of all." This *probatio* looks familiar to us, of course. Here is the identity of the one God who is the focus of the debate between Irenaeus and his opponents. The *probatio* then leads to a *refutatio*. The second article of the faith is

the Word of God, the Son of God, Christ Jesus our Lord, who was revealed by the prophets according to the character of their prophecy and according to the nature of the economies of the Father, by whom all things were made and who, in the last times, to recapitulate all things, became a man amongst men, visible and palpable, in order to abolish death, to demonstrate life, and to effect communion between God and man.

Notice how Irenaeus focuses on Christ's presence throughout the economy of salvation. In order to understand Christ one needs to understand his revelation through the prophets, his revelation in the flesh, and his recapitulation in the end times. Finally, the third article of the faith is "the Holy Spirit, through whom the prophets prophesied and the patriarchs learnt the things of God and the righteous were led in the path of righteousness, and who, in the last times, was poured out in a new fashion upon the human race renewing man, throughout the world, to God."[13] Following Ephesians 1:10, we say that Christ recapitulates all things. But here Irenaeus discusses the role the Spirit plays in renewing man to God.

Christ is the recapitulation of the scriptures, which is another way of saying that Christ is the recapitulation of the economy of salvation. We should remember, though, that in the *Demonstration*, Irenaeus focuses his attention only on the writings of the Old Covenant. We

13. *Demonstration* 6.

could say that Christ's life is the embodiment of the Old Covenant, the way the Old Covenant is played out in a single human life. As Irenaeus says, the only thing new that Christ brings in the New Covenant is himself. But in bringing himself Christ opens the covenant to all who follow him. This, then, *is* the New Covenant. Human beings are regenerated through baptism and this regeneration takes place through these three articles, "granting us regeneration unto God the Father through His Son by the Holy Spirit."[14] Irenaeus's language here is suggestive. Baptism takes place through the three articles. Irenaeus is not concerned for the "three persons" of the Trinity. Instead, he is interested in how the Father, Son, and Spirit work in the economy of salvation as that economy is recorded in scripture.

We can put this another way. The faith, received at baptism, enables the baptized to become the *homo vivens*, who understands himself in the economy of salvation that the scriptures record. Because Irenaeus makes his argument in the *Demonstration* on the basis of texts from the Old Covenant, it is worth bringing this argument together with the similar argument that Irenaeus makes in the fourth book of *Adversus Haereses*. That book, as we recall, also focused on the economy of Christ's incarnation and on prophecy. My discussion of Book Four spent some time on Irenaeus's famous dictum that the living human being is the glory of God. Life, Irenaeus clarified there, is the vision of God. And this vision only comes about through a proper interpretation of the scriptures. Thanks to baptism, the Christian can share Christ's vision of the economy of salvation.

Baptism, we could say, seals the *Demonstration* just as it seals the believer. Near the end of the text, Irenaeus draws on Genesis 1:28. This scriptural verse concluded the *Adversus Haereses*. "'He appeared on earth and conversed with men' mixing and blending the Spirit of God with the handiwork of God, that man might be according to the image and likeness of God."[15] As we would expect, Irenaeus ends the main body of his text with a focus on recapitulation and salvation, and he does so by stressing the work of the Son with the Father and the Holy Spirit. This would be a fitting way to end the text, just as it was a fitting

14. *Demonstration 7.*
15. *Demonstration 97.*

end to the *Adversus Haereses*. Instead, Irenaeus tells Marcianus that what he has written is "the preaching of the truth," "the character of our salvation," and "the way of life which the prophets announced and Christ confirmed and the apostles handed over."[16] The church now hands it down to all her children. This preaching, character, and way of life *are* the faith. The interpretation of the scriptures occurs in the way Christians live their lives. This is why the witness of the martyrs is so prominent in Irenaeus's thought.

In the end, the problem with Valentinus, Ptolemy, Marcion, and the rest is that they "despise the Father or do not accept the Son—they speak against the economy of His Incarnation—or they do not accept the Holy Spirit, that is they despise prophecy." To say this is to say that these teachers neither accept nor understand baptism, which is to say they do not understand the scriptures. If they do not understand the scriptures, they cannot live the scriptures, and they cannot be those living human beings who behold the vision of God. Irenaeus does not oppose these teachers because he wants them to burn or he desires purity. He wants everyone sealed with baptism to partake in the vision that the scriptures offer. After all, he is a rhetor, and a Christian rhetor at that.

Where does that leave us as scholars of "religion," as scholars of late antiquity, and as scholars of Christian theology? For starters, we need to acknowledge that we all work in Irenaeus's shadow in ways so profound that they are easy to miss. The fact that we can talk coherently about the Bible—as a text that begins with the Book of Genesis and ends with the Book of Revelation—shows Irenaeus's imprint. No Christian author before him did that. Even acknowledging the study of "biblical literature" and extra-canonical sources relies on some understanding of the Bible and of canonicity. As we have seen, these understandings of the Bible and of the canon come directly, for Irenaeus, from an understanding of baptism and the faith in the Father, Son, and Holy Spirit that baptism imparts. Thus we must remember that all of the many deeply important discussions that we as scholars have about the many and various strands of early Christianity are founded upon these fundamental Irenaean insights.

---

16. *Demonstration* 98.

This is especially the case when it comes to our understanding of Irenaeus's opponents. The wealth of scholarship that has arisen since the discovery of the Nag Hammadi texts has shown how Irenaeus's opponents were a varied lot, but, as we have seen, Irenaeus knew this already. And truthfully, the discoveries at Nag Hammadi show little about what Irenaeus might have encountered in Lyon. There are times when this scholarship has a tinge of "detect and overthrow."[17] The scholarship often ends up reenacting the same policing techniques that scholars mistakenly attribute to Irenaeus. The exegete from Lyon often gets lost in the caricature. These policing techniques often lose sight of the true site of disagreement between Irenaeus and his opponents. The scholarship on the various authors once called "Gnostic" could focus more on how those authors were engaged in questions of scriptural interpretation. Again, sociology works as the operative discipline, rather than literary studies.[18] My study, obviously, does not engage with the interpretations of Irenaeus's opponents. But if we were to shift the scholarly discussion to consider how Irenaeus and his opponents understood the same texts, we would be doing precisely what Irenaeus saw himself doing.

This study has placed Irenaeus's *Adversus Haereses* in the context of traditions of Greek and Roman rhetoric. In particular I have shown that the structure of Irenaeus's argument is Irenaeus's argument, and he bases that structure on the faith. I hope this structural study might entice scholars who work on the Nag Hammadi texts to engage in work that would examine how those authors structured their arguments and what theological bases might have inspired those structures. This avenue of research would also help make connections between Christian and "pagan" sources in the first centuries of the

17. There are moments in Karen King's work where I find this to be the case, especially in the conclusion of her *What Is Gnosticism?*

18. I want to emphasize again that I do not dispute the value of such studies. Two excellent recent works come to mind: Todd S. Berzon, *Classifying Christians: Ethnography, Heresiology, and the Limits of Knowledge in Late Antiquity* (Berkeley: University of California Press, 2016), and Geoffrey S. Smith, *Guilt by Association: Heresy Catalogues in Early Christianity* (New York: Oxford University Press, 2015). Works that do engage with literary studies include Catherine M. Chin, *Grammar and Christianity in the Late Roman World* (Philadelphia: University of Pennsylvania Press, 2008).

common era. I signaled some of this in my discussion of Irenaeus and the Second Sophistic. Although there have been many superb studies on rhetoric and the New Testament, even these studies do not quite examine what, if any, theological rationale might have lain behind the rhetorical choices the authors make.

In all of this, I suppose I am offering a plea to scholars to take the texts of the late antique world seriously *as texts*. They should be understood as texts before they are understood as "religious" documents or as pieces of data used to construct a picture of life in the first or second or third century of the common era. These texts, of course, were produced in specific communities and the more we know about the social conditions of those communities the better. My study has been an attempt to think through Irenaeus's argument as he presents it as an argument. Even those scholars who agree that Irenaeus is first and foremost an interpreter of the scriptures do not always pay enough attention to how Irenaeus presents his interpretation.

If scholars of religion and scholars of late antiquity would do well to attend to the structure and—for lack of a better term—"theology" of the texts they study, Christian theologians could pay more attention to the literary aspect of all theology. Moreover, thanks to Irenaeus, theologians can remember that all their theological investigations ultimately rest on the faith. This faith is the first principle from which all theological work flows. But to say that faith is the first principle is certainly not to say that it can be left behind, that a theologian might start from faith but somehow move beyond it. The faith, as Irenaeus presents it throughout the *Adversus Haereses* and which structures the *Adversus Haereses*, both begins and ends with the interpretation of scripture. It helps the Christian who reads scripture to understand that he is himself part of the economy of salvation that the scriptures recount. Indeed, as I have tried to argue, for Irenaeus the faith is, in part, a literary device that undergirds both one's interpretation of the scriptures and, through baptism, inducts one into an interpretative community. Without the faith, one cannot interpret properly. Without the faith, one cannot seek a deeper understanding.

I have already noted that Irenaeus does not see his work as merely a literary study. The structure and argument of the *Adversus Haere-*

ses are at the service of a vision that, Irenaeus hopes, will transform human beings. If they were pressed, I have no doubt that Christian theologians today would share Irenaeus's goal of helping their audiences recognize the transformation that God offers and has already begun. But the question is whether they structure their arguments in such a way that the faith is ever-present in what they write. As we have seen repeatedly, according to Irenaeus, to ask if the faith is present is to ask if the scriptures are present. My point here is not to chastise but to recognize the challenges that reading Irenaeus and thinking with Irenaeus present.

As I understand him, Irenaeus presents a challenge to us today. He challenges scholars to look beyond caricatures of him as a Grand Inquisitor who seeks to burn heretics. He challenges critics to understand the interplay between structure and argument in texts. He challenges historians to shift their focus from Christian exegetes as philosophers to Christian exegetes as rhetors. He challenges theologians to structure their own arguments in accord with the faith. If scholars take up the challenges he presents, they would be unusual historically. After all, for all of the deep influence Irenaeus has had, caricatures of him have sprung up so easily because he has more often been mentioned than read. He is not quoted as often as someone like Justin, let alone Augustine. If we lack many of the details of Irenaeus's legacy because of texts that are completely lost to us or exist only in translation, what remains—however fragmentary—asks us to rethink our assumptions about the scholarship surrounding his time and about Christian theology itself. For Irenaeus, the faith that structures his argument ultimately is his argument. This faith allows the *homo vivens* to see the vision of salvation that the Father offers through the Son who interprets him and in the Holy Spirit that joins the community of believers.

APPENDIX

Outline of the *Adversus Haereses*

1. Book One

1.1 *Probatio*, 1–8: God
    1.1.1 *Probatio* of *Probatio*, 1–3
    1.1.2 *Refutatio* of *Probatio*, 4–5
    1.1.3 *Recapitulatio* of *Probatio*, 6–8
    1.1.4 Theological Methodology, 9–10
1.2 *Refutatio*, 11–21: Scripture/Economy
    1.2.1 *Probatio* of *Refutatio*, 11–12
    1.2.2 *Refutatio* of *Refutatio*, 13–20
    1.2.3 *Recapitulatio* of *Refutatio*, 21
    1.2.4 Theological Methodology, 22
1.3 *Recapitulatio*, 23–31: Christ/Salvation
    1.3.1 *Probatio* of *Recapitulatio*, 23–25
    1.3.2 *Refutatio* of *Recapitulatio*, 26–29
    1.3.3 *Recapitulatio* of *Recapitulatio*, 30–31

2. Book Two

2.1 *Probatio*, 1–10: God
    2.1.1 *Probatio* of *Probatio*, 1–4
    2.1.2 *Refutatio* of *Probatio*, 5–9
    2.1.3 *Recapulatio* of *Probatio*, 10–11
2.2. *Probatio*, 12–19: Aeons
    2.2.1 *Probatio* of *Probatio*, 12–13
    2.2.2 *Refutatio* of *Probatio*, 14–19
2.3 *Refutatio*, 20–28: Scripture/Economy
    2.3.1 *Probatio* of *Refutatio*, 20–24
    2.3.2 Theological Methodology, 25–28

2.4 *Recapitulatio*, 29–35: Christ/Salvation
    2.4.1 *Probatio* of *Recapitulatio*, 29–30
    2.4.2 *Refutatio* of *Recapitulatio*, 31–32
    2.4.3 *Recapitulatio* of *Recapitulatio*, 33–35

3. Book Three

3.1 *Probatio*, 1–8: God
    3.1.1 *Probatio* of *Probatio*, 1–2
    3.1.2 *Refutatio* of *Probatio*, 3–4
    3.1.3 *Recapitulatio* of *Probatio*, 5–8
3.2 *Refutatio*, 9–15: Scripture/Economy
    3.2.1 *Probatio* of *Refutatio*, 9–11
    3.2.2 *Refutatio* of *Refutatio*, 12–13
    3.2.3 *Recapitulatio* of *Refutatio*, 14–15
    3.2.4 Theological Methodology, 16–18
3.3 *Recapitulatio*, 19–25: Christ/Salvation
    3.3.1 *Probatio* of *Recapitulatio*, 19–22
    3.3.2 *Refutatio* of *Recapitulatio*, 23
    3.3.3 *Recapitulatio* of *Recapitulatio*, 24–25

4. Book Four

4.1 *Probatio*, 1–20: God
    4.1.1 *Probatio* of *Probatio*, 1–8
    4.1.2 *Refutatio* of *Probatio*, 9–16
    4.1.3 *Recapitulatio* of *Probatio*, 17–19
    4.1.4 Theological Methodology, 20
4.2 *Refutatio*, 21–35: Scripture/Economy
    4.2.1 *Probatio* of *Refutatio*, 21–24
    4.2.2 *Refutatio* of *Refutatio*, 25–31
    4.2.3 *Recapitulatio* of *Refutatio*, 32–35
4.3 *Recapitulatio*, 36–41: Christ/Salvation
    4.3.1 *Probatio* of *Recapitulatio*, 36
    4.3.2 *Refutatio* of *Recapitulatio*, 37
    4.3.3 *Recapitulatio* of *Recapitulatio*, 38–41

5. Book Five

5.1 *Probatio*, 1–14: God
    5.1.1 *Probatio* of *Probatio*, 1–7
    5.1.2 *Refutatio* of *Probatio*, 8–11
    5.1.3 *Recapitulatio* of *Probatio*, 12–14
5.2 *Refutatio*, 15–24: Scripture/Economy
    5.2.1 *Probatio* of *Refutatio*, 15–19
    5.2.2 *Refutatio* of *Refutatio*, 20
    5.2.3 Theological Methodology, 21–22
    5.2.3 *Recapitulatio* of *Refutatio*, 23–24
5.3 *Recapitulatio*, 25–36: Christ/Salvation
    5.3.1 *Probatio* of *Recapitulatio*, 25–26
    5.3.2 *Refutatio* of *Recapitulatio*, 27–28
    5.3.3 *Recapitulatio* of *Recapitulatio*, 29–36

Outline of *Demonstration of the Apostolic Preaching*

Preface, 1–7
Probatio, 8–30
Refutatio, 31–42a
Recapitulatio, 42b–98
Conclusion, 98–100

SELECTED BIBLIOGRAPHY

Ancient Sources

Anaximenes. *Ars Rhetorica: Quae Vulgo Fertur Aristotelis Ad Alexandrum*. Berlin: De Gruyter, 2010.

Aristotle. *The "Art" of Rhetoric*. Translated by John Henry Freese. Cambridge, Mass.: Harvard University Press, 1959.

Cicero, Marcus Tullius. *De Oratore I–III*. Edited by Augustus S. Wilkins. London: Bristol Classical Press, 2002.

Eusebius. *The Ecclesiastical History*. Translated by Kirsopp Lake. New York: G. P. Putnam's Sons, 1926.

Holmes, Michael W. *The Apostolic Fathers: Greek Texts and English Translations*. Grand Rapids, Mich.: Baker Books, 1999.

Irenaeus of Lyon. *Against the Heresies: Book 1*. Translated by Dominic J. Unger and John J. Dillon. ACW 55. New York: Paulist Press, 1992.

———. *Against the Heresies: Book 2*. Translated by Dominic Unger and John Dillon. ACW 65. Mahwah, N.J.: Paulist Press, 2012.

———. *Against the Heresies: Book 3*. Translated by Dominic Unger and Irenaeus Steenberg. ACW 64. Mahwah, N.J.: Paulist Press, 2012.

———. *Contre Les Hérésies: Livre I*. 2 vols. SC 263–64. Paris: Cerf, 1979.

———. *Contre Les Hérésies: Livre II*. 2 vols. SC 293–94. Paris: Cerf, 1982.

———. *Contre Les Hérésies: Livre III*. 2 vols. SC 210–11. Paris: Cerf, 2002.

———. *Contre Les Hérésies: Livre IV*. 2 vols. SC 99–100. Paris: Cerf, 1965.

———. *Contre Les Hérésies: Livre V*. 2 vols. SC 152–53. Paris: Cerf, 1969.

———. *Eis Epideixin Tou Apostolikou Kerugmatos = The Proof of the Apostolic Preaching: With Seven Fragments: Armenian Version*. Turnhout: Brepols, 1974.

———. *Irenaeus's Demonstration of the Apostolic Preaching: A Theological Commentary and Translation*. Translated by Iain M. Robinson MacKenzie. Burlington, Vt.: Ashgate, 2002.

———. *On the Apostolic Preaching*. Translated by John Behr. Crestwood, N.Y.: St. Vladimir's Seminary Press, 1997.

Justin Martyr. *The First and Second Apologies*. New York: Paulist Press, 1997.

Musurillo, Herbert. *The Acts of the Christian Martyrs*. Oxford: Clarendon Press, 1972.

Philostratus. *The Lives of the Sophists*. Loeb Classical Library. Cambridge, Mass.: Harvard University Press, 1961.

Plato. *Opera: Volume I: Euthyphro, Apologia Socratis, Crito, Phaedo, Cratylus, Sophista, Politicus, Theaetetus*. 3rd edition. New York: Clarendon Press, 1995.

Plutarch. *De Gloria Atheniensium*. Translated by Jean-Claude Thiolier. Paris: Presses de l'Université de Paris-Sorbonne, 1985.

Quintilian. *The Orator's Education*. Translated by D. A. Russell. Cambridge, Mass.: Harvard University Press, 2001.

Theophilus of Antioch. *Ad Autolycum*. Translated by Robert Grant. Oxford Early Christian Texts. Oxford: Clarendon Press, 1970.

Modern Sources

Abramowski, Luise. "Irenaeus Adv. Haer. Iii.3.2: Ecclesia Romana and Omnis Ecclesia and Ibid. 3.3. Anacletus of Rome." *JTS* 28, no. 1 (1977): 101–4.

Adamopoulo, Themistocles. "Sophia, the Creator and the Created Cosmos: Early Christian Cosmogonic and Cosmological Polemics." *Phronema* 8 (1993): 33–48.

Aland, Barbara. "Fides und Subiectio: zur Anthropologie des Irenäus." In *Kerygma und Logos: Beiträge zu den geistesgeschichtlichen Beziehungen zwischen Antike und Christentum*, edited by Adolf Ritter, 9–28. Göttingen: Vandenhoeck and Ruprecht, 1979.

———. "Polemik Bei Irenäus Von Lyon: Strategie — Ertrag — Wirkung." In *Polemik in der frühchristlichen Literatur: Texte und Kontexte*, edited by Oda Wischmeyer and Lorenzo Scornaienchi, 579–602. Berlin: De Gruyter, 2011.

Anderson, Graham. *The Second Sophistic: A Cultural Phenomenon in the Roman Empire*. New York: Routledge, 1993.

Andia, Ysabel de. "L'hérésie et sa réfutation selon Irénée de Lyon." *Augustinianum* 25, no. 3 (1985): 609–44.

———. *Homo Vivens: Incorruptibilite et divinisation de l'homme selon Irenee de Lyons*. Paris: Etudes augustiniennes, 1986.

Andre, J. M. "Les ècoles philosophiques aux deux premiers siecles de l'empire." *Aufstieg und Niedergang der romischen Welt* 36, no. 1 (1987): 5–77.

Audet, Th-André. "Orientations théologiques chez saint Irénée: le contexte mental d'une gnôsis alēthēs." *Traditio* 1, no. 1 (1943): 15–54.

Bacq, Philippe. *De l'ancienne à la nouvelle alliance selon s. Irénée: unité du livre iv de l'Adversus Haereses*. Paris: Lethielleux, 1978.

Balthasar, Hans Urs von. *The Glory of the Lord: A Theological Aesthetics*, vol. 2: *Studies in Theological Style: Clerical Styles*. Translated by John Kenneth Riches. Edinburgh: T and T Clark, 1986.

Bandstra, Andrew J. "Paul and an Ancient Interpreter: A Comparison of the Teaching of Redemption in Paul and Irenaeus." *Calvin Theological Journal* 5, no. 1 (1970): 43–63.

Barnes, Michel Rene. "Irenaeus's Trinitarian Theology." *Nova et Vetera* 7, no. 1 (2009): 67–106.

Behr, John. *Asceticism and Anthropology in Irenaeus and Clement*. New York: Oxford University Press, 2000.

———. *The Way to Nicaea*. Crestwood, N.Y.: St. Vladimir's Seminary Press, 2001.

———. *Irenaeus of Lyons: Identifying Christianity*. New York: Oxford University Press, 2013.

Bengsch, Alfred. *Heilsgeschichte und Heilswissen: Eine Untersuchung zur Struktur und Entfaltung des theologischen Denkens im Werk "Adversus Haereses" des Hl. Irenäus Von Lyon*. Leipzig: St. Benno-Verlag, 1957.

Benjamins, H. S. "Die Apostolizität der kirchlichen Verkündigung bei Irenäus von Lyon." In *Apostolic Age in Patristic Thought*, edited by A. Hilhorst, 115–29. Leiden: Brill, 2004.

Benoit, André. *Saint Irénée: introduction à l'étude de sa théologie*. Paris: Presses universitaires de France, 1960.

Bergmeier, Roland. "'Koniglosigkeit' als nachvalentinianisches Heilspradikat." *Novum Testamentum Novum Testamentum* 24, no. 4 (1982).

Berrouard, M. F. "Servitude de la loi et liberté de l'évangile selon saint Irénée." *Lumière et vie* 61, no. 1 (1963): 41–60.

Berthouzoz, Roger. *Liberté et grâce suivant la théologie d'Irénée de Lyon: Le débat avec la gnose aux origines de la théologie chrétienne*. Paris: Cerf, 1980.

Bertrand, Dominique. "L'eschatologie de saint Irénée." *Théophilyon* 16, no. 1 (2011): 113–48.

Berzon, Todd S. *Classifying Christians: Ethnography, Heresiology, and the Limits of Knowledge in Late Antiquity*. Berkeley: University of California Press, 2016.

Bingham, D. Jeffrey. *Irenaeus' Use of Matthew's Gospel in Adversus Haereses*. Leuven: Peeters, 1998.

———. "Knowledge and Love in Irenaeus of Lyons." *Studia Patristica* 36 (2000): 184–99.

———. "Himself within Himself: The Father and His Hands in Early Christianity." *Southwestern Journal of Theology* 47, no. 2 (2005): 137–51.

———. "Irenaeus of Lyons." In *Routledge Companion to Early Christian Thought*, edited by D. Jeffrey Bingham, 137–53. London: Routledge, 2010.

Blackwell, Benjamin C. "Paul and Irenaeus." In *Paul and the Second Century*, edited by Michael Bird and Joseph Dodson, 190–206. New York: T and T Clark, 2011.

Blanchard, Yves Marie. *Aux sources du canon, le témoignage d'Irénée*. Paris: Cerf, 1993.

Blowers, Paul M. "The Regula Fidei and the Narrative Character of Early Christian Faith." *Pro Ecclesia* 6, no. 2 (1997): 199–228.

Borg, Barbara. *Paideia: The World of the Second Sophistic*. Berlin: Walter de Gruyter, 2004.

Boulluec, A. Le. *La notion d'hérésie dans la littérature grec (IIe–IIIe siècle)*. Paris: Etudes augustiniennes, 1985.

Bousset, Wilhelm. *Jüdisch-christlicher Schulbetrieb in Alexandria und Rom: literarische Untersuchungen zu Philo und Clemens von Alexandria, Justin und Irenäus*. Göttingen: Vandenhoeck and Ruprecht, 1915.

Bowersock, G. W. *Greek Sophists in the Roman Empire.* Oxford: Clarendon Press, 1969.

———. *Approaches to the Second Sophistic.* University Park, Penn.: American Philological Association, 1974.

———. *Hellenism in Late Antiquity.* Ann Arbor: University of Michigan Press, 1990.

Boyle, M. O'Rourke. "Irenaeus's Millenial Hope: A Polemical Weapon." *Recherches de théologie ancienne et medieval* 36, no. 1 (1969): 5–16.

Boys-Stones, George R. *Post-Hellenistic Philosophy: A Study of Its Development from the Stoics to Origen.* Oxford: Oxford University Press, 2001.

Brakke, David. *The Gnostics: Myth, Ritual, and Diversity in Early Christianity.* Cambridge, Mass.: Harvard University Press, 2010.

Braun, Willi. *Rhetoric and Reality in Early Christianities.* Waterloo: Wilfrid Laurier University Press, 2005.

Brauw, Michael de. "The Parts of the Speech." In *Companion to Greek Rhetoric*, edited by Ian Worthington, 187–202. London: Blackwell, 2007.

Briggman, Anthony. "Revisiting Irenaeus Philosophical Acumen." *VC* 65, no. 2 (2011): 115–24.

———. *Irenaeus of Lyons and the Theology of the Holy Spirit.* New York: Oxford University Press, 2012.

Brown, Peter. *The World of Late Antiquity: From Marcus Aurelius to Muhammed.* London: Thames and Hudson, 1971.

Brown, Robert F. "'On the Necessary Imperfection of Creation': Irenaeus' Adversus Haereses iv, 38." *Scottish Journal of Theology* 28, no. 1 (1975): 17–25.

Brox, Norbert. "Irenaeus and the Bible." In *Handbook of Patristic Exegesis: The Bible in Ancient Christianity*, edited by Charles Kannengiesser, 483–506. Boston: Brill, 2004.

Cameron, Averil. *Christianity and the Rhetoric of Empire: The Development of Christian Discourse.* Berkeley: University of California Press, 1991.

Campenhausen, Hans. "Irenäus und das Neue Testament." *Theologische Literaturzeitung* 90, no. 1 (1965): 1–8.

Canlis, Julie. "Being Made Human: The Significance of Creation for Irenaeus' Doctrine of Participation." *Scottish Journal of Theology* 58, no. 4 (2005): 434–54.

Carey, Christopher. "Epideictic Oratory." In *Companion to Greek Rhetoric*, edited by Ian Worthington, 236–50. London: Blackwell, 2007.

Chin, Catherine M. *Grammar and Christianity in the Late Roman World.* Philadelphia: University of Pennsylvania Press, 2008.

Clarke, Graeme W. "Irenaeus Adv Haer 4 30 I." *Harvard Theological Review* 59, no. 1 (1966): 95–97.

Colson, Jean. *Saint Irénée: aux origines du christianisme en Gaule.* Paris: Ouvriıres, 1993.

Conzelmann, Hans. *Gentiles, Jews, Christians: Polemics and Apologetics in the Greco-Roman Era.* Minneapolis, Minn.: Fortress Press, 1992.

Cribiore, Raffaella. *Gymnastics of the Mind: Greek Education in Hellenistic and Roman Egypt.* Princeton, N.J.: Princeton University Press, 2001.

d'Ales, A. "Le mot oikonomia dans la langue théologique de saint Irénée." *Revue des études grecques* 32, no. 1 (1919): 1–9.

Donovan, Mary Ann. "Alive to the Glory of God: A Key Insight in St Irenaeus." *Theological Studies* 49, no. 2 (1988): 283–97.

———. "Irenaeus: At the Heart of Life, Glory." In *Spiritualities of the Heart: Approaches to Personal Wholeness in the Christian Tradition,* edited by Annice Callahan, 11–22. Mahwah, N.J.: Paulist Press, 1990.

———. *One Right Reading?: A Guide to Irenaeus.* Collegeville, Minn.: Liturgical Press, 1997.

Dunderberg, Ismo. *Beyond Gnosticism: Myth, Lifestyle, and Society in the School of Valentinus.* New York: Columbia University Press, 2008.

Dunning, Benjamin. "Virgin Earth, Virgin Birth: Creation, Sexual Difference, and Recapitulation in Irenaeus of Lyons." *Journal of Religion* 89, no. 1 (2009): 57–88.

Ebneter, Albert. "Die 'Glaubensregel' des Irenaeus als Oekumenisches Regulativ." In *Unterwegs zur Einheit,* edited by Johannes Branchtschen, Heinrich Stirnimann, and Pietro Selvatico, 588–608. Freiburg: Universitaetsverlag, 1980.

Elsner, Jasi. *Roman Eyes: Visuality and Subjectivity in Art and Text.* Princeton, N.J.: Princeton University Press, 2007.

Enslin, Morton Scott. "Irenaeus: Mostly Prolegomena." *Harvard Theological Review* 40, no. 3 (1947): 137–65.

Évieux, Pierre. "Théologie de l'accoutumance chez saint Irénée." *Recherches de science religieuse* 55, no. 1 (1967): 5–54.

Faivre, A. "Irénée, premier théologien 'systématique'?" *Recherches de science religieuse* 65, no. 1 (1991): 11–32.

Fakasfalvy, D. "Theology of Scripture in St Irenaeus." *Revue Bénédictine* 78, no. 3–4 (1968): 319–33.

Fantino, Jacques. *L'homme, image de Dieu, chez saint Irénée de Lyon.* Paris: Cerf, 1986.

———. *La théologie d'Irénée: Lecture des ecritures en réponse à l'exégèse gnostique: une approche trinitaire.* Paris: Editions du Cerf, 1994.

———. "Ordre social et politique, temps et eschatologie: la lecture de l'apocalypse par Irénée." *Studies in Religion/Sciences religieuses* 37, nos. 3–4 (2008): 481–96.

Farmer, William Reuben. "Galatians and the 2d Century Development of the Regula Fidei." *Second Century: A Journal of Early Christian Studies* 4, no. 3 (1985): 143–70.

Ferguson, Everett. "Irenaeus' Proof of the Apostolic Preaching and Early Catechetical Instruction." *Studia Patristica* 18, no. 3 (1989): 119–35.

Ferguson, Thomas C. K. "The Rule of Truth and Irenaean Rhetoric in Book 1 of *Against Heresies.*" *VC* 55, no. 4 (2001): 356–75.

Ferlay, P. "Irénée de Lyon exégète du quatrième évangile." *Nouvelle Revue Théologique* 106, no. 1 (1984): 222–34.

Foster, Paul. "Who Was Irenaeus? An Introducution to the Man and His Work." In *Irenaeus: Scripture, Life, Legacy,* edited by Sara Parvis and Paul Foster, 13–24. Minneapolis, Minn.: Fortress, 2011.

Fowler, Ryan Coleman. "The Platonic Rhetor in the Second Sophistic." PhD diss., Rutgers University, 2008.

Frend, William Hugh Clifford. *Martyrdom and Persecution in the Early Church: A Study of a Conflict from the Maccabees to Donatus.* Grand Rapids, Mich.: Baker Book House, 1981.

Galtier, Paul. "Ab his qui sunt undique Irénée, Adv Haer, Iii, 3,2." *Revue d'histoire ecclésiastique* 44, nos. 3–4 (1949): 411–28.

Gilliard, Frank D. "Apostolicity of Gallic Churches." *Harvard Theological Review* 68, no. 1 (1975): 17–33.

Glasson, J. F. "The Temporary Messianic Kingdom and the Kingdom of God." *JTS* 41, no. 4 (1990): 517–25.

Gleason, Maud. *Making Men: Sophists and Self-Presentation in Ancient Rome.* Princeton, N.J.: Princeton University Press, 1995.

Goldhill, Simon. "Rhetoric and the Second Sophistic." In *The Cambridge Companion to Ancient Rhetoric,* edited by Erik Gunderson. Cambridge: Cambridge University Press, 2009.

Gouilloud, André. *Saint Irénée et son temps: deuxième siècle de l'église.* Lyon: Briday, Libraire-Éditeur, 1876.

Gounelle, Rémi. "L'ultime combat de Dieu: le face à face infernal du Christ et du Diable." *Foi et vie* 110, no. 2 (2011): 36–47.

Graham, Susan. "'Zealous for the Covenant': Irenaeus and the Covenants of Israel." PhD diss., University of Notre Dame, 2001.

———. "Irenaeus and the Covenants: 'Immortal Diamond.'" *Studia Patristica* 40 (2006): 393–98.

Grant, Robert M. "Irenaeus and Hellenistic Culture." *Harvard Theological Review* 42, no. 1 (1949): 41–51.

———. *Irenaeus of Lyons.* New York: Routledge, 1997.

Greer, Rowan A. "The Dog and the Mushrooms: Irenaeus's View of the Valentinians Assessed." In *Rediscovery of Gnosticism,* edited by Bentley Layton, 1:146–71. Leiden: Brill, 1980.

Gunderson, Erik, ed. *The Cambridge Companion to Ancient Rhetoric.* New York: Cambridge University Press, 2009.

Hadot, Pierre. *Philosophy as a Way of Life: Spiritual Exercises from Socrates to Foucault.* Edited by Arnold Davidson. New York: Wiley-Blackwell, 1995.

Hahn, Johannes. *Der Philosoph und die Gesellschaft: Selbstverstandnis, offentliches Auftreten und populare Erwartungen in der hohen Kaiserzeit.* Stuttgart: Steiner, 1989.

Harnack, Adolf von. *History of Dogma.* Translated by Neil Buchanan. New York: Russell and Russell, 1958.

Hefner, Philip J. "Saint Irenaeus and the Hypothesis of Faith." *Dialog* 2, no. 4 (1963): 300–306.

——. "Theological Methodology and St Irenaeus." *Journal of Religion* 44, no. 4 (1964): 294–309.

Hill, Charles E. *Regnum Caelorum: Patterns of Millennial Thought in Early Christianity.* 2nd edition. Grand Rapids, Mich.: Eerdmans, 2001.

——. *From the Lost Teaching of Polycarp: Identifying Irenaeus' Apostolic Presbyter and the Author of Ad Diognetum.* Tübingen: Mohr Siebeck, 2006.

——. "'The writing which says ...' The Shepherd of Hermas in the Writings of Irenaeus and the Shepherd of Hermas." *Studia Patristica* 65, vol. 13 (2013): 127–38.

Hitchcock, F. R. Montgomery. "Loofs' Asiatic Source (I.Q.A.) and the Pseduo-Justin De Resurrectione." *Zeitschrift für die neutestamentliche Wissenschaft* 36, no. 1 (1937): 35–60.

——. "Loofs' Theory of Theophilus Von Antioch as a Source of Irenaeus." *JTS* 38, no. 150 (1937): 254–66.

Hoffman, Daniel L. "Irenaeus, Pagels, and the Christianity of the Gnostics." In *Light of Discovery*, edited by John Wineland, 65–82. Eugene, Ore.: Pickwick, 2007.

Holsinger-Friesen, Thomas. *Irenaeus and Genesis: A Study of Competition in Early Christian Hermeneutics.* Winona Lake, Ind.: Eisenbrauns, 2009.

Houssiau, A. *La christologie de saint Irénée.* Louvain: Publications Universitaires de Louvain, 1955.

Jacobsen, Anders-Christian. "The Philosophical Argument in the Teaching of Irenaeus on the Resurrection of the Flesh." *Studia Patristica* 36 (2001): 256–61.

Jazdzewska, Katarzyna Anna. "Platonic Receptions in the Second Sophistic." PhD diss., Ohio State University, 2011.

Jonas, Hans. *The Gnostic Religion: The Message of the Alien God and the Beginnings of Christianity.* Boston: Beacon Press, 1963.

Joppich, Godehard. *Salus Carnis: eine Untersuchung in der Theologie des Hl. Irenäus von Lyon.* Münsterschwarzach: Vier-Türme-Verlag, 1965.

Jorgensen, David W. *Treasure Hidden in a Field: Early Christian Reception of the Gospel of Matthew.* Berlin: Walter de Gruyter, 2016.

Kalvesmaki, Joel. "The Original Sequence of Irenaeus, against Heresies 1: Another Suggestion." *Journal of Early Christian Studies* 15, no. 3 (2007): 407–17.

Kennedy, George. *The Art of Persuasion in Greece.* Princeton, N.J.: Princeton University Press, 1963.

——. *The Art of Rhetoric in the Roman World.* Princeton, N.J.: Princeton University Press, 1972.

——. *New Testament Interpretation through Rhetorical Criticism.* Chapel Hill: University of North Carolina Press, 1984.

——. *Classical Rhetoric and Its Christian and Secular Tradition from Ancient to Modern Times.* Princeton, N.J.: Princeton University Press, 1989.

——. *A New History of Classical Rhetoric.* Princeton, N.J.: Princeton University Press, 1994.

——. *Progymnasmata: Greek Textbooks of Prose Composition and Rhetoric.* Atlanta: Society of Biblical Literature, 2003.

Kereszty, R. "The Unity of the Church in the Theology of Irenaeus." *Second Century* 4, no. 2 (1984): 202–18.

King, Karen L. *What Is Gnosticism?* Cambridge, Mass.: Harvard University Press, 2003.

Kinneavy, James. *Greek Rhetorical Origins of Christian Faith.* New York: Oxford University Press, 1987.

Lampe, Peter. *From Paul to Valentinus: Christians at Rome in the First Two Centuries.* Minneapolis, Minn.: Fortress Press, 2003.

Lanne, Emmanuel. "'"Église de Rome" a gloriosissimis duobus apostolis Petro Et Paulo Romae fundatae et constitutae ecclesiae' (Adv Haer iii 3:2)." *Irénikon* 49, no. 3 (1976): 275–322.

Lausberg, Heinrich. *Handbook of Literary Rhetoric: A Foundation for Literary Study.* Translated by Matthew T. Bliss. Edited by David E. Orten and R. Dean Anderson. Leiden: Brill, 1988.

Lawson, John. *The Biblical Theology of St. Irenaeus.* London: Epworth Press, 1948.

Levesque, G. "Consonance chrétienne et dissonance gnostique dans Irénée Adversus Haereses iv 18,4 à 19,3." *Studia Patristica* 16, no. 2 (1985): 193–96.

Lewis, Nicola Denzey. "*Apolytrosis* as Ritual and Sacrament: Determining a Ritual Context for Death in Second-Century Marcosian Valentinianism." *Journal of Early Christian Studies* 17, no. 4 (2009): 525–61.

Loewe, William P. "Irenaeus' Soteriology: Transposing the Question." In *Religion and Culture: Essays in Honor of Bernard Lonergan, S.J.*, edited by T. Fallon and P. Riley, 167–79. Albany: State University of New York Press, 1987.

Löhr, Winrich A. "Gnostic Determinism Reconsidered." *VC* 46, no. 4 (1992): 381–90.

Long, A. A. *Hellenistic Philosophy: Stoics, Epicureans, Sceptics.* New York: Scribner, 1974.

Loofs, Friedrich. *Theophilus von Antiochen Adversus Marcionem und die anderen theologischen Quellen bei Irenaeus.* Leipzig: J. C. Hinrichs, 1930.

MacDonald, Nathan. "Israel and the Old Testament Story in Irenaeus's Presentation of the Rule of Faith." *Journal of Theological Interpretation* 3, no. 2 (2009): 281–98.

Mambrino, J. "'Les deux main de Dieu' dans l'oeuvre de s. Irénée." *Nouvelle revue théologique* 79 (1957): 355–70.

Manohar, Christina. "The Salvific Work of God Is a Pedagogic Process: Insights from St Irenaeus." *UBS Journal* 1, no. 1 (2003): 57–65.

Markschies, Christoph. *Valentinus Gnosticus?: Untersuchungen zur valentinianischen Gnosis mit einem Kommentar zu den Fragmenten Valentins.* Tübingen: J. C. B. Mohr, 1992.

Marrou, Henri Irénée. *Histoire de l'éducation dans l'antiquité.* Paris: Seul, 1948.

May, Jordan Daniel. "The Four Pillars: The Fourfold Gospel before the Time of Irenaeus." *Trinity Journal* 30, no. 1 (2009): 67–79.

McCue, James F. "Conflicting Versions of Valentinianism: Irenaeus and the

Excerpta Ex Theodoto." In *Rediscovery of Gnosticism*, edited by Bentley Layton, 1:404–16. Leiden: Brill, 1980.

McGuire, Anne M. "Valentinus and the Gnōstikē Hairesis: Irenaeus, Haer I,Xi,1 and the Evidence of Nag Hammadi." *Studia Patristica* 18, no. 1 (1985): 247–52.

Meijering, E. P. "Irenaeus' Relation to Philosophy in the Light of His Concept of Free Will." In *Romanitas et Christianitas*, edited by W. Den Boer, 221–32. Amsterdam: North-Holland, 1973.

Meijering, Roos. *Literary and Rhetorical Theories in Greek Scholia*. Groningen: E. Forsten, 1987.

Minns, Denis. *Irenaeus*. Washington, D.C.: Georgetown University Press, 1994.

———. *Irenaeus: An Introduction*. New York: T and T Clark, 2010.

Mongrain, Kevin. *The Systematic Thought of Hans Urs Von Balthasar: An Irenaean Retrieval*. New York: Crossroad, 2002.

Moringiello, Scott D. "The Pneumatikos as Scriptural Interpreter: Irenaeus on 1 Cor. 2:15." *Studia Patristica* 65, no. 1 (2013): 105–18.

———. "Allegory and Typology in Irenaeus of Lyon." *Studia Patristica* 93, no. 19 (2017): 255–64.

———. "Teaching the Rule of Faith in Love: Irenaeus on 1 Cor 8:1." In *Irenaeus and Paul*, edited by Todd Still and Davie Wilhite. Waco, Tex.: Baylor University Press, forthcoming.

Mutschler, Bernhard. *Irenäus als johanneischer Theologe: Studien zur Schriftauslegung bei Irenäus von Lyon*. Tübingen: Mohr Siebeck, 2004.

Nautin, Pierre. *Lettres et écrivains chrétiens des iie et iiie siècles*. Paris: Éditions du Cerf, 1961.

Nielsen, J. T. *Adam and Christ in the Theology of Irenaeus of Lyons: An Examination of the Function of the Adam-Christ Typology in the Adversus Haereses of Irenaeus, against the Background of the Gnosticism of His Time*. Assen: Van Gorcum, 1968.

Noormann, Rolf. *Irenäus als Paulusinterpret: zur Rezeption und Wirkung der paulinischen und deuteropaulinischen Briefe im Werk des Irenäus von Lyon*. Tubingen: J. C. B. Mohr (Paul Siebeck), 1994.

Norris, Richard A. "The Transcendence and Freedom of God: Irenaeus, the Greek Tradition and Gnosticism." In *Early Christian Literature and the Classical Intellectual Tradition*, edited by William Schoedel and Robert Louis Wilken, 87–100. Paris: Editions Beauchesne, 1979.

———. "Irenaeus and Plotinus Answer the Gnostics: A Note on the Relation between Christian Thought and Platonism." *Union Seminary Quarterly Review* 36, no. 1 (1980): 13–24.

———. "Irenaeus' Use of Paul in His Polemic against the Gnostics." In *Paul and the Legacies of Paul*, edited by William S. Babcock, 79–98. Dallas, Tex.: Southern Methodist University Press, 1990.

———. "Theology and Language in Irenaeus of Lyon." *Anglican Theological Review* 76, no. 3 (1994): 285–95.

———. "The Insufficiency of Scripture: Adversus Haereses 2 and the Role of Scripture in Irenaeus's Anti-Gnostic Polemic." In *Reading in Christian Communities: Essays on Interpretation in the Early Church*, edited by Charles A. Bobertz and David Brakke, 63–79. Notre Dame, Ind.: University of Notre Dame Press, 2002.

———. "Who Is the Demiurge? Irenaeus' Picture of God in Adversus Haereses 2." In *God in Early Christian Thought*, edited by Andrew McGowan, Brian E. Daley, SJ, and Timothy J. Gaden, 9–36. Leiden: Brill, 2009.

Olson, Mark William. *Irenaeus, the Valentinian Gnostics, and the Kingdom of God (A. H. Book V): The Debate about 1 Corinthians 15:50*. Lewiston, N.Y.: Mellen Biblical Press, 1992.

Orbé, Antonio. "San Ireneo y el regimen del Milenio." *Studia Missionalia* 32, no. 4 (1983): 345–72.

———. *Teología de San Ireneo, V 1: Comentario al libro 5 del Adversus Haereses*. Biblioteca de Autores Cristianos. Madrid: Editorial Católica, 1985.

———. *Teología de San Ireneo, V 2: Comentario al libro 5 del Adversus Haereses*. Madrid: Editorial Católica S A, 1987.

———. *Teología de San Ireneo, V 3: Comentario al libro 5 del Adversus Haereses*. Madrid: Editorial Católica, 1988.

———. "Gloria Dei Vivens Homo (Analisis De Ireneo, Adv Haer Iv,20,1–7)." *Gregorianum* 73, no. 2 (1992): 205–26.

Osborn, Eric F. *Irenaeus of Lyons*. Cambridge: Cambridge University Press, 2001.

Overbeck, Winfried. *Menschwerdung: Eine Untersuchung zur literarischen und theologischen Einheit des Fünften Buches 'Adversus Haereses' des Irenäus von Lyon*. Bern: P. Lang, 1995.

Pagels, Elaine H. "Conflicting Versions of Valentinian Eschatology: Irenaeus' Treatise vs the Excerpts from Theodotus." *Harvard Theological Review* 67, no. 1 (1974): 35–53.

———. *The Gnostic Paul: Gnostic Exegesis of the Pauline Letters*. Philadelphia: Fortress Press, 1975.

———. "Irenaeus, the 'Canon of Truth,' and the Gospel of John: 'Making a Difference' through Hermeneutics and Ritual." *VC* 56, no. 3 (2002): 339–71.

Parvis, Sara, and Paul Foster, eds. *Irenaeus: Life, Scripture, Legacy*. Minneapolis, Minn.: Fortress Press, 2012.

Pelland, Gilles. "Le décalogue dans la théologie d'Irénée de Lyon (Aduersus Haereses iv, 14, 1s)." In *Décalogue au miroir des Pères*, edited by Rémi Gounelle and Jean-Marc Prieur, 93–106. Strasbourg: Université Marc Bloch, 2008.

Perkins, Pheme. "Irenaeus and the Gnostics. Rhetoric and Composition in Adversus Haereses Book One." *VC* 30, no. 3 (1976): 193–200.

Pernot, Laurent. *Rhetoric in Antiquity*. Translated by W. E. Higgins. Washington, D.C.: The Catholic University of America Press, 2005.

Presley, Stephen O. *The Intertextual Reception of Genesis 1–3 in Irenaeus of Lyons*. Leiden: Brill, 2015.

Reynders, B. "Paradosis. Le progrès et l'idée de tradition jusqu'à saint Irénée." *Recherches de théologie ancienne et medieval* 5, no. 2 (1935): 155–91.

———. "La Polémique De Saint Irénée." *Recherches de théologie ancienne et medieval* 7, no. 1 (1965): 5–27.

Richter, Gerhard. *Oikonomia: Der Gebrauch des Wortes Oikonomia im neuen Testament, bei den Kirkenvätern und in der theologischen Literatur dis ins 20. Jahrhundert.* Berlin: Walter de Gruyter, 2005.

Rordorf, Willy. "Was Heisst; Petrus und Paulus Haben die Kirche in Rom 'Gegruendet': zu Irenaeus Adv Haer iii,1,1;3,2,3." In *Unterwegs zur Einheit*, edited by Johannes Branchtschen, Heinrich Stirnimann, and Pietro Selvatico, 609–16. Freiburg Schweiz: Universitaetsverlag, 1980.

Rougé, Jean, and Robert Turcan, eds. *Les Martyrs De Lyon (177)*. Colloques Internationaux du Centre National de la Recherche Scientifique, no. 575. Paris: Éditions du C.N.R.S, 1978.

Sagnard, Francois. *La gnose valentinienne et le témoignage de saint Irénée*. Paris: Vrin, 1947.

Scherrer, Thierry. *La glorie de Dieu dans l'oeurve de saint Irénée*. Rome: Editrice Pontifica Universita Gregoriana, 1997.

Schoedel, William R. "Philosophy and Rhetoric in the Adversus Haereses of Irenaeus." *VC* 13, no. 1 (1959): 22–32.

———. "Theological Method in Irenaeus (Adversus Haereses 2:25–28)." *JTS* 35, no. 1 (1984): 31–49.

Secord, Jared. "The Cultural Geography of a Greek Christian: Ireaneus from Smyrna to Lyons." In *Irenaeus: Life, Scripture, Legacy*, edited by Sara Parvis and Paul Foster, 25–34. Minneapolis, Minn.: Fortress, 2012.

Slusser, Michael. "How Much Did Irenaeus Learn from Justin?" *Studia Patristica* 40 (2006): 515–20.

Smith, Geoffrey S. *Guilt by Association: Heresy Catalogues in Early Christianity.* New York: Oxford University Press, 2015.

Sobosan, Jeffrey G. "Role of the Presbyter: An Investigation into the Adversus Haereses of Saint Irenaeus." *Scottish Journal of Theology* 27, no. 2 (1974): 129–46.

Steenberg, M. C. "The Role of Mary as Co-Recapitulator in St Irenaeus of Lyons." *VC* 58, no. 2 (2004): 117–37.

———. *Irenaeus on Creation the Cosmic Christ and the Saga of Redemption*. Leiden: Brill, 2008.

———. "Irenaeus on Scripture, Graphe, and the Status of Hermas." *St. Vladimir's Theological Quarterly* 53, no. 1 (2009): 29–66.

Thomassen, Einar. *The Spiritual Seed: The Church of the "Valentinians."* Leiden: Brill, 2006.

Tiessen, Terrance L. *Irenaeus on the Salvation of the Unevangelized*. Metuchen, N.J.: Scarecrow Press, 1993.

Tosaus Abadía, José Pedro. *Cristo y el universo: estudio lingüístico y temático de Ef 1:10b, en Efesios y en la obra de Ireneo de Lión*. Salamanca: Universidad Pontificia de Salamanca, 1995.

Tremblay, Real. "Le Martrye Selon Saint Irénée De Lyon." *Studia Moralia* 16, no. 2 (1978): 167–89.

Tripp, David H. "The Original Sequence of Irenaeus Adversus Haereses I: A Suggestion." *Second Century: A Journal of Early Christian Studies* 8, no. 3 (1991): 157–62.

Usher, Stephen. "Sumbouleutic Oratory." In *A Companion to Greek Rhetoric*, edited by Ian Worthington, 220–35. Oxford: Blackwell, 2007.

Vallée, Gérard. *A Study in Anti-Gnostic Polemics: Irenaeus, Hippolytus, and Epiphanius*. Waterloo: Wilfrid University Press, 1981.

Walker, Jeffrey. *Rhetoric and Poetics in Antiquity*. Oxford: Oxford University Press, 2000.

Wanke, Daniel. *Das Kreuz Christi bei Irenaeus von Lyon*. Berlin: Walter de Gruyter, 2000.

Webb, Ruth. *Ekphrasis, Imagination and Persuasion in Ancient Rhetorical Theory and Practice*. Burlington, Vt.: Ashgate, 2009.

Wendt, Hans Hinrich. *Die christliche Lehre von der menschlichen Vollkommenheit*. Göttingen: Vandenhoeck and Ruprecht, 1882.

Whitmarsh, Tim. *The Second Sophistic*. Oxford: Oxford University Press, 2005.

Whittaker, John. "Platonic Philosophy in the Early Centuries of the Empire." *Aufstieg und Niedergang der romischen Welt* 36, no. 1 (1987): 81–123.

Wiegel, James B. "The Trinitarian Structure of Irenaeus' Demonstration of the Apostolic Preaching." *St. Vladimir's Theological Quarterly* 58, no. 2 (2014): 113–39.

Wilken, R. L. "The Homeric Cento in Irenaeus' Adversus Haereses I,9,4." *VC* 21, no. 1 (1967): 25–33.

Williams, Michael A. *Rethinking "Gnosticism": An Argument for Dismantling a Dubious Category*. Princeton, N.J.: Princeton University Press, 1996.

Wingren, Gustaf. *Man and the Incarnation: A Study in the Biblical Theology of Irenaeus*. Philadelphia: Muhlenberg Press, 1959.

Woolf, Greg. *Becoming Roman: The Origins of Provincial Civilization in Gaul*. Cambridge: Cambridge University Press, 1998.

INDEX

Abraham, 114, 121, 126, 175

Acts of the Apostles, 39, 92, 94

Acts of the Martyrs, 5

Adam, 103, 115, 155, 163, 168

aeon, 28–30, 58–61, 81, 88, 108

allegory, ix, 57, 68, 171, 178, 179

anakephalaiosis, 100, 144–46

Antichrist, 130, 145, 170, 174, 175

Apostles, 9, 16, 26, 28, 29, 31–36, 48, 51, 56, 62, 67, 71, 73, 75, 79, 80–86, 89–91, 94, 97, 98, 102–4, 119, 122, 124, 132, 134, 145, 146, 151, 156, 158, 162, 168, 170, 180

Aristotle, xvii, xviii, 9, 12, 13, 14, 17, 18, 21, 35, 76, 77, 144

Asia, 4, 5

authority, 84

Bacq, Phillipe, 109n3, 110n4

Balthasar, Hans Urs von, xv, 78n7

baptism, 34, 47, 182, 185, 187, 188

Barbeliotes, 46

Basilides, 46, 83

Behr, John, viin10, 3n3, 35, 80n16, 82n20

Bingham, D. Jeffrey, 31n23, 82n21, 87n39, 143n3

bishop, xiii, 83

Cainites, 46

canon, 35

Carpocrates, 46

Cerinthus, 46, 83

Cerdo, 46, 98

church, 14, 36, 37, 46, 56, 71, 96, 104–6, 122, 127–29, 133, 148, 163, 174, 181, 184

Cicero, Marcus Tullius, 78

Clement of Alexandria, 59

Clement of Rome, 86

Commandments, 116

Corinthians, First letter, 43, 47, 48, 65, 69, 83, 95, 113, 115, 129, 133, 137, 141, 142, 150, 152, 163, 166

creation, 1, 27, 28, 47, 56, 57, 90

cross, 127, 132

Daniel, 170

David, 129

deliberative speech, 11, 12, 13, 15, 16, 69, 71, 76, 103, 105, 117, 138, 140, 143, 144, 156, 170

delight, 39, 105, 126

Demiurge, 98

Demonstration of the Apostolic Preaching, 181–88

Deuteronomy, 166

Devil. *See* Satan

Donovan, Mary Ann, 109n3

Ebionites, 46

economy, 36, 38, 41, 51, 61, 97, 98, 101, 110, 124, 125, 133, 160, 187

economy of salvation, 1, 9, 12, 16, 21, 23, 24, 31, 32, 40, 41, 47, 49, 67, 88, 92, 97,

The Rhetoric of Faith: Irenaeus and the Structure of the Adversus Haereses
was designed in Minion with Mr Eaves Sans display type and composed by Kachergis
Book Design of Pittsboro, North Carolina. It was printed on 60-pound House Natural
Smooth and bound by Sheridan Books of Chelsea, Michigan.